The Art *of*

FIRST
IMPRESSIONS

for

POSITIVE
IMPACT

8 WAYS TO SHINE BRIGHT TO
TRANSFORM RELATIONSHIP RESULTS

SUSAN YOUNG

Library of Congress-in-Publication-Data: 2017912687
Young, Susan
The Art of First Impressions for Positive Impact: 8 Ways to Shine Bright to Transform Relationship Results, by Susan Young

Published by *ReNew You Ventures*
Editing by Elizabeth Dixon
Co-Editing by Judy Dippel, www.JLDWrites.com
Contributions by Julie Escobar, www.SpeakersChoiceConsulting.com
Book Design by Kendra Cagle, www.5LakesDesign.com
Back Cover Photography by Rhonda Schaefer, www.RhondaClicks.com

ISBN-10: 0-9985561-1-4
ISBN-13: 978-0-9985561-1-6

To learn more about Author, Speaker Susan Young, explore her other resources, or hire her to speak for your live events, please visit: www.SusanSpeaks.com

This book is dedicated to my cherished mother

Ann Chandley Cullison

You are my first best friend and shining role model.
You taught me grace, dignity, love, and how to
nurture relationships. Thank you.

I love you forever.

Contents

Foreword. ix
First & Foremost xi
Let the Transformation Begin xix

1

THE ART OF **BEING**

1. Authenticity. 5
2. Personal Integrity 13
3. Passion 19
4. Love & Generosity 27
5. Healthy Self-Esteem 35
6. Dignity & Grace. 41
7. Charisma & Charm. 47
8. Confidence & Command 51

2

THE ART OF **PREPARATION**

1. Mastering Your Mindset 63
2. Emotional Intelligence. 69
3. Prepare for Success 75
4. Your Personal Brand. 79
5. Dress to Impress. 85
6. Healthy Habits & Hygiene 97
7. Punctuality Plus 105
8. Expertise, Experience & Education 109

3

THE ART OF **BODY LANGUAGE**

1. Energy & Aura 123
2. Approachability 131
3. Mirror, Mirror 137
4. Eye Contact 141
5. Smiling & Expressions of Emotion 147
6. Poise, Postures & Gestures 157
7. Orientation & Proximity 167
8. Handshakes, Hugs & Other Touching 171

4

THE ART OF **ACTION**

1. Just Be Nice 185
2. Be Brave 191
3. Manners Matter 197
4. Polish the Gold 205
5. Service Beyond Self 211
6. Take the Initiative 219
7. Mix, Mingle & Glow 229
8. Be Fully Present & Engaged 233

5

THE ART OF **COMMUNICATION**

1. Mindful Awareness 243
2. Conversation Starters. 251
3. Active Listening. 255
4. Voice Value. 265
5. Using Names 269
6. Wise with Your Words 275
7. Communication Styles. 279
8. Savvy Socializing & Synchronicity 287

6

THE ART OF **CONNECTION**

1. Building Trust & Rapport. 299
2. Personable & Friendly 305
3. Interested & Interesting. 309
4. Be a Discovery Expert 315
5. Commonality & Camaraderie. 319
6. Make Others Feel Important. 323
7. Use Fun & Humor. 327
8. Discretion & Good Judgment 333

7

THE ART OF **A POSITIVE LASTING IMPRESSION**

1.   Happy Endings. 345
2.   Share It Forward 349
3.   Humility & Gratitude 355
4.   Class, Tact & Diplomacy. 361
5.   Play Well with Others 365
6.   Follow-Up & Follow-Through 369
7.   Reputation & Respect. 375
8.   Make Moments Memorable. .379

8

THE ART OF **NURTURING YOUR NETWORK**

1.   Cultivate Your Connections. .389
2.   Warm Referrals & Repeat Business. 395
3.   Networking to Expand Your Influence 403
4.   Join New Groups & Organizations 409
5.   Volunteer Your Time & Talent. 415
6.   With a Little Help from Your Friends. 423
7.   Make Deposits in the Love Bank. 430
8.   Friendships for a Lifetime. 437

Bringing It Full Circle 445
Acknowledgements 447
About Susan Young. 449

Foreword

BY SHEP HYKEN

Few things are more important to us than how we are perceived and received by others—personally and professionally. Since meeting new people will continue to be a significant part of your life experience, it pays to learn powerful, purposeful, and effective ways to improve your first impressions. That said, "You never have a second chance to make a first impression." It's not known who said it first, but it has been attributed to Oscar Wilde, Will Rogers, and even Yogi Berra. Whoever said it doesn't really matter. It's a catchy phrase. And, if you only meet a person once, it is valid. However, my belief is that you do have a second chance to make a first impression. Even a third—or one-hundredth—or more!

Yes, upon meeting someone you make a true first impression. Then in subsequent meetings or encounters, you make a first impression that sets the tone for whatever interaction is to follow. It may be a co-worker you see every day. A customer you see once a month. Or, a family member you come home to every night after work. Each time you have an interaction, you have the opportunity to make your first impression a positive lasting one—and it is under your control. And Susan will help you bring it full circle.

So, with all of the impressions we leave with people during our lifetime, it's worth our time to know our strengths and weaknesses. What better way to figure out what to do and how to do it, than through Susan Young's book, *The Art of First Impressions for Positive Impact*. She shines a light on what is important and influential for positive engagement and interaction. I sincerely believe her book could become standard training for businesses and organizations alike. And when utilized personally, readers will have the tools to transform the relationships in their lives for the better.

I met Susan almost twenty years ago when she attended her first National Speakers Association's convention in Dallas, Texas. The positive impression she made on me that very day continues to be the lasting impression which I enjoy, respect, and admire now. Since that first meeting, and each and every time I've met with her, she radiates with charisma and charm; always smiling, always positive and always dressed like a star. Her energy, positivity, authenticity, and love for people have been consistently genuine and heartfelt. She walks the talk with dignity and discretion—encouraging others to do the same. As a positive role model for making a great first impression, Susan is a living example of her topic.

As a customer service expert, I work with companies who want to build loyal relationships with their customers and employees. I believe that positive first impressions are indeed an art form that forms the basis for every relationship, business interaction, marketing brand, and customer service experience we have. These first and lasting impressions are crucial for winning the hearts and minds of your customers and have the power to make or break your success in life and business.

In *The Art of First Impressions for Positive Impact,* Susan brings together thirty years of knowledge and experience to help you identify, enrich, and deliver the everlasting elements for building healthy relationships. You have the power to make amazing first impressions by learning, practicing, and living the concepts Susan has provided for you, served on a silver platter, in this book, in wonderful detail.

—Shep Hyken

Customer Service Expert and *New York Times* and *Wall Street Journal*
Bestselling Author of *The Amazement Revolution*
www.Hyken.com

First & Foremost
What's in It for You?

Universally, what do most people want? Think about it. How about you . . . what do YOU want? To make new friends? Build social confidence? Have more fun? Be a stronger leader? Expand your influence? Get the job of your dreams? Grow your business? Nurture your network? Be your best self? Find happiness and fulfillment while engaging others? The list is long and unique to each of us. *The Art of First Impressions for Positive Impact* is your go-to guide for achieving all of this and more.

Like it or not, your life—what works well and what doesn't—is largely the result of the first impressions you have created along the way.

---

66 *With every new encounter, impressions are made and opinions are formed in only a matter of seconds. The instant imprint you make on someone can impact them, and you, for a lifetime.* 99

You can increase your opportunities and improve your outcomes by making these opening moments with people more meaningful, memorable, and successful. *The Art of First Impressions for Positive Impact* will show you how by raising your awareness and giving you the tools that will soon become second nature.

Research has shown that it takes only one to seven seconds to make a first impression. In these few seconds, people will formulate an entire opinion about you—your service, your company, your credibility, your competence, your trustworthiness, and your likability.

Human resource directors and hiring managers tell me they usually know within the first thirty seconds of a job interview whether or not the person is even a viable candidate.

You may ask, "Why is a first impression so important?" Because these brief seconds can be the make-or-break, live-or-die, or yes-or-no basis for building rapport, earning trust, winning friends, or making the sale. These "seconds" will often determine your outcomes—good, bad or indifferent.

Whether a first impression is made by way of a mere glance, a warm smile, a visit to your website, your poise and speech, or a formal introduction, it sets the stage for your relationships, personally and professionally. Regardless of the venue, there are skills you can learn and special qualities you can adopt that will help you optimize your encounters. Applying these skills will ensure a positive experience to help you . . . **Shine Bright and Stand Apart from the Crowd!**

Ask Yourself

What impresses you when you meet someone new? What is it about some people that makes you remember them for the rest of your life, even though your interaction lasted only a few moments? What qualities do you notice about people who walk into a room and shine so brightly they captivate everyone there? How do their personalities bring out the best in others?

How do they inspire and encourage people to become their best selves? What is it about their style, their attitude, and their essence that enchants and delights us? *The Art of First Impressions for Positive Impact* will help you create the same positive results in your life.

Make Your Mark

Throughout your life, thousands of people will cross your path. Some you will remember fondly. Some you will remember negatively. Others will slip by unnoticed, perhaps because they were neutral, unengaged or, quite frankly, unimpressive.

What can you do, beginning TODAY, to be the one who makes your mark and leaves others in awe?

There are times when making a great first impression is essential and you need to do everything in your power to be diligent, deliberate, and dedicated to making the connection count (seeking a prized job, signing a new client, meeting a prospective in-law, being considered for a jury). There will be other times, however, when your efforts can be more relaxed to encourage easy engagement and comfortable connections. Knowing the distinct difference begins with awareness and ends with mastery.

Up Your Game

To 'up your game' means, simply, to make the effort to improve what you are doing—to amplify, boost, or strengthen your talents or performance.

When it comes to positive impressions, is there a magic formula to follow? A secret recipe? Not really, even though it may sometimes feel like it. However, there are skills, tools, and mindsets that can empower you to optimize how you present who you are to the world. Making a great first impression combines multiple ingredients to create a successful outcome.

In this book, I have made it easy for you to go to any chapter and find tools to "up" your game—and help you not only get in but stay in.

---

66 Applied in ways that are authentic to you, these concepts are powerful and can positively impact and influence every type of relationship. 99

In a perfect world, it would be great for you to take everything you find here and put it all into action. You may find that you already do a large percentage of the things I share, naturally and intuitively. But just as importantly, *The Art of First Impressions for Positive Impact* will also **expose the blind spots and address the gaps** where you might be at a loss for how to move the needle to achieve better outcomes.

Most books written about making a positive first impression are limited to the business-minded and address the questions . . .

- How can sales people make more sales?
- How can people deliver better service and earn loyalty from customers?
- How can business people discover and open new doors of opportunity?
- How can you go up to total strangers at networking events and begin a conversation?

The Art of First Impressions for Positive Impact will answer these questions and more—addressing both your business and personal relationships—as well as your perception of yourself. The unique and special difference in this book compared to others is that it provides a universal appeal to help people from all walks of life—at any age and any place—adopt and apply lessons for social success. What you receive from this book will be determined by where you are and what you need.

The Art of First Impressions for Positive Impact Can Help If . . .

- You want to make new friends.
- You want to be heard above the noise.
- You want to feel accepted, included, and embraced.
- You want to make a positive and memorable impression.
- You want to be a part of something larger than yourself.

- You want to improve your self-esteem and self-image.
- You want to feel more socially courageous and confident.
- You want to approach people with comfort and ease.
- You want to inspire, motivate, and encourage others.
- You want to have influence and inspire your team.
- You want to stretch beyond your comfort zone to create a daring adventure or experience.
- You want to stand up, stand out, and be well remembered.

The Art of First Impressions for Positive Impact Will Empower You To . . .

- Deliver exceptional customer service.
- Interview for a new position or start a new job.
- Build your business and expand your territory.
- Make more sales and be more profitable.
- Deliver a commanding performance in meetings and speeches.
- Optimize networking events and opportunities.
- Earn repeat business, customer loyalty, and referrals.
- Refine your personal and professional branding to position you as special, unique, and memorable.
- Collaborate well in teams and get the best out of your people.
- Lead effectively, earn respect, and encourage cooperation.
- Exude the integrity, humility, and confidence of a leader.
- Make a positive lasting impression to build relationships for life.

WHY 8 Chapters?

The Art of First Impressions for Positive Impact features **8 Parts.** This is done not by accident, but by intention—a deliberate numerological metaphor, representing infinity—as well as balance, order, prosperity, and many ideals beyond!

The number 8 is well-rounded, circular, continuous, consistent, connected—and eternal. These are the same outcomes you can create and enjoy when you turn a positive first impression into a constructive and lasting one.

Yes, "First Impressions" is in the title; however, wouldn't you like to make this the ongoing theme for life? To continually enjoy and reap the benefits of leaving a positive impression in nearly all your encounters for years to come? Positive impressions have staying power, so make them great. **You can transform your connections and your relationship results!**

Why "ART?"

Art represents creative expression, flexibility, fun, and individual interpretation. As with "Art," first impressions are not rigid or carved in stone. Rather they are agile and adaptable, depending on the inspiration, the artist, the observer, the medium, and the circumstance.

Every one of your first encounters begins with a "blank canvas" which provides you with unlimited opportunities to color your world in the ways you most desire. We are each a work in progress—special and unique. By learning and living the "Art of First Impressions," you can design a masterpiece of which you can be proud.

8x8 Will Make You Great!

In each of the 8 Parts, you will discover 8 Arts filled with game-changing concepts that you can apply right away—beginning today! Seek to develop mastery in the . . .

1. *The Art of Being*
2. *The Art of Preparation*
3. *The Art of Body Language*
4. *The Art of Action*
5. *The Art of Communication*
6. *The Art of Connection*
7. *The Art of a Lasting Positive Impression*
8. *The Art of Nurturing Your Network*

Whether you adopt one over-arching principle or sixty-four specific techniques, everything comes together for good to make you more aware, better prepared, and empowered on your journey. The book is formatted in bite-sized pieces so that no matter where you turn, you will find valuable tips and tools which you can read quickly and implement in your life immediately.

The Art of First Impressions for Positive Impact has the tools to help you prevent and avoid social mishaps, lost business, rejection, low self-esteem, failure, career complacency, and lifelong frustration. When you become aware of how to be intentional in your efforts, you will enjoy greater success by connecting in positive ways. These principles and practices are enduring. Knowing how to make a great first impression will enable you to more easily achieve your goals and live out your hopes and dreams to become a happier, more content you.

Let the Transformation Begin

"YOLO"—you only live once! Making an excellent first impression may seem old-fashioned to some, but the realities of life confirm that the first impression is a lasting one—impactful enough to change your life and even outlive you altogether. Your success and legacy, personally and professionally, are built through the impressions you make one encounter at a time. They matter—why? Because YOU matter!

Like you, I have my own reality show—it's my life. And even though it's not on TV (yet), it's watched by many people. It has drama, laughter and tears, disappointments and dreams. It has inspired me and made me more resilient. By living everyday life and working as a professional speaker for almost twenty years, I recognize the need to modernize the conventional wisdom of making outstanding and authentic first impressions at every opportunity.

The significance of first impressions has really hit home for me twice in my life—when I moved to new cities where I did not know anyone. Both times, I had left behind the comforting familiarity of family, friends, and an established life where people knew and trusted me. I was thrust into totally new environments where it was up to me to design a new reality and create fulfilling experiences. There was always uncertainty and the risk of the unknown, but ever the optimist, I also felt a degree of confidence that everything was going to be okay.

I did not always enjoy such social or personal confidence. Somehow, I survived high school, as well as the self-doubt, fragile self-esteem, and feelings of inferiority that accompany it for most of us. College bound, I yearned for the secrets to success which would help me to make new friends, find my place in the world, and forge a rewarding path.

Thank You, Mr. Carnegie!

As fate would have it, someone introduced me to Dale Carnegie's *How to Win Friends and Influence People* when I was only seventeen. His book was a game-changer that serves me 'til this day! I read the book from cover to cover multiple times, absorbing the wisdom it contained.

---

66 The discovery that making great first impressions can be a learned skill helped me to understand that we can and do have power over how we affect and impact others and on how well we are received in this world. 99

Over the next couple of decades, my success in life, business, and relationships could be attributed directly to many of Dale Carnegie's concepts, and for that I am grateful.

In my late thirties, I was recruited by a Fortune 300 company to explode an untapped territory where our competitors dominated and had a stronghold in the marketplace. Knowing that it would take every ounce of **winning friends and influencing people** to knock down doors, I had to take my social skills to a new level. It was then that I discovered Seth Godin's *Purple Cow Marketing.* In short, he encouraged me to differentiate myself and my services to stand apart from the herd and be remarkable. You can do the same.

By combining Dale Carnegie's time-tested tools with Seth Godin's edgy "purple cow marketing" philosophy, I was empowered to help my clients achieve their goals, which inevitably did the same for my company and me. In my first year, I quadrupled my territory and received the award for "Most New Accounts Signed" for the entire state of Florida.

This stuff really worked! They were lessons well learned, just as the concepts I share with you in this book will help you lay the groundwork for making terrific impressions and special connections.

How This Book Began

Some years back, when I launched my professional speaking website www.SusanSpeaks.com, I needed to create a short e-book that I could offer for free to visitors and prospective clients. What better gift could there be than to help people succeed in all types of relationships?

Over the course of a few years, my little e-book grew and evolved as I did. The book you now hold in your hands is the end result—providing you with the best of my experience, observations, interviews, and research. I am humbled and excited to finally bring this information to my audiences in book form.

The Gift That Keeps Giving . . .

A couple of years ago, I moved one thousand miles north to Madison, Wisconsin to be with my life love, Daniel. Yet again, I found myself starting from scratch and not knowing anyone.

We are always in a state of change—**reviewing, redoing,** and **renewing,** as taught in my book, *Release the Power of Re³,* aren't we?

This time, I took deliberate and thoughtful steps to practice what I was preaching. Not only did I become a keen observer to notice who was making a positive impression on me and why, but I walked the talk and lived every lesson you will read about in this book. Applying these principles has helped me make new friends whom I love dearly, build a successful business, and design an enriching life.

In writing *The Art of First Impressions for Positive Impact,* I wanted to "share it forward" and be for others what Dale Carnegie had been for me. You will find this book to be a dynamic resource, a modern guide, and helpful companion—not only to teach you how you can win friends and influence people, but how you can show up to life feeling great inside, looking great outside, and being sensational at whatever level you seek or goal you wish to conquer.

I hope you will see this as an adventure in learning to positively influence your first impressions! After reading this book yourself, I encourage you to help others by sharing it with your sales people, your customer service team, an upcoming graduate, a friend who is moving, and any others who come to mind. These real-life strategies can benefit EVERYONE.

Are you creating, maintaining, and retaining the relationship results you want? Would you like to know how to better optimize your outcomes and make the best first impressions possible?

For some, a **positive** state of being comes quite naturally, but for others it does not. Even so, we all can benefit when we have a guide and mentor to help us walk the high road to create the results we desire. And sometimes, we need to be thrown a lifeline! The pages that follow will meet you on your journey wherever you may be.

---

66 My greatest desire is to provide you with the guidance, support, and ideas to present your best self in any venue or situation. 99

You will learn to communicate without barriers, express your message authentically, activate the law of attraction, and optimize the positive perceptions of others. Reading *The Art of First Impressions for Positive Impact* will serve to help your relationship transformations begin!

1

The *Art* of

BEING

8 WAYS TO OPTIMIZE
YOUR PRESENCE & ESSENCE
FOR POSITIVE IMPACT

The Art of BEING

Attitude. Personality. Mindset. Spirit. Essence. Perspective. Regardless of how you define your state of being, your mental, intellectual, emotional, and spiritual approaches are the basis for your existence and how you experience life.

Your way of **being** impacts your happiness and outcomes—the wisdom of your choices, your confidence and courage, your self-esteem, how you are perceived and received by others, and the quality of your relationships. The more positively centered and grounded you are in your authentic being, the more people may be drawn to you.

The Art of Being lays the foundation for this entire book, as well as your first impressions, because if you get this part wrong not much else matters. All other efforts may be diminished or wasted. Someone who is being gracious, kind, and passionate is more likely to achieve what they want in life than someone who is being petty, cruel, or resistant. Your way of being sets the tone for how people relate to you, behave toward you, and engage. How is it working for you?

Becoming the person you want to be draws from being your best and doing your best as you allow your personality, passions, and purpose to shine through. *The Art of Being* encompasses . . .

1. *Authenticity*
2. *Personal Integrity*
3. *Passion*
4. *Love & Generosity*
5. *Healthy Self-Esteem*
6. *Dignity & Grace*
7. *Charisma & Charm*
8. *Confidence & Command*

1. AUTHENTICITY

"Be yourself. Everyone else is already taken."
—Oscar Wilde

Being authentic is key to living a happy life and enjoying healthy relationships. I list authenticity first because if we miss this vital component of our unique way of being, everything else in this book becomes irrelevant.

ASK YOURSELF: Are you being real? When people meet you, are you straight up and natural—the real deal? If you are, then you will appreciate what it means to approach life always being YOU.

Standing in your personal truth enables you to transcend social layers of happenstance and get to the heart of matters—revealing what is raw and real.

Your goal, then, is to never be anything less than real or to clone yourself from another. Why would you be anything other than your unique and best self?

---

66 Life's most amazing moments between people are built on trust, communication, acceptance, and love. 99

As we observe and experience varying degrees of difficulty, negativity, loss, hurt, anxiety, and fear in life, we yearn for the reassurance that our relationships are safe. The days of the pushy salesmen and self-serving narcissists are over. That type of behavior quickly alienates and pushes people away because it offends and can't be trusted.

People must believe that you are real and are who you say you are, otherwise they will not want to do business with you, much less make the effort to move forward in starting and building a relationship.

When I meet someone who is truly genuine, I am drawn to their personality and find them easier to approach, engage, and interact with. I know that what I see is what I get. They have no hint of false pretense, nor do I worry about hidden agendas.

Authentic people are instantly more likable and trustworthy, which makes building rapport with them a pleasure. In their presence, we feel accepted for who we are without judgment or criticism. We crave real people and are delighted when we find them.

My dear friend Marnie Tate once shared, "An aura of authenticity is one of the finest qualities that a person can project. When I meet these sincere people and they look me in the eye—they have me."

Own Your Truths

"If you are your authentic self, you have no competition."
—Scott Stratten

Own your truths—all of them. Be honest. Be genuine. Be straight forward. Be refreshing! We gravitate towards such people, don't we? Allow your natural personality to shine through without pretending to be someone you're not, or you may be stuck with that label forever. Walking in alignment with your integrity will help keep you on the right track.

There is a reason that the words **natural, wholesome,** and **organic** resonate throughout our culture today. Aim to be natural and truly who you are one-hundred percent of the time.

We've all met people who are beautiful on the outside, however, when they open their mouths to speak, they have nothing of substance to contribute. And other times we meet folks who appear rather plain, yet when they speak from a heart of service, love, compassion, and wisdom, they instantly become respected favorites.

Authenticity is the litmus test for the honesty, transparency, and trust which are necessary for healthy relationships. You have met phonies—fake people who appear plastic and put on airs trying to impress other people. The person they present to the world is not the person who resides inside.

My friend Tina Hallis, Ph.D. (ThePositiveEdge.org) is a professional speaker who specializes in positivity in the workplace. One day after presenting her "Positive Psychology" workshop, an audience participant approached and asked her, "What about authenticity? Sometimes I don't feel like being positive. What if I feel authentically mad, bad, or negative? Is that okay?"

Tina responded, "Of course it is okay! You need to honor where you are and it is not always about being happy. Your negative feelings are there for a reason, too."

Authenticity respects the ebb and flow between positive and negative. The people who really know you will understand that you are not always going to be in a happy place and an occasional bad mood is acceptable. By authentically sharing when things aren't right you allow the people you care about to offer the support you may need.

The Challenge for the People Pleaser

"Always be a first-rate version of yourself and not a
second-rate version of someone else."

—Judy Garland

The challenge of being authentic for people pleasers is that we *really* want people to like and accept us. Being vulnerable, however, requires that we come to terms with the fact that not everyone is going to like us, and that it is okay. Not everyone needs to like us.

ASK YOURSELF: Do you really want people to like you for something that you're not? It takes a lot of energy to pretend to be someone else for the sake of pleasing others.

Teenagers especially go through this when they are trying to be accepted and fit in. As a lifetime people pleaser, I remember trying to mold myself into the person I thought other people wanted me to be— all for the sake of being liked and accepted. As a young girl, I allowed my self-esteem to be determined by others' opinions, and I devoted incredible energy tuning in to how everyone else felt. I wanted to win them over to the "Susan Fan Club," and when I failed, I was devastated.

Why did I think that the mask was a better portrayal than my authentic self? We can get hidden under layers of illusion, can't we?

I love to make people happy, choose to be positive, and usually have a joyful heart. Do you? While you would think my energy, enthusiasm, and passion would be great virtues, it annoys the hell out of some folks. I especially irritate negative, cynical spirit suckers who may think my eternal optimism is unrealistic and insincere. Oh well. I don't want to shut down and stop being happy to accommodate someone else. I've gotten to a point in life to understand that not everyone is going to like me. After all, I don't always like everyone either. That's life!

After I hit fifty, a friend of mine said, "Susan, this a great place to be because everything is either a "Hell yeah!" or a "Hell no!" I said, "You're right! You really can say no without regrets." Being my authentic self frees me to live out my priorities. I feel the relief. I don't waste time any longer saying yes to someone else's priorities just to receive their accolades and acceptance.

Additionally, being authentic means accepting other people for who they are in their own individuality.

---

66 *Authenticity isn't just about saying "this is who I am"—it is also about being flexible enough to recognize and appreciate the uniqueness in others—honoring the mutual respect for being authentic and true.* 99

Embracing Imperfection

"I know of nothing more valuable, when it comes to the all-important virtue of authenticity, than simply being who you are."
—Charles R. Swindoll

I am a recovering perfectionist, and like all in recovery, I do better some days than others! I have a friend who strives for perfection in all things. I have no idea how she does it. She always looks amazing. She is the whole package! Regardless of whether she is exercising, at the grocery store, or sweating in the sun at her child's ball game, she looks 'all together.' Being so darned perfect all the time makes a lot of people feel uncomfortable. They think she's wearing a mask and they don't think she is authentic, real. Even though she is genuinely very nice, they are intimidated by her need for personal perfection.

ASK YOURSELF: Do you generally feel uncomfortable around people whom you perceive to be perfect? Is there really such a thing as the perfect person? The perfect weight? The perfect shade of skin? Of course not! Our flaws are often what differentiate us from each other, and no person is perfect.

Brené Brown, Ph.D. is a respected thought leader who teaches the power of vulnerability and authenticity, bringing deeper understanding to our inner shame. If you have never seen her TED Talks, do yourself a favor and listen to her meaningful messages today. She gives everyone permission to simply be themselves. She quickly earns trust, respect, and affection through her own wholesome sincerity and transparent imperfections.

Dr. Brown shares, "Authenticity is the daily practice of letting go of who we think we are supposed to be embracing who we are." Why are we so critical of ourselves? We would all endure a lot less suffering if we would simply love and accept ourselves in all our imperfections.

In their book, *Forget Perfect!* authors Lisa Earle McLeod and Jo Ann Swan celebrate imperfection by providing a true and likely scenario. Imagine that you have just woken up. You have bad breath, messy hair, and are still in your pajamas with smeared make-up. You decide to sneak outside to grab your newspaper. As you are tiptoeing quietly down your sidewalk, you realize that you have locked yourself out of your house.

Which neighbor will you go to go to ask for help? The one to the left, who is perfectly coifed without a hair out of place, has an immaculate yard, the perfect children, the perfect husband, the perfect figure, and more . . . *at least seemingly.* Or will you knock on the door of the neighbor to your right with four kids, dogs barking, a messy house, a sink full of dishes, and baby throw-up on her shoulder?

If you are like me, you would go to the neighbor whose life is real, authentic, messy, and in my opinion—*amazing*. Why? Because she is authentic. She is so secure in her beautifully imperfect self that she would welcome you with open arms, no judgment, and complete acceptance.

---

66 *Authentic people are so comfortable in their own skins they make us more comfortable in our own.* 99

Interestingly, being yourself allows others to be themselves. Even with crazy imperfections, being a bona fide genuine person is the best any of us can be—messy flaws and all!

As I mentioned earlier, moving to the Midwest from Florida was a major life change for me. The transition, however, was made easier by the authentic and friendly attitudes of the people who live here. "Midwest Nice" is true! I have repeatedly experienced their sincere kindness, caring, low-key attitude, and acceptance.

When my friend Jackie lived in a rich section of Atlanta, she felt pressured to wear the right shoes, drive the right car, sport the right hairstyle, and dress a certain way to fit in and be accepted. When she moved to Madison, she found that it didn't matter how she showed up. As long as she showed up as her real and authentic self she would be warmly embraced.

Admittedly, there will be times when you must interact on a superficial level and adjust your behavior to fit in, to go along to get along. Not everyone is always going to like you. What impresses one person may turn another away. To thine own self be true. Living in alignment with your true self enables you to cultivate transparency and unshakable authenticity.

2. PERSONAL INTEGRITY

"To give real service you must add something which cannot be bought or measured with money, and that is sincerity and integrity."

– Douglas Adams

Integrity is a most valued human quality. Your integrity is your personal code of honor which has the power to build your reputation or destroy it, establish credibility or crumble it—in one swift move. Your personal integrity, defined as being honest and having strong moral principles, communicates whether (or not) you can be trusted. Integrity, once tarnished, or broken, is hard to recover.

Think of the people whom you love, like, trust, and admire. Isn't their integrity the golden thread which elevates them to a higher standard in your eyes and in your heart? Being able to depend on a person's integrity lays a solid foundation for a relationship built on trust, both in business and in life.

Your Character Blueprint

My first career out of college was in real estate, where I specialized in new home construction. It was rewarding to help clients find their land, design their homes, monitor construction, and work to bring it all to completion. Being involved in the process from start to finish brought me great fulfillment as I watched their vision become their reality.

Their home blueprints always came in the same sequential order. The first page illustrated the new home's exterior, complete with roof lines, windows, siding, landscaping, and doors. The second page featured the floor plan's walls, and diagram specifics like the placement of cabinets, fireplaces, plumbing, appliances, and more. As we would progress to the third page, we would dig deeper into the electrical wiring to see what the interior walls would hold inside. Finally, on the last and final page, you would find the design for the foundation.

This last page was never fancy. As a matter of fact, it was rather plain, humble, and simple. The irony, however, is that the foundation was the most essential element in the entire construction process. Yet, the exterior **first impression** is how most would judge the value of the home—similar to what we do when meeting new people.

When a foundation is built following sound structural principles, with solid, high-quality materials, anything that is layered on top is more secure, durable, and resilient. However, if the foundation is poorly designed and constructed with low-quality materials, everything layered on top can easily come tumbling down and become worthless.

---

   66 *As with construction, your personal integrity is the firm foundation upon which you can build a strong character, rewarding life, and healthy relationships.* 99

Building a Rock-Solid Foundation

For this Florida resident, hurricanes were a potential threat my entire life. When Hurricane Ivan hit the Gulf Coast in 2006, it devastated Northwest Florida. This treacherous hurricane stripped thousands of homes down to their foundations. Because of the chaos and destruction, the foundations were often all that remained.

This metaphor illustrates what happens in the human experience when our lives are ravaged by the storms of life. Through change and challenge, if our personal foundations are built with quality virtues of character and integrity, we are more resilient, healthy, and ultimately more impressive.

Throughout the history of mankind, the virtues embraced by humanity have remained true, unwavering, and consistent. While many may claim that these virtues are old-fashioned, they are essential materials for building a solid and worthwhile foundation for your life that will never go out of style:

• Integrity	• Reverence
• Honesty	• Work ethic
• Diligence	• Compassion
• Charity	• Persistence
• Justice	• Wisdom
• Courage	• Humanity
• Patience	• Morality
• Kindness	• Decency
• Humility	• Goodness

ASK YOURSELF: What do each of the words above really mean to you? Which ones are your strengths? Which ones might you need to improve upon? If more than one, work on one at a time, in order of personal priority.

The Illusion of External Appearances

Our modern-day society is often so consumed with external appearances that living a virtuous life may sound boring and dull. You know the ones! They are the people who invest all their focus, energy, and effort into how they look and what they own. While having a strong character foundation may not sell newspapers, increase TV ratings, or make a person famous, it's essential for building a life that is meaningful and matters.

When you take the high road to living a virtuous life, you are fortified by knowing that regardless of what life throws your way or what storms may rage, you are grounded in goodness. In this, you secure not only your own integrity, but you secure it in the eyes others.

Knowledge Without Integrity has No Value

"The greatness of a man is not in how much wealth he acquires, but in his integrity and his ability to affect those around him positively."

– Bob Marley

Have you ever known a person who was highly intelligent, yet their lack of character destroyed your impression of them? Even though they may have been accomplished, articulate, and knowledgeable, their words became impotent and irrelevant. It was hard to take their word at face value, wasn't it?

Years ago, I worked with a person who was incredibly bright, very industrious and creative—like a fox. He used the best (and the worst) of his talents to be a top producing salesman, but . . . there was a cost. He would do anything and everything it took to make the sale. He bent the truth, manipulated the facts, and told bold-faced lies.

Month after month, his selling success was evident. However, in the eyes of the people around him, he was failing at his game. He could not be trusted and we simply learned to keep him at arm's length so that we would not get burnt in the process. He created a dual reputation for talent and dishonesty. Making money and being prosperous is a wonderful place to be, but not at the expense of your ethics, integrity, and reputation. It is simply not worth it. It nixes any chance of creating trusted working relationships.

UN-Impressives

A lack of integrity shows up in unlimited ways including:

- Cheating
- Dishonesty
- Bold-faced lies
- Stealing credit
- Deceitfulness
- Fraudulent behavior

- Underhandedness
- Corruption
- Breaking promises
- Representing one thing and being another
- Pandering to what a person wants to hear even though you do not believe it yourself
- Stretching the truth to fit your story
- Exaggerating the facts in hopes to impress
- Manipulating others for your personal gain

ASK YOURSELF: Is there any way, as mentioned above, in which you are being UNimpressive? If you answer yes, make a fresh start today by choosing to avoid that behavior.

"Integrity is doing the right thing, even when no one is watching."
—C. S. Lewis

3. $\mathcal{P}$ASSION

Desire. Enthusiasm. Purpose. Pleasure. Delight. Peace. Power. However you define passion, it is at the heart of your motivation. Feeling passion fuels your spirit and feeds your joy. It's a catalyst for action and provides you with the emotional stamina to stick with it, regardless of the obstacles. Every day should have threads of passionate pursuits within it.

What turns you on, tunes you in, and lights your fire? Think of the times in your life when you have been deeply passionate about something. Whether it is for your family, a cause, a person, an adventure, a hobby, a career, a love for music, or even going to the beach—your deep passion for it helps you tap into your unique personal power to live and love your life out loud.

❝ *When passion is lit, the fire permeates your being with the positive expectation that all is well and everything will turn out great.* ❞

To be truly satisfied that your life is well-lived, the object of your passion is something you feel you must *be, do,* or *have.* What lights your fire?

My friends Rolf and Monika have a passion for fine wines. Ron and Joy have a passion for boating. Kathy has a passion for painting. Daniel has a passion for staying fit. My mother has a passion for her flower gardens. I have a passion for speaking. As you see, it is not just about the object of your focus or desires—it is the compelling emotion, fulfillment, and intense enthusiasm that it engenders.

Passion Inspires Excellence

"Passion is the genesis of genius."
—Anthony Robbins

Are you impressed when you meet people who are filled with passion and conviction? Their energy is contagious and can make us all want "some of what they're having!" When a person exudes passion, it is evident that they love what they are doing. Their passion projects an aura of confidence and decisiveness.

Whether they are passionate about business, pets, paddle boarding, golf, or videography, when they share their passions, their fervor makes them all the more fascinating.

What are they doing that you would like to do too? How can you emulate their energy and enthusiasm? If their marriage is happy and passionate, ask "What can I learn from them?" If they share ideas and exhibit expertise, ask "How can I take what I have learned from them and be the best at what I do?"

Passion inspires us to be to be better in our own pursuits and situations. We are motivated by people that share our passion and provide living evidence that it (whatever your passion) can be done.

Passion Fosters Participation

"Passion is what you feel when you get a glimpse of your potential."
—Unknown

Do you want to gain buy-in for your ideas or win people to your way of thinking? Sharing your passion with others will not only enlighten them to your dedication and commitment, it can enable you to garner their participation, collaboration, cooperation, and endorsement.

Passion Empowers Persistence

I love the adage "Obstacles are what you see when you take your eyes off the prize." When we are deeply passionate about something, the obstacles or challenges are diminished by sheer will and desire. When you want something badly enough, it does not matter whether it is going to be easy. The passion will push you forward. When people are not passionate about their goals, everything is more of a struggle.

❝ *Passion is the fire that gets us moving and keeps us motivated regardless of what roadblocks impede the way.* ❞

I once served on the Board of Directors for a Boys and Girls Club. At the time, we were funding, planning, and building a new six-million-dollar facility. It was a major undertaking with continuous challenges. Our passion for serving children transcended the difficulties we were facing with fund-raising, permitting, groundbreaking, construction, and more. Passion kept our hope alive, and today the new center is a reality.

Alignment

"A great leader's courage to fulfill his vision comes from passion, not position."
—John Maxwell

When your passion is aligned with your purpose, you are unstoppable! It is in that zone of high octane congruence that you are turned on and "cooking with gas." Passionate people are great about discovering what lights their fire and going for it. They might be encouraged by others who share their passion, but they don't rely on others to tell them what they need to do or how they need to do it.

I once took a corporate position that was so completely disconnected from my passions, integrity, and dreams, that I became physically ill from the misalignment and developed an ulcer. Needless to say, I chose to leave. Thank God! Although this job would have given me a great income, my friend Julie McCarthy reminds me—**it is better to receive a paycheck of the heart.** When we hold true to our passions, we are authentic and living in alignment with our integrity and our passion-filled calling.

Passion gives you direction. It's an inner compass that links you to action. When you choose a career that is aligned with your passion, the work becomes irrelevant because the fulfillment outweighs everything.

As you can guess, one of my greatest passions in life is empowering others with tools to live their best lives. As a lifelong student of the motivational and self-improvement genre, my passion for speaking was ignited at the early age of twenty-two. The passion never wavered and finally, fifteen years later, I started my own company to speak professionally. It was the alignment of my passion that kept the embers burning because, believe me, the obstacles were many.

Working for a company may provide a more consistent and predictable income, however, I wouldn't enjoy the reward of motivating the masses and seeing lives changed for the better. I'm dedicated to living in alignment with my passion. It makes me remarkably happier in more ways than one.

Passion Can Ignite Your Business Success

"I have always found, in business development, that passion is the number one factor in making a good first impression. You can promise excellent service, great pricing, and flawless products, but none of that will be believed in your first meeting. . . unless you believe passionately in it yourself. Learn what makes you different than the other companies in your space—and show your passion."

—David Sears, Print Resource

I love the saying "If you're not passionate about your business, neither am I." As a national speaker, I work with companies who want to engage their customers, and it is common to see varying degrees of passion among their employees. When they lack passion, it is nearly impossible to deliver excellent customer service. Doesn't it make you less inclined to want to do business with them as well?

One interaction can make or break the experience—forever! When an employee, a team, or a company is passionate about their products and services, I am more inclined to bring them my business. Aren't you? It can't be taught to all, but people who deliver exceptional work, merely by relaying their passion through what they say and do in the workplace, are priceless.

A motivated workplace is key to getting the best out of your people. When employees are motivated and love what they do you will see higher productivity, less turnover, healthier communication, increased loyalty, and a happier environment. As the adage says, **you will never reach the peak of your potential unless you love what you are doing.** Put the right people in the right positions. Create the space for them to develop and deliver their strengths and talents. If you want to improve performance and productivity, set a vision that inspires and delights.

Passion Transcends Words

> *"Passion is energy. Feel the power that comes from focusing on what excites you."*
> —Oprah Winfrey

This speaks volumes! At the end of a transformational workshop I attended in Ft. Lauderdale, Florida, we were each asked to stand in front of the group, tell our story, and share how the lessons learned over the weekend had positively impacted our lives.

A young man from South America stood up and tried earnestly to explain, in broken English, what an extraordinary shift he had experienced. He was incredibly passionate, but we could not understand what he was trying to say. Without speaking in his native language, he struggled to express his depth of passion.

The workshop leader then asked him to speak his heart in Spanish. The passion with which he shared his feelings bordered on ecstasy. Even though we could not understand his words, we understood his heart and felt his extraordinary passion. We were all covered in goosebumps, and with tears in our eyes, gave him a standing ovation! Obviously, there's more than one way to communicate. Talk about first impressions!

Like all good things, if taken to the extreme, zeal can nullify or contradict a good intention. Is there a fine line between passion and being nuts? How can such a powerful emotion hinder or hurt us? Passion can go to the "dark side" when . . .

- It becomes addictive and elicits negative behaviors.
- Hyper-excitement begins to annoy some people.
- You get so riled up you spew spittle.
- Uncontrolled enthusiasm runs amok and becomes obnoxious.
- Force-feeding your passion onto others alienates people.
- Over-zealousness borders on obsession.
- It goes past the realm of reality—is not grounded in truth.
- It is one-sided and not mutual and awkwardness ensues.

What Happens When Passion Leaves You?

Life isn't always easy and can be wrought with challenges. Have you ever lost your passion? Years ago, I was going through a very hard time in life, striving to adapt and flourish in times of crisis and chaos. I turned to a counselor for solutions and guidance. It felt like my passion had died and I did not know how to recapture my joy to move past the pain. He said "Susan your joy has never left you. You simply have sensory blockages that have buried your joy. It is still a part of your being and remains intact." He was right. I simply needed to excavate it by being resilient, resolving the blockages, and healing. As soon as I did, the passion, and joy, burst forth.

We've all been there. What is blocking your joy? What is preventing you from living your passion? We've all been through pain and needed to be resilient to keep moving forward.

---

66 *Think about the things in life that elicit passion in you and make you happy.* 99

My cherished friend Marnie Tate recently published her first book, *A Passion for Living.* Through agony, ecstasy, trials, and tribulations, Marnie overcame and moved through life's challenges with humor, passion, and positive expectancy. She shares her story of how passion was the golden thread that wove her life together to be happy, successful, and fulfilled. Her passions are varied and she approaches them all with a profound gratitude for living and a zest for life. She inspires us all to live in that state of grace by living our passion.

Passion is Contagious

Passionate personalities are attractive and magnetic. In his book, *The Passion Centered Person*, Gary Zelesky shares, "When you follow your passion—or more accurately, when you turn it loose to run free, dragging you behind like a Great Dane owner barely holding onto the leash—you will create opportunity. People will come into your life attracted by your vision and excitement."

Do you have a dream or desire that is burning a hole in your soul? What provides warm satisfaction and brings you simple pleasure? Whether it's a hot cup of cappuccino on a cold winter morning, taking a walk with your dog, coaching your child's baseball team, making more sales, or planning your next vacation, it doesn't matter. Fan that flame. Feed its energy. It will make your life more fun and more rewarding. Your passion is contagious so learn it, love it, and live it.

4. $\mathcal{L}$ove & $\mathcal{G}$enerosity

"Everybody can be great . . . because anybody can serve. You don't have to have a college degree to serve. You don't have to make your subject and verb agree to serve. You only need a heart full of grace. A soul generated by love."

—Martin Luther King Jr.

It Starts with the Heart

Love is one of our most profound emotions and enduring qualities for living a life that matters. This feeling of warm personal attachment and deep affection is what connects, unifies, and binds our humanity. Approaching others with a loving heart enables you to be more caring, compassionate, and empathetic. What's not to love about that?

Do you genuinely love people? Or at least make an effort to *like* them? Your first impressions will be made easier and more successful when you **start with your heart.**

---

66 *Love is the universal language that transcends countries, borders, barriers, and differences.* 99

It's an expression and experience that we all understand. Yes, we know and learn love from our parents, children, mates, families, and friends. However, love extends far beyond the people whom we know and it makes us a part of something much greater than ourselves.

Love Is in the Air

Love is not only one of the greatest blessings in your personal life, but when it is extended professionally, the possibilities are endless.

Decades ago, Southwest Airlines understood that putting their heart into the center of their business would nurture loving and loyal relationships with customers for life. Because of their genuine love and caring for people, they have become one of the most profitable and successful airlines in aviation history. Their heart logo exemplifies their mission and is integrated throughout their branding. Southwest Airline's vision statement clearly communicates their intentions:

> *"We're putting our heart on our airplanes as a message to the world: We care deeply about our people and customers, and we push ourselves to always exceed their expectations of what an airline with low fares can offer.*
>
> *The Southwest spirit has always been perseverant, courageous, and caring. Our new look embodies that spirit, boldly proclaiming what sets us apart."*

Do you feel the love? Who wouldn't want to do business with a company like that? Their loving first impressions secure positive lasting impressions for loyalty, referrals, and repeat business. How can you integrate love into your vision, intentions, and actions? When you **start with your heart,** giving comes easily.

Reciprocity & the Joy of Giving

> 66 *When you graciously accept something from someone else, you are giving to them in return. By accepting their gift, you're allowing them to act upon what is in their heart.* 99

Begin asking how you may be of service and you will soon discover that the true gift is in your giving. When in doubt, give it out. Regardless of what is happening in your life, there is always someone else worse off that needs your help. Helping another person will instantly shift your energy. As you go from being self-absorbed to focusing on others, miracles seem to happen. And incredible impressions are made.

The best-selling book *The Go-Giver* has become a household name and launched a world-wide movement. Its authors Bob Burg and John David Mann encourage businesses and individuals to shift their focus from *getting* to *giving*. They share that "The principles of the "Go-Giver Way," affirm that when you come from a place of authenticity, are welcoming and open, and create value for others, you will touch lives and grow your network of meaningful relationships." The "Law of Reciprocity" is activated and everyone wins. It's important.

Doesn't it feel great when someone does something nice for you? Especially when you're not expecting it? The irony is that they are getting as much joy by giving as you are by receiving.

❝ *It's simple. You enrich your life when you enrich the lives of others.* ❞

For others to be generous requires that a person accept their generosity for the cycle to be completed. There are people who say "No, don't get me anything" or "Thank you anyway, but I will take care of it on my own," not realizing that they may be denying the other person's joy of giving.

If You Want to Get Rich in Life

When I was an undergraduate student in Florida State University's Business School, I didn't have a clue as to what I wanted to do with my life. I thought business school was a good idea because I wanted to make a lot of money to become financially secure. So, there I was, sitting in my first class on my first day of my junior year in "Real Estate Feasibility."

My professor, Dr. John Lewis, walked in and began by saying, "If you want to be rich, find out what people want and give it to them!" My thoughts flowed . . . *That's me! I want to be rich! What does everyone need? A house! What pays big commissions? Real estate. Cha-Ching, Bada-Bing!*

From his one comment, I decided to get my degree in marketing and real estate. When I graduated from college, I went straight into real estate and became a professional Realtor. For the next sixteen years, I enjoyed a multi-million-dollar producing real estate career in Tallahassee, Florida. It was made possible only by my putting my client's needs before my own and delivering dedicated service.

The epiphany came years later when I realized that when Dr. John Lewis said, "If you want to get rich in life, find out what people want and give it to them!" he was not talking about money. It had absolutely nothing to do with money. It was about service to others. So, what do people want?

    ❝ *You and I may have never met, but I already know so much of what you want: to be happy and feel valued. We want love, connection, respect, confidence, health, vitality, passion, kindness, and success.* ❞

We all want these things. When you generously provide them for others, the universe will generously return them right back to you. When you come to life from a heart of service, you may be surprised by the blessings you will receive.

Many people, however, have never discovered the power generated from a heart of service. They show up to life projecting a right of entitlement in which their needs are their first priority and they will do whatever it takes to forward their own agenda without any concern for how it impacts others. This behavior pushes people away, creates barriers for trust and communication, and leaves a bad impression.

Networking as a Place to Give, Not Get

My friend Joe Sweeney is *The New York Times* Best Selling Author of the book *Networking is a Contact Sport*. He encourages readers to reframe how they approach networking. "Begin to see networking as a place to give, rather than to get." When you come from this mindset, you will receive more than you ever expected.

If you're always taking, you will inevitably experience resistance and struggle. Without realizing it, you may be creating a firewall that is blocking you from receiving exactly the things you most desire.

Have you ever been to a networking event where someone approaches and shoves their business card at you? They don't ask who you are, what you do, why you are there, or even try to find any common ground. They are so focused on self-promotion that your needs, interests, and services are irrelevant. What a major turn-off and bad first impression!

After reading Joe's book, I started testing a few of his ideas with business contacts and acquaintances. Instead of asking for a referral or asking when I might be able to come train their team, I would simply ask, "How may I be of service? What are the problems and challenges that you're experiencing that I might have a solution for?" It is a refreshing and different way to approach relationships, and people appreciate it. Don't know what to say? Simply ask the other person questions.

Isn't it a delight when a new acquaintance asks, "How may I help you? What can I do to help you on your journey? What type of referrals do you need for your business?" They make a much more positive impression and seal the deal when they take the time to follow up and deliver on the needs you share.

Serving Your Community

Another friend, Brian Haugen, exemplifies a heart of service. He has served, volunteered, and managed special projects in his community for years. From being an Army Green Beret in service to our country, to being the Destin, Florida Chamber of Commerce President, Brian brings a passion for helping others.

He says, "You can walk into a room and know instantly who the people are that are simply out for themselves. I have a lot of folks in my business who ask me about my keys to success. And I will say we are heavily involved in Chambers of Commerce. And it always floors them. 'Really? You have had success in your Chamber?' The reason that people don't have success is because they go there always expecting others to give them something."

Networking events need to be so much more than just a place to gather business cards. He served on a Chamber actively for years before he ever gained a prospect.

---

66 *If you can establish yourself in the community as a giver, those people with whom you associate yourself will extend your branding far beyond you.* 99

His service has been the most important principle to succeed in business. The impression he leaves, to those who barely know him and to those who know him well, is that of an authentic and generous person.

How May I Be of Service?

When I first met my friend Michelle Reddington, I was very impressed. She was the co-owner and publisher of BRAVA Magazine in Wisconsin. It was evident from the beginning of our new friendship that she comes to life with a heart of service. She's genuinely living in alignment with serving women. She empowers women through her popular magazine—providing style, substance, and education to help each woman become the best person she can be. Michelle is authentic, brilliant, charming, and engaging.

You know who the men and women are in your life that represent these fine qualities. Take a minute to think about and appreciate them. They make an instant and positive impression that makes you say, "Yes! I like that person. I would like to get to know them better!" Are you projecting this gracious heart of service?

Messengers of Hope

"I slept and I dreamed that life is all joy. I woke and I saw that life is all service. I served and I saw that service is joy."

—Kahlil Gibran

When I attended my first National Speakers Association convention in 2001, I was struck by the outrageously passionate, generous, and friendly people whom I met there. Their genuine positivity and enthusiasm made me feel like I had come home to the 'mother ship' for all that is good in this world. I intuitively knew I had found my people!

Imagine putting 2,000 motivational speakers and world-changers under one roof at the same time—it felt as if the entire building was levitating. I soon learned that the high vibration for positive energy was being fueled by something greater than ourselves—the Spirit of Cavett.

Seeing that I was a first- timer, complete strangers would approach me with a warm welcome and an earnest offer to help me succeed.

No question was off limits and everyone would share their advice and guidance with unconditional generosity. I had never attended such an event before or since.

You see, NSA was founded in 1973 by a man named Cavett Robert. His vision for our organization was to create a place where professional speakers could come together to collaborate, exchange ideas, share best practices, refine their craft, encourage excellence, and learn from one another.

Mr. Robert once said, "a desire to help others is our most noble attribute; it gives immortal momentum to life and is our only certain path to heaven." He lived by example and encouraged speakers to create a bigger pie so that everyone could have a bigger slice. Now, over forty-four years later, our association continues to embody his spirit and servant's heart philosophy.

A few years ago, our brilliant member Simon T. Bailey (simontbailey.com) delivered an impactful and profound presentation on the main stage for an annual convention. He cited startling statistics for the number of meetings, conferences, summits, and events being held every year world-wide. He not only reaffirmed that our business is big enough for everyone to enjoy success, but that in our negative world today, messengers of hope are needed now more than ever.

Speakers, coaches, consultants, though-leaders, experts, and authors who dedicate their professional lives for the love of humanity and the betterment of society are making a positive difference in the lives of millions. These messengers of hope make our entire world a better place through their love and generosity.

"A candle loses nothing by lighting another candle."
—James Keller

5. HEALTHY SELF-ESTEEM

"You're always with yourself, so you might as well enjoy the company."
—Diane Von Furstenberg

There will never be another you! It's true. Did you notice that this chapter is entitled "Healthy Self-Esteem" not "High Self-Esteem?" There is a distinct difference that is worth noticing.

Being healthy, balanced, and positive is key to making a positive first impression. A **high self-esteem**, however, can quickly deteriorate into egotism, arrogance, and an over-confidence that can backfire and turn people off.

Your **healthy self-esteem** is one of the most significant and powerful drivers in your life. It drives your perceptions, attitudes, opinions, relationships, communications, and your decisions.

---

66 *How you think and feel about yourself sets the tone for how other people feel about you too. When you feel great about you, personal qualities radiate that make you more attractive and compelling to others.* 99

While developing a healthy self-esteem is a lifetime learning process, you can take daily steps to enjoy a confident sense of well-being.

When you have a healthy self-esteem, qualities such as likeability, confidence, trustworthiness, compassion, sense of humor, empathy, and optimism all serve to make you more interesting and successful. But unfortunately, we sometimes get in our own way . . .

Self-Talk & Your Inner Critic

"Low self-esteem is like driving through life with your hand-brake on."
—Maxwell Maltz

I can . . . I can't. How do you speak to yourself? Do you ever feel as though you have an angel on one shoulder and a devil on the other? And they continually argue over your self-worth, competence, and personal value? Which one usually wins the debate?

Your inner critic is that voice in your head that second-guesses your choices, doubts your abilities, judges your appearance, criticizes you at every turn, and tries to convince you that you are never good enough.

That voice is mean, unforgiving, punishing, and downright hurtful. When you allow it to run roughshod over your happiness and emotional well-being, it can wreak havoc on your peace of mind and leave you feeling anxious, fearful, and depleted.

This demoralizing self-talk leads to a self-destructive mindset, making everything in life more difficult. Not only that, how you feel about yourself oozes out of your pores and makes a bad impression on others.

We all can give in to our inner critic. I don't know about you, but I would never allow anyone to speak to me the way I speak to myself! I wouldn't be their friend! If you wouldn't want to hang out with someone who was constantly bashing you with a barrage of belittling insults, why would you allow them to live in your head?

Well, I have great news! You can take your power back and silence the criticism and lies NOW! How?

- Notice what your inner critic is saying, and issue a **cease and desist!** Regain control. Resist, and refuse to listen.
- Disrupt your thinking by saying, "Cancel! Cancel!" thereby interrupting the negative thought patterns. This not only has a psychological effect, but a physiological one, as well.

- Replace your negative mind chatter with positive affirmations and positive thinking.
- Take deliberate steps to retrain your brain and turn your inner critic into an enthusiastic, devoted fan.
- Become your own best friend—smile and say "I love you" to yourself occasionally.

❝ Focusing your energy on the things you don't like about yourself is self-sabotage and defeating. When you re-direct all that energy into a more positive direction, you will feel the shift instantly to improve your self-esteem and attitude. ❞

Brendon Burchard once wrote, "A life filled with silly social drama and gossip indicates that a person is disconnected from purpose and lacking meaningful goals. People on a path of purpose don't have time for drama." Isn't that the truth? The people we know who have healthy self-esteem don't waste their positive energy feeding the negativity of tearing down others, or themselves.

Self-respect

"Our self-respect tracks our choices. Every time we act in harmony with our authentic self and our heart, we earn our respect. It is that simple. Every choice matters."
—Dan Coppersmith

It is hard to earn the respect of others when you do not respect yourself. Others may find it difficult to enjoy your company if you do not enjoy your own.

Popularity does not equal respect. It is not only kids who will do what they think they must to fit in and be popular—adults do it too. Wouldn't you rather have the respect of your friends and colleagues than succumb to pressure to do and say things that are out of character in order to feel accepted? You can overcome this habit simply by learning to say "no."

Healthy self-esteem rests upon a strong foundation of core values and an inclination to act and speak in alignment with those values. Living in integrity with one's principles that are held in high regard engenders respect—both from others and self.

Imposter Syndrome

"To establish true self-esteem, we must concentrate on our successes and forget about the failures and the negatives in our lives."

—Denis Waitley

It is human nature for self-doubt to occasionally creep in and take up residence. It happens to even the most successful people among us. In the 1970's, social psychologists Dr. Pauline R. Clance and Suzanne A. Imes recognized that many high-achieving individuals were unable to internalize their accomplishments despite evidence to the contrary. Their observations led them to name this unique phenomenon "The Imposter Syndrome."

We all go through times of self-doubt, times when we may question our abilities and hope we can live up to the expectations of others.

Have you ever. . .

- Experienced fear that others might find out that you are not as smart, confident, or capable as you project yourself to be?
- Had feelings of phoniness?
- Felt like a fraud?
- Given credit for your success over to dumb luck or great timing?

What we often forget is that most everyone else has dealt with the same struggles and uncertainties. You get to pick your response when this doubt creeps in. Will you allow it to undermine your confidence, or instead, choose to look at it objectively?

With an objective eye, take an inventory of your successes and enlist the honest feedback of a trusted and respected mentor or peer. Chances are they see you in a better light than you see yourself! Remind yourself of the many victories you've achieved and build healthier self-esteem and perceptions on those.

Love, Accept, and Believe in Yourself

"You have been criticizing yourself for years, and it hasn't worked.
Try approving of yourself and see what happens."

—Louise L. Hay

Be mindful to love and appreciate yourself and become your own champion. This healthy and loving relationship will be felt when people meet you. Bestselling author Louise Hay shares that a lack of self-acceptance is the cause of most of our suffering. You will be stuck with you for the rest of your life so learn to be your own best friend. Take a moment, look at yourself in the mirror, and say, "I love you." It feels awkward at first. Do it anyway. Begin a great friendship with YOU!

UN-Impressives

I once heard the phrase, "What you are speaks so loudly, I can't hear what you're saying." When a person has unhealthy self-esteem, it shows in the way they walk, talk, and behave. Even without meaning for it to, their low self-esteem is evident when they:

- Whine and complain.
- Bully others to exert power and control.
- Find humor at the expense of others.
- Criticize, condemn, and judge others.

- Reject compliments.
- Justify and defend their shortcomings.
- Make excuses and blame others for their problems.
- Overcompensate for their self-doubt by bragging or over sharing—or in contrast, always saying they're sorry.
- Emotionally withdraw.
- Underperform.
- Focus on the negatives.
- Gossip and disparage others to feel better about themselves.

10 Ways to Build a Healthy Self-Esteem

1. Take care of yourself—mind, body, and spirit.
2. Use positive self-talk and affirmations.
3. Learn something new.
4. Surround yourself with positive people who bring out your best.
5. Be your own best friend.
6. Focus on what you want more of.
7. Learn from your mistakes and do things better next time.
8. Always do your best and the rest will take care of itself.
9. Set goals that give you purpose and direction.
10. Do something kind and considerate for others.

"Tell me how a person judges his or her self-esteem, and I will tell you how that person operates at work, in love, in sex, in parenting, in every important aspect of existence—and how high he or she is likely to rise. The reputation you have with yourself—your self-esteem—is the single most important factor for a fulfilling life."
—Nathaniel Branden

6. Dignity & Grace

"The ideal man bears the accidents of life with dignity and grace,
making the best of circumstances."

—Aristotle

A book about first impressions would not be complete without discussing dignity and grace. Do you see them as a state of emotional and spiritual being or a physical projection of courage and class? Perhaps they describe both. The radiance of dignity and grace creates a profound elegance which exists whether anyone is watching or not.

Dignity

"Dignity does not consist in possessing honors, but in deserving them."

—Aristotle

Dignity brings a quiet smile as I think of my own mother. I'm sure you have someone that immediately comes to mind as well. It is that quiet strength which reflects one's deep honor and self-respect. Likened to "still waters run deep," a dignified person is able to call upon their wisdom and experience to discern a situation and expertly navigate it with grace. Grounded by healthy self-esteem and personal self-worth, this admirable character quality can inspire awe and reverence.

Dignity is an inherent value and human virtue which represents the best of mankind. When I asked Daniel what dignity meant to him, he shared, "Dignity is a gracious pride without narcissistic projection. It portrays a calm confidence and awareness regardless of the environment or circumstances."

Indeed. Think of the people whom you have known who have endured unspeakable hardship, heartbreaking loss, or great adversity. Perhaps you are one of them. In spite of the circumstance, a person who abides in dignity and grace will use the lessons learned as ballast for their ship as they sail through stormy waters—taking the wisdom gained from life and using it to anchor their confidence.

When Pride is on the Good Side

"There are two kinds of pride, both good and bad. 'Good pride' represents our dignity and self-respect. 'Bad pride' is the deadly sin of superiority that reeks of conceit and arrogance."

—John C. Maxwell

Arrogant pride has given the word "pride" a bad rap. When it is all about ego, conceit, and superiority, of course pride will be off-putting and make a bad impression. It can destroy trust and shatter teams. One who behaves that way probably doesn't feel proud when alone—there's something lacking.

One of my friends was a Realtor in a luxurious residential lakefront development in the South. The high-priced properties resulted in high-dollar commissions, creating lucrative opportunities for the agents. They had one particular agent who was the consistent top producer month after month. Unfortunately, with his remarkable success came great ego and pride. He became such an arrogant prima donna that he alienated the entire office and negatively affected morale, leaving the broker no choice but to ask for his resignation. Yes, pride can go to the dark side.

However, *gracious* pride is a powerful motivator and an exceptional quality. It drives a person to strive for excellence, keep promises, not give up, be more resilient, maintain optimism, and hold their head high while enduring challenge and change. *Gracious* pride is a wonderful quality when it is used for good; it brings out the best in you and encourages the best in others.

66 *Dignity is pride's barometer.* 99

Grace

Grace is a demeanor which comes naturally to some but more difficult for others. The good news is that with awareness and practice, even the most awkward people can learn how to be both fluid and purposeful in their bearing. A wonderful place to start is to seek role models who exemplify this way of being and try their style on for size.

I remember one such role model very well. Grace Kelly was a beautiful American actress who fell in love with and married the Prince of Monaco in the 1950s. As a young child, I remember admiring her real-life fairy tale. Her name matched her countenance as she became an international role model of grace and dignity for the entire world to see. Her simple elegance and refinement defined her aura and her era. For you men, flash back to Cary Grant. He exemplified masculine grace.

Grace is also an attitude of generosity toward our fellow humans. We are not easily offended and do not look to judge and label others. With a spirit of graciousness we are amiable, benevolent, and charitable.

UN-Impressives

A loss of dignity and grace occurs when a person:

- Speaks ill of others.
- Behaves badly, irrationally, or inappropriately.
- Makes decisions which lack integrity, discretion, or self-respect.
- Boasts, brags, and broadcasts about how great they are.
- Compromises their virtue and their values, leading to shame and disgrace.
- Acts without considering the impact it has on others.
- Lowers their standards to a point of humiliation or flagrant disregard.
- Injures, cajoles, or interrupts others.

- Loses self-control.
- Is impaired by drugs, alcohol, anger, or ego.

How Do You Restore Dignity Once It Has Been Lost?

"Don't judge me by my past, I don't live there anymore."
—Unknown

People sometimes make mistakes, do stupid things, and lose their dignity in the process. Whether from intentional actions, carelessness, or outright arrogance, a loss of dignity teaches people how to perceive you—and that perception may be that you are goofy, foolish, or unwise.

Can a tarnished, undignified reputation be re-polished? Can trust be re-earned? Can you turn a poor first impression into a better one? Once lost, can dignity be restored? Perhaps. The following steps offer a start:

- Be honest with yourself through self-assessment and reflection.
- Accept complete responsibility for your actions.
- Address the problem and take the action necessary to solve and eliminate it.
- Apologize and make amends to the people you may have disappointed, hurt, or offended.
- Forgive yourself for your transgression.
- Change directions. No matter how far you go down the wrong path, always turn back.
- Focus on the qualities that you love about yourself.
- The proof is in the pudding. Prove your dignity, integrity, grace, trustworthiness, dependability and more through your thoughts, words, deeds, and actions.
- Dignity is a lot easier to get back if you had it in the first place!

10 Ways to Exude Dignity & Grace

1. Stay humble.
2. Live in integrity.
3. Maintain calm composure.
4. Exercise tact and discretion.
5. Think before you speak.
6. Listen thoughtfully, respond appropriately.
7. Be in touch with your spirituality and how you view the world.
8. Treat others with respect and understanding.
9. Stand for justice, freedom, and honor.
10. Don't participate in gossip and people bashing.

Your level of dignity impacts everything in your life. It affects the quality of your internal world for how you see, feel, and think about yourself. It impacts the quality of your external world in your relationships, communications, and interactions. It impacts how you are perceived and received when making a first impression. Living as a role model in dignity encourages others to do the same.

"We need to give each other the space to grow, to be ourselves, to exercise our diversity. We need to give each other space so that we may both give and receive such beautiful things as ideas, openness, dignity, joy, healing, and inclusion."

—Max de Pree

7. Charisma & Charm

"Charming people have the ability to make us feel as though we've known them forever—even if we've only just met them thirty minutes ago. They bring an easy sense of familiarity and intimacy that we don't often feel with other people especially with people we've only just met . . . but it feels so natural that we never think about it."

—DrNerdLove.com

Charisma and charm are endearing qualities which go hand in hand to make others feel "lighter, happier, and a little in love" when they are around you. People with this gift exude a delightful demeanor—an attractive likability that enwraps you in their warmth. When they are authentically engaged, their positive impressions create memorable moments and leave a lasting impact.

Physical beauty becomes irrelevant because their exuberance and engagement bring out the beauty in you. They seem to possess a heightened sensitivity to the feelings of others—delivering gentle manners, gracious compliments, and sincere interest.

Aren't you naturally drawn to those people who are genuinely glad to meet you and eager to hear your point of view? It is not simply in the words they speak—they show their interest both verbally and non-verbally. They emanate an essence of caring, love, and compassion towards the people they know, and generously extend their aura to the new people they encounter.

Their engaging manner is grounded in consideration as they seek to get along well with others. People who exhibit charisma and charm are also said to be alluring, bewitching, captivating, magnetic, fascinating, enchanting, and seductive.

What is their secret? How do they do it? Where did they learn how to be so pleasant and engaging? If charisma and charm are such valuable behaviors, why don't more people put into them practice for improving outcomes?

Nature or Nurture?

There are differing opinions as to whether charisma and charm are innate qualities which we are born with or learned personality styles. I believe it is a combination of both. Young children demonstrate a propensity for this enthusiasm. However, smart adults realize that they can get further in life when they develop these special traits.

My Grandma Lorene Cullison exemplified gracious hospitality and charm. As one of my most significant role models, she demonstrated to me at an early age that you will attract more bees with honey than vinegar and life is lovelier when you make others feel valued. She had an intuitive sense of harmony and her first instinct was to nurture and put others at ease. These lessons have undoubtedly helped me succeed in life and love—and in networking while forging new relationships and business. It can do the same for you.

18 Qualities of Charisma and Charm

Charisma (presence, poise, magnetism) and charm (enchantment, attraction, fascination) are behaviors which can be learned and practiced. Whether you adopt one new quality or ten, you can begin to embody and apply these qualities to positively grow the presence of character, your reputation, influence, and effect. People who exhibit these favorable characteristics tend to be:

1. Patient.
2. Respectful and fair.
3. Open-minded for new adventures.
4. Sincerely interested in others.
5. Engaging conversationalists.
6. Creative and curious.
7. Easily humored with an infectious laugh.
8. Joyful and happy in most situations.
9. Complimentary and look for positives.

10. Knowledgeable about how to use physical touch appropriately.
11. Able to admit their mistakes or make an apology.
12. Able to grow from failure and find gifts in the pain.
13. Action-oriented and self-motivated.
14. Kind and considerate without expecting anything in return.
15. Able to refrain from judging and condemning others.
16. Willing to show vulnerability.
17. Able to remember names and small details.
18. Adaptable to change, people, and situations.

Prince Charming

The romantic Prince Charming archetype from fairy tales and folklore portrays a sense of heroism, good looks, good manners, and quiet courage. Fairness and justice for all! Not only can he make others swoon, but Prince Charming inspires courage, admiration, leadership, and confidence.

These people do exist and are a pleasure to know. Their keen communication skills are attentive to what you want, what you are thinking, saying, or not saying. They want to hear how you are and what you've been up to.

In his article, "The Charm of You," for *Oprah Magazine*, Peter Smith, writes, "At its best, highest form, charm is a show of generosity and moral goodness, an extension of the self toward others that permits them to shine. By helping others relax and unfold, charm allows you to shine too."

When Charisma & Charm Go to the Dark Side

"If you go around charming the socks off of people there are going to be a lot of cold feet!"
—Unknown

Is it possible to be too charming? Absolutely! When it is insincere and overzealous, it can badly backfire. Misused and abused by men or women, charm can destroy trust, ruin a reputation, be annoying, alienate others, and make a person generally unlikable. These offenders behave in a charming way only when they want something like money, sex, promotion, position, or personal gain. Crafty and conniving charmers, use their wiles for . . .

- Gaining an upper hand or an unfair advantage.
- Manipulating people, situations, and details in their favor.
- Hiding their agenda for a secondary gain.
- Using other people without concern, bother, or gratitude.
- Hiding their dishonest motives and intentions.
- Making up for a lack of integrity, confidence, and self-esteem.

The key is to keep charisma and charm positive and underpinned with sincere and good intentions. Psychology Today defines charisma as "the ability to attract, charm, and influence the people around you." While it may seem to be a mysterious, ineffable quality—charisma is enhanced and enriched by a person's attitude and confidence, their aims and optimism, expressive body language, and natural effervescence.

---

66 Your charisma and charm can make your moments more memorable for amazing first impressions. 99

---

8. CONFIDENCE & COMMAND

"With confidence, you can reach truly amazing heights; without confidence, even the simplest accomplishments are beyond your grasp."

—Jim Loehr

What do confidence and command look like when you see them? Moving one step past a healthy self-esteem, they project an air of authority, respect, and deliberate intention. Confidence is silent, cool, self-assurance. Developing a commanding presence is essential for leadership and a powerful impact.

There can be a fine line between being confident and cocky. True confidence is not something that can always be determined by a first impression. It may take a few interactions to detect whether a person is full of false bravado or if they are the "real McCoy."

Confidence and command earn this authority by accomplishing uncommon things which elevate one's expertise. "The best captains are not made on calm seas" is a relevant statement which recognizes that when a person has been in the trenches they have the experience to back up their command. Their prowess inspires faith in their abilities and affirms they can indeed "put their money where their mouth is." Their confidence gives those they lead the assurance that their words and their actions are reliable.

In our natural world, it is the strongest of the species that claim their space, seek out new territories, explore their surroundings, and learn how to survive and thrive. It is those same qualities that enable us to apply confidence and command to transcend the mediocre and achieve outstanding results.

Confidence in Communications

My friend Suzanne Gaddis, Ph.D. is an international speaker and the CEO of www.CommunicationsDoctor.com. Years ago, she worked as a communications trainer and consultant for an organization whose director had recently resigned. The assistant director was automatically moved into the open position. However, there was a problem. The new director had enormous talent and a rich education, BUT, she had no confidence. Despite her skills, her team saw her as weak. She did not exert the confidence and command needed to unify and lead her people. People who show weakness appear vulnerable and less decisive. Confidence, or lack thereof, significantly changes the dynamics of communication and the ability to lead.

Once the new director received communications coaching and became more confident in herself and her new position, she began to earn the trust and respect of her teams. As she began to exude confidence and command, her people took her more seriously in her new role, which enabled her to get the job done.

We tend to listen to the people who believe in their own words as opposed to those who don't. When we feel their conviction, they earn our buy-in. Whereas, we lose confidence in those who speak from weakness or with little conviction. Even something as simple as ending a sentence with the tone of a question mark rather than a period can diminish a person's authority and credibility.

Low Self-Confidence

"Low self-confidence isn't a life sentence. Self-confidence can be learned, practiced, and mastered—just like any other skill. Once you master it, everything in your life will change for the better."

—Barrie Davenport

When you feel low self-confidence, it is usually the result of the negative thoughts your inner critic whispers in the darkness of your mind. When your inner critic undermines your confidence, inner conflict, anxiety, and agitation take over. It tells you that you are not good enough, smart enough, handsome enough, worthy enough, or basically just plain NOT enough. It takes a toll on your self-confidence, doesn't it?

As these thoughts repeatedly turn over, whatever you choose to tell yourself becomes a self-fulfilling prophecy. If your self-talk leans toward the negative, the continual bashing will become debilitating.

What to do? Notice when negativity spins in your head and disrupt it immediately before it has a chance to take hold and stick. Even the smartest and most successful of people will experience lower self-confidence occasionally, but the difference is that they deliberately shift out of it and refuse to stay there.

Qualities of Self-Confident People. They . . .

- Inspire confidence in others; they would much rather build people up than tear them down.
- Are proud of their accomplishments, but can remain humble without bragging.
- Face their fears head-on and are willing to take risks.
- Know that obstacles are only temporary setbacks.
- Tend to be optimistic thinkers and focus on the positives.
- Respect and believe in themselves.
- Don't make their self-esteem, self-image, happiness, or self-confidence dependent on another person's approval, validation, or acceptance.
- Take the initiative to move forward in the direction of their dreams.
- Act calmly and rationally when thrown curve balls.
- Are mindful about spending their time, energy, and interests on things that truly matter.

Leveraging Learning Curves

Building confidence is an ongoing process and something that can be accomplished over time. Just because you may not feel confident about doing something now does not mean you will not master it later with ease. As you jump new hurdles, you gain greater confidence.

Confidence can be achieved like any other practiced skill.

The first time Susanne delivered a public presentation her knees knocked together. She fought back a gag reflex as she was trying to choke down her fear. She had never done it before and speaking was far beyond her comfort zone. She is now a highly sought after speaker who loves every moment on stage and continues to blossom in her craft.

---

66 You will build confidence by continuing to put yourself into new and innovative situations where you can learn new skills, grow your education, test your strengths, and improve your abilities. 99

Just because you don't know how to do something now does not mean you can't learn how to do it later. If you are lacking confidence in something, just keep trying and don't give up.

Yes, learning curves can be painful, exhausting, trying, scary, and intimidating. How did you learn to ride a bike? One pedal, one balance, one turn, and one step at a time.

Confidence is not a goal or a final ending point where you arrive and then stop once you reach it. Rather, it is the satisfaction and reward you achieve by stretching to, and beyond, the best of your abilities.

14 Ways to Project Confidence and Command

Building self-confidence is like building a muscle. Your confidence grows in response to your intensity of usage and the level of performance you require from it. If you don't use it, you may lose it. Stretch, flex, live, and build!

1. Think and act positively by focusing on the positives in yourself, other people, and situations.
2. Steer clear of negativity and set boundaries so that when people bring it on, you can engage your force-field to deflect their distracting energy.
3. Use your body language and posture to project confidence. Shift your physiology into a more powerful pose or position and your mindset will follow.
4. Make and maintain eye contact.
5. Speak slowly, articulately, clearly, and deliberately.
6. Dress confidently in clothes that make you feel great about yourself. When you look better you feel better.
7. Embrace change and practice flexibility. It will make you more agile in adapting to new people and situations.
8. Be prepared for all things that matter.
9. Set goals and create a clear sense of purpose and direction.
10. Get outside your comfort zone. Stretch beyond your norm and try new things.
11. Walk the talk and project confidence. If at first you don't feel confident, fake it until you make it.
12. Identify confident people whom you admire and respect and notice what they do differently to project such confidence. Learn by observing role models.
13. Practice positive and affirming self-talk.
14. Nurture a balanced perspective and don't "sweat the small stuff."

"It all boils down to how you present yourself. Do you "look the part?" Do you carry yourself with confidence? Do you ACT the part? Do you speak the part? If you can, then you are developing Command Presence, which will make your job a LOT easier."

—Chief Ronald Richards
Forest City Fire Department, Forest City, PA

8 WAYS TO **MASTER**
The Art of BEING

1. *Authenticity.* Be honest. Be genuine. Get raw and be real. Own your truth and let your natural personality shine through.

2. *Personal Integrity.* Integrity is a most worthy human value. Reinforce it. It is a solid foundation, built on honesty, morality, virtue, decency, and trustworthiness.

3. *Passion.* Passion is at the heart of your motivation. Let it fuel your spirit and feed your joy. It is your catalyst for courageous pursuits—and it will provide you the stamina to stick with it.

4. *Love & Generosity.* You enrich your life when you enrich the lives of others. The gift is in the giving—in your family, community, business, and network.

5. *Healthy Self-Esteem.* Being healthy, balanced, and positive is key to making a positive first impression. How you feel about yourself sets the tone for how other people feel about you too.

6. *Dignity & Grace.* Dignity is a quiet strength which reflects deep honor and self-respect. It is a gracious pride without narcissistic projection which portrays a calm awareness and generosity of spirit regardless of circumstances.

7. *Charisma & Charm.* These endearing qualities make others feel "lighter, happier, and a little in love" when they are around you. People with this gift exude a delightful demeanor—an attractive likability that enfolds you in their warmth.

8. *Confidence & Command.* Confidence is silent, humble self-assurance. Moving one step past a healthy self-esteem, confidence projects an air of authority, trust, and respect—a commanding, respected presence.

2

The *Art* of

PREPARATION

8 WAYS TO PLAN WITH
PURPOSE & INTENTION
FOR POSITIVE IMPACT

The *Art* of **PREPARATION**

If you want to be successful, how you show up to life matters. What steps can you take to **prepare** before meeting others to ensure that when you do show up, you are bringing your very best to the table? Wouldn't you like to arrive to any event or situation with a sense of confidence and ease that things are as they need to be? Get ready to take on the world from a position of personal power, strength, and intention!

Your first impressions will often occur within a limited window of opportunity—and if you blow it—the opportunity may be lost forever. Benjamin Franklin is credited with saying, "By failing to prepare, you are preparing to fail." Why leave your success up to dumb luck or accident when you can take a stand, make a plan, and be proactive in your pursuits and possibilities?

Prime yourself for success and demonstrate to others that you are diligent, reliable, and trustworthy. Care enough to take deliberate steps and get ready through thoughtful discipline, research, organization, and effort. It will impress others and give you the winner's edge to live and give your best. Begin by asking yourself if you are currently showing up to your life, your business, and your relationships in a way that is cultivating an extraordinary life.

1. *Mastering Your Mindset*
2. *Emotional Intelligence*
3. *Prepare for Success*
4. *Your Personal Brand*
5. *Dress to Impress*
6. *Healthy Habits & Hygiene*
7. *Punctuality Plus*
8. *Education, Expertise & Experience*

1. MASTERING YOUR MINDSET

"I think anything is possible if you have the mindset and the will and desire to do it and put the time in."

—Roger Clemens

Your mindset serves as the operating system for your entire life's experience. To say your mindset is critical to your success is a gross understatement—it is the underpinning! It brings together your attitude, perceptions, experience, interpretations, opinions, beliefs, values, and understanding to determine how you think, act, walk, talk, behave, and engage.

---

66 *Your internal thoughts determine your outer world.* 99

One would think that if people truly wanted to live incredible lives, they would do everything in their power to create a mindset which helped them get there. Right?

Unfortunately, that is often not the case. More people continue to be and do exactly the things in life that prevent them from getting what they want or from waking up excited about their day.

Since your mindset can make you or break you, how is it going? As Dr. Phil McGraw would ask, "How's that working for you?" Is it representing you well or does it need a complete overhaul? Ask a trusted friend or colleague to answer that question for you if you feel a bit uncertain. Discuss how you might improve it.

The Law of Cause and Effect

The Law of Cause and Effect is as active in your life as the Law of Gravity. It teaches us that for every action there is a reaction. **If you**

do nothing, you'll have nothing. If you do something spectacular, you will have something spectacular. Mindsets work the same way. Some call it Karma; I prefer to think of it as **Be. Do. Have.**

ASK YOURSELF: Do you yearn for loving, loyal relationships? Would you like to feel a calm confidence when you walk into a room full of strangers, knowing that you can start a new conversation with anyone? Would you like to be able to engage easily with others? Do you want to be happy?

We all want these things, don't we? But we often forget that the reason we do not have them is because we are not being and doing what it takes to have them. As a matter of fact, many people go through life complaining, whining, and obsessing so much about what they don't have that they are doing exactly what it takes to block it.

Learn to leverage the Law of Cause and Effect to your advantage in positive ways! If you want to have the confidence, engagement, positive feedback, connection, and reward in your relationships, start being and doing what it takes to make it happen. Create and nurture a mindset that works for you rather than against you. Strive to be . . .

- Optimistic rather than pessimistic.
- Forgiving rather than a grudge holder.
- A possibility thinker rather than an impossibility thinker.
- Hopeful rather than resigned and doubtful.
- Healthy rather than dis-eased—emotionally, physically, and spiritually.
- Happy rather than downhearted or miserable.
- Pleased and accepting rather than angry.
- Proactive rather than passive or a procrastinator.
- Brave rather than reluctant or afraid.
- Active rather than lethargic.
- Determined rather than wavering or lazy.
- Positive rather than negative.

There are more qualifiers that fall under "Mindset" than you could ever imagine.

Fill in the blanks for yourself:

I want to be _____ rather than _____.

What you think about, you bring about. Your thoughts, beliefs, and interpretations initiate and largely determine how you experience your reality. They filter how you see everything in your world—and here is the clincher—**_you_ get to choose!** This mindset buffet is filled with possibilities that can feed your heart, mind, and soul if you will simply serve yourself and go for it! Choose wisely, my friends, choose wisely.

When you make a deliberate effort to keep your thoughts positive, and authentically feel that way, more positive outcomes are inevitable.

Use The Power of Positivity to Strive, Thrive & Soar

> *"Once you replace negative thoughts with positive ones, you'll start having positive results."*
>
> —Willie Nelson

You wear your attitude. It is highly visible to every person you meet, and in the way you act, live, and love. Your attitude is hard to conceal; it's evident before you ever say hello. It's the outward expression of your internal perceptions, self-esteem, and current thoughts. Mindset and attitude are so tightly intertwined they almost mean the same thing!

Your attitude is the one thing in this world you have complete control over. You have full command. As empowering as that truth can be, there are some days we let down and give in to a bad attitude. Nevertheless, when you wake each day, it is your choice if you are going to use your attitude to your advantage or let it work against you.

The motivational master and world-changer Zig Ziglar, taught "Your attitude determines your altitude" and "How you get up in the morning determines how you get up in life."

If you want to fly high and go amazing places, your attitude is crucial. Put yourself in the driver seat by designing the best attitude possible to help you get where you need and want to go.

Throughout my life, I have been blessed with a positive and resilient attitude. I grew up with an alcoholic father and he tested my disposition in more ways than you might imagine. Knowing I couldn't depend on him for positive reinforcement, I clung to my positive attitude like a life preserver to give me the strength for positivity and self-reliance. Otherwise, I would have sunk into the depths of low self-esteem and worthlessness. A positive attitude was my saving grace and it became a habit by choice, day-in and day-out.

---

66 At times, maintaining a positive attitude and outlook takes great risk, courage, toughness, and flexibility. It is not easy to stay positive in a cynical and negative world. 99

Remain vigilant and try diligently not to succumb to the soul-sucking, mind-numbing, ill-mannered attitudes that seem so prevalent in the world today.

I have known many people who have been incredibly successful in life. It was not necessarily because they had immense talent, brilliance, an expensive education, or exemplary skills. It was because they had an extraordinary attitude to take on life with love, passion, conviction, consistency, and hard work. What they all had in common was getting their minds right and becoming positive thinkers—which activated their potential to achieve remarkable things and build strong relationships.

Why a Positive Attitude is One of the BEST GIFTS

Henry Ford said, "Think you can or think you can't; either way you'll be right." Clearly, developing a positive attitude is one of the most transformational things you can do to shift your mindset, improve your disposition, manifest good things, and attract quality people into your life. The benefits you will enjoy have a multiplier effect which can exponentially impact your personal well-being. A positive attitude will . . .

- Make you more fun to be around!
- Bring more happiness and joy into your life.
- Help you be more inspiring and motivating to others.
- Empower you to proactively adapt to change.
- Enable you to embrace new opportunities with a positive expectancy.
- Stimulate creative thinking and constructive problem-solving.
- Elevate your energy and invigorate your tasks.
- Edge out cynicism and pessimism.
- Build your courage, confidence, and self-esteem.

A positive attitude feels a heck of a lot better than a negative one! Years from now you will be able to celebrate a life well lived with no regret. Did I just describe you? If not, and if you *choose* to make some needed changes, the list below will begin your attitude upgrade journey.

16 Ways to Develop a Positive Attitude

The attitude upgrade starts here . . .

1. Believe in your power to make happiness a choice—do so every day, until it becomes a lifelong habit.
2. Surround yourself with positive people who ignite your energy and spirit.
3. Share your happiness with others.

4. When adversity hits, reframe the challenge and find lessons learned; acknowledge gifts that have come from the pain.
5. Stretch your imagination to a new dimension, be hopeful and flexible, and believe in new possibilities.
6. Smile generously at others and their smiles will be returned right back to you.
7. Don't participate or allow yourself to be dragged into other people's dramas, complaints, or gossip.
8. Strive to see the best in others, situations, and experiences.
9. Be a source of positive energy and inspiration for others.
10. Celebrate the success of others.
11. Love, accept, and believe in yourself.
12. Wake up early, do your best, practice self-care, and finish strong.
13. Become a lifelong learner. Read books, watch videos, and listen to audio to learn new ways to live your best life now.
14. Take a moral inventory of ways you may be self-sabotaging and then take proactive steps to change.
15. Be mindful of the words in your mind and in your mouth. Choose to use an affirming and positive vocabulary. Your actions will follow suit.
16. Exercise and get moving to pump up your endorphins and elevate your mood. Take an adult recess.

You are the only one who can choose your attitude for you. Remember that your attitude towards life determines life's attitude toward you. At any moment you can choose to change everything for the better.

"With everything that has happened to you, you can either feel sorry for yourself or treat what has happened as a gift. Everything is either an opportunity to grow or an obstacle to keep you from growing. You get to choose."
—Dr. Wayne W Dyer

2. $\mathcal{E}$MOTIONAL $\mathcal{J}$NTELLIGENCE

"Emotional intelligence emerges as a much stronger predictor of who will be most successful, because it is how we handle ourselves in our relationships that determines how well we do once we are in a given job."

—Daniel Goleman

The Art of First Impressions for Positive Impact is based on the premise that when you become self-aware and learn how to shine bright as your best self, you can transform your relationships in life and in business. Absolutely everything associated with your success is relationship based and emotionally connected.

Developing your emotional intelligence will allow you to explore new depths of understanding in yourself and others. It will give you insight as to why people behave as they do and assist you in areas you may wish to improve. All the elements of greater emotional awareness can weave together to ensure you make a positive impact.

The term "Emotional Intelligence" was originally coined in 1990 by Yale psychologists John D. Mayer and Peter Salve. Emotional intelligence marks one's ability to perceive, understand, control, and evaluate his emotions. Ironically, its two founders differ in opinion as to whether EI is genetic or can be taught. I have built my entire career empowering people with tools such as these, so I believe the latter to be true.

❝ *Haven't you known people who seem to have a "sixth sense" super power when it comes to connecting, communicating, and understanding others?* ❞

They always know the right things to say to make us feel that we matter. I promise, by the time you finish reading this section, your raised awareness of this concept will make you more emotionally intelligent!

Research has shown that your EQ (Emotional Quotient) is a stronger indicator of your success in life than your IQ (Intelligence Quotient). Your EQ is your capacity to recognize, discriminate, and label emotions accurately and interpret them to help guide your thinking and behavior.

In his best-selling book, *Emotional Intelligence: Why EQ Can Matter More Than IQ,* Daniel Goleman shares the five dimensions of being an Emotionally Intelligent person. While considering these dimensions of Emotional Intelligence, you will see where I have elaborated on each from my own observation and research. I hope you will recognize what you are doing right and areas in which you can improve.

1. **Self-awareness . . .**

    Your capacity to understand and express your own emotions—you are in touch with your strengths and weaknesses and realize where you might like to make improvements. You trust your instincts and can identify how certain thoughts, feelings, people, and situations make you feel. You can hold yourself accountable for your behavior, failures, decisions, and successes.

2. **Self-regulation . . .**

    You have developed your ability to keep your emotions and impulses under control. Just as your body has self-regulating mechanisms, like perspiring to cool you down and shivering to warm you up, you can regulate your emotions according to the circumstances. You abstain from over-reacting, and you know how to set boundaries and how to say "no." You think before you speak and exercise discretion. You have an ability to manage stress as it happens and remain calm through chaos.

3. **Self-motivation . . .**
    You can focus your emotions to improve performance and productivity. You know how to light your own fire and sustain your activities to accomplish your goals.

4. **Empathy for Others . . .**
    You can perceive, identify, and understand the wants, needs, emotions, and viewpoints of others. You are excellent at managing relationships, listening, and being sensitive to other's feelings.

5. **Social Skills . . .**
    You can connect and engage with others easily. You generally like people and are easy to talk to, making you an excellent communicator. Your great collaborative abilities make you an excellent team player and master of relationships. You have a knack for managing disputes and reaching resolutions.

Didn't it feel good to read the descriptions of your qualities as if you already have achieved a high EQ? If every point resonated with you—congratulations! You are well on your way to positive and successful impressions! If not, you will get helpful tips below for increasing your EQ to your advantage.

14 Ways to Develop Your Emotional Intelligence

"When our emotional health is in a bad state, so is our level of self-esteem. We have to slow down and deal with what is troubling us so that we can enjoy the simple joy of being happy and at peace with ourselves."
—Jess Scott

1. Ask yourself, "How am I feeling?"
2. Listen to your gut and tune into your intuition.
3. Connect your thoughts to your feelings to your behaviors.

4. Pay attention to your physiological responses and emotional reactions.
5. Observe how you react to other people's behavior.
6. Write your thoughts and feelings down.
7. Read body language and look for unspoken messages.
8. Try on someone else's shoes and walk around them for a while to better understand their perspective.
9. Read books, attend seminars, and study emotional psychology to increase your knowledge.
10. Listen without interrupting.
11. Delay gratification by not acting impulsively.
12. Deliberately decide to respond thoughtfully.
13. Practice positivity in thoughts, words, and actions.
14. Learn to give without expecting anything in return.

UN-Impressives

*"Wise men speak because they have something to say;
Fools because they have to say something."*

—Plato

People who lack emotional intelligence, may . . .

- Become irritated and frustrated with themselves or others quickly when things don't go their way.
- Defend their limitations, poor choices, or unhealthy habits.
- Demonstrate narcissism and lack consideration for others.
- Trivialize other people's emotions and feelings.
- Blame other people for their problems and refuse to accept personal responsibility.
- Jump to conclusions and make judgments before having all the information.
- Be apathetic, indifferent, or lack sympathy for others.
- Show an absence of emotion in an emotionally charged

environment.
- Always look for why something can't be done, focusing on the challenge rather than the solution.

A person who draws upon healthy emotional intelligence when interacting with others demonstrates poise and maturity that helps make everyone present feel at ease, supported, and valued.

I encourage you to take this list seriously. Work to improve any area above that resonated. It can't be denied—and that is emotional intelligence!

9 Ways to Be Socially Intelligent

1. Patiently allow others to interrupt you for conversational clarity.
2. Leave a conversation making your partner feel good about himself.
3. Make sure every person in the group is involved in the conversation.
4. Allow people to finish jokes, even if you're heard them a million times.
5. Break the uncomfortable silence when nobody else will.
6. Try to be friendly to others even if you're in a bad mood.
7. Change the subject when someone else feels uncomfortable.
8. Be sensitive to other people's communication apprehension.
9. Give people an experience, not just a conversation.

Not only are Social Skills one of the five dimensions for Emotional Intelligence, but when a person enjoys a higher EQ, they have a keen understanding for how to best navigate social situations. Being more socially intelligent serves to make a better first impression every time.

3. $\mathcal{P}$REPARE FOR $\mathcal{S}$UCCESS

"There are no secrets to success. It is the result of preparation, hard work, and learning from failure."

—Colin Powell

Don't you love the sense of personal power you feel when you've got your act together? When your life is in order, you're organized, and you have everything you need? Whether you're delivering a sales presentation to a new client, going on a trip, speaking in front of a thousand people, or handling a customer complaint, when you are prepared, you are more empowered to do your best and perform at a higher level. It feels great! Preparation will not only fortify your confidence to approach life from a position of strength, but it will impress other people as well.

There are few things more important than being prepared—for an interview, an important meeting, selling your home, a new baby—the list goes on. Even if what you're preparing for does not happen, your efforts aren't for naught. With preparation comes knowledge of each situation, as well as the confidence to handle every new encounter with more grace and ease than the time before.

Without proper readiness, we're subject to a 'flub,' or a costly mistake which might have been easily prevented with some simple homework beforehand. Failing to do so deteriorates credibility and reputation, leaving us vulnerable to an unfavorable impression. Dumb luck and flying by the seat of your pants can only get you so far in life.

Knowledge is Power

Living in the age of the Internet and being a part of the information generation, we have unlimited access to an unprecedented wealth of knowledge and learning. We have no excuse to show up to an appointment, a sales call, a date, or an important meeting without learning everything we can to tip the odds in our favor.

Knowledge imparts a sense of authority. It will help you stand out and give you an edge over your competition. Being prepared and sharing your knowledge earns the confidence of those who are interviewing you, depend on your expertise, or seek you out for solutions, answers, or presentations. Give yourself and others the gift of your brilliance to deliver a more compelling and memorable presentation.

Doing Your Homework

Homework doesn't end when you receive a diploma. Often, it's just the beginning of your learning. Doing your homework and being well prepared for appointments is one of the most powerful ways to set yourself apart from your competition to gain and retain new clients.

---

66 *If there is someone whom you would really like to impress, learn as much as you can to be informed, enlightened, and aware about them before you meet.* 99

By performing a simple Google search, a website review, a visit to their LinkedIn profile, or a media release search on the person you are about to meet, you can find out where they've been, what they care about, and where they're going. Whether you learn an interesting fact about a hobby they enjoy, the breed of their dog, or something you both have in common, it will show that you took the time to research and that you care about them as a person.

Referencing this information will better enable you to ask relevant questions and link their answers to your product or service to create a win-win situation.

Know Before You Go

Doing your research ahead of time shows that you care about your client and your reputation. By making the extra effort to learn about the person and their business, you become very appealing and much more memorable.

Know your audience. What do *they* need to hear from you? Years ago, I attended a large corporate event where the guest speaker was a famous basketball coach. We were all eager to hear his message; his fame and reputation had preceded him.

Sadly, he had not done any research about the audience, the business, or the company before delivering his presentation. His speech did not resonate remotely with us and, as a result, we felt jaded. He obviously did not care enough to do his homework. He left us feeling unimpressed and disappointed. It was easily preventable and a disastrous misstep, especially for a seasoned professional.

Never Come Empty Handed

Whether you are staying in someone's home as a house guest, attending a dinner party, or visiting a sick friend, when you bring a "hostess gift" or a thoughtful token, you are providing a gesture of kindness which will extend far beyond your visit.

When I was the Northwest Florida Agency Manager for Fidelity National Title Insurance, I would visit my clients on a regular basis. It gave me joy to make them happy by walking into their business with a bouquet of flowers, a box of chocolates, a bag of sandwiches, or a box of cookies. It wasn't about the value of the items; it was about presenting a thoughtful gesture that made them feel appreciated. Discover an interest, a passion, a preference or need your client has, and take the time to give them some small item related to it.

Just in Case . . .

My friend Megan Watt (dreamcatalystlabs.com) is a wonderful

speaker and she has a 'bag of tricks' that she makes sure to take every time she presents. It is filled with extra cables and wires, and cords and batteries. She has handouts, snacks, water, and electronics. She has everything she needs at her fingertips. This level of preparation enables her to give a fantastic performance without panicking if things don't go as expected.

PowerPoint is such an integral part of my own keynotes that I not only load them onto my laptop, but email them to myself then save them on a thumb drive in the event that something unexpected happens. It is better to be safe than sorry, especially when people are depending on you.

Making Lists

Being prepared not only reduces our stress level and keeps us from looking stupid, but it builds the confidence that other people have in us that we are dependable, reliable and can be counted upon. It prevents us from getting tripped up by unexpected glitches and surprises. Discover what works best work for you—hard copy lists, Siri on your iPhone, Evernote, visual reminders, or even calendars. Whatever your style, utilize technology to your advantage. Store the *stuff* that is overflowing in your brain—it's too easy to forget!

Remember the 5 P's

Prior Planning Prevents Poor Performance

4. Your Personal Brand

"Regardless of age, regardless of position, regardless of the business we happen to be in, all of us need to understand the importance of branding. We are CEOs of our own companies: Me Inc. To be in business today, our most important job is to be head marketer for the brand called You."

—Tom Peters in "The Brand Called You"

What is YOUR personal brand? How are you packaging your unique talents, style, personality and/or products to represent who you are, what you do, and how you show yourself to the world?

ASK YOURSELF: How do you want others to perceive you? How do you "show and tell" your interests, your skills, your work, or your company?

Whether it is in the way you walk, talk, dress, or behave, your personal brand impacts how people react and respond to you. It is the essence of what makes you likable, knowable, and trustworthy. And it is what can make you memorable and sought after in the marketplace.

It is no longer a matter of IF you have a personal brand—it is a question of "How is it working for you?" Does it best express your intentions, your uniqueness, and your service offering? Is it helping or hindering your progress and success in business?

Is it proving to serve your needs with positive impact? Is it paving the way for a great first impression on people when they meet you, think of you, speak of you, or even see you on the Internet? If not, it's time for a change, and it is perfectly within your control.

Your Unique Selling Proposition

We used to think of brand awareness as being the magic bullet that would make or break a company and the success of its product. However, the word "brand" has now taken an individualized and highly personalized shift toward how you are perceived in the minds of others. For many people and companies, the only place they are seen by others "in person" is on the Internet. A stand-out, consistent brand is imperative.

Project your "brand" to be remarkable and memorable. Whether through a positioning statement, product placement, advertising campaign, service, a logo, mission, or message, your brand is what makes you and/or your company remarkable—or not.

A "brand" identifies how you are unique and different. It is an attention-getter to help you stack up against your competitors. It also shares with us what we can expect by doing business with you.

---

66 *Is YOUR brand consistent with your desired outcomes?* 99

Whether you are in business or simply want to be remembered positively, frankly consider these things: What makes you feel special and significant? What makes you unforgettable? When people see or think of you, what image do you think comes to mind?

Since nothing stays the same, the great news is that, at any moment, you have the ability and power to move the needle in the direction of your dreams and create a brand that best represents you. You can re-design your life, learn a new skill, update your appearance, offer a new service, or even change your attitude. You can always create the space to **review, redo,** and **renew** as I teach in my book *Release the Power of Re³* (releasethepowerofre3.com). If you feel it is time to refresh your brand, take a moment to rethink your relevance and apply my 3-step formula.

My friend and professional speaking consultant, Lois Creamer (bookmorebusinessnow.com), has built her career teaching professional speakers how to promote their brands to optimize their business. The elevator speech is alive and well. Can you summarize your brand in one statement? She helps speakers craft, draft, and refine their "positioning statement," which succinctly says, "Here's who I am, what I do, and how I can help you."

Crossing the Great Differential Divide

When my friend Jenna Atkinson (jennaatkinsonconsulting.com) worked in the financial industry, she quickly observed that the reason twenty percent of the brokers were doing eighty percent of the business was because they had positioned themselves as experts. They clearly differentiated why they were the best choice to work with. As a result, when she left her Fortune 200 employer to start her own company, she made it her mission to teach individuals how to personally brand themselves to maximize their opportunities, expand their influence, build long-lasting relationships, and increase sales. As the founder of "Growth Bomb Elite" she helps entrepreneurs explode their business by reaching higher levels of success in their careers and lives. And branding lays the foundation.

Stand Apart from the Crowd

Daniel, my life love, is the Chiropractic Chief of Staff at a multi-disciplinary clinic in Madison, Wisconsin. He is an old-fashioned gentleman with a bodybuilder's physique. Though living in Wisconsin for the past twenty-six years, he has never lost his Mississippi dialect. When people meet him, receive his kindness, see his healthy attitude and physique, and hear that Southern drawl, there is no doubt that his manners, dialect, and even his muscles make him memorable. He definitely stands apart from the crowd! His brand evolved simply by him being himself. He's proof that outstanding branding is as easy as letting your genuine self shine through.

As an additional example, I'm known for always wearing colorful dresses, no matter what—rarely jeans or pants. I've never given it much thought, but I realize now that it's part of my personal brand; it sets me apart. It's my style and what I feel most comfortable in.

When I moved from sunny Florida to seasonal Wisconsin, I still wore my sundresses—people chuckled at me, but I just added a brightly colored sweater to complement. When sandals became a problem, my new friends encouraged me to switch to boots. Now my climatization is complete, but my style and brand remain the same.

Purple Cow Cool

In his book *Purple Cow Marketing,* Seth Godin introduces a wise parable about cows to illustrate the power of branding. Imagine that you are taking a long country drive and as you continue down the highway you see fields and fields of cows. Brown cows, beige cows, black cows, and white cows. They become quite predictable because they all look like what you would expect of cows.

And then suddenly . . . you see a PURPLE cow! What is this purple creature? Out of sheer surprise, awe, and curiosity, you jam on your brakes, hop out of the car, jump over the fence and run up to this amazing sight that is a purple cow. You have never seen anything like it before. It is memorable and unique; it has stopped you in your tracks!

How does this apply to you? Being a purple cow in your field enables you to stand apart from the herd. Being a purple cow makes a memorable impression.

In the old days, I would look in the Yellow Pages and see the purple cows that stood out from other businesses. As another example, for decades, realtors all advertised in the Homes and Lands Real Estate advertising magazine the same way—with thumbnail photos of the front of the house and the driveway. And then one day, much to the delight of the public, realtors started advertising the interiors and views of the homes. They became the purple cows and encouraged more showings (and sales!) in the process.

The world is shifting. It is a noisy, busy, distracted place plying us with information overload and 24/7 technology vying for our attention. If that were not enough, we cross the paths of thousands of people throughout our lives who often go unnoticed and unremembered.

How can you stand apart from the herd? How can you start to be noticed so people will remember you? How can you be heard above the noise?

---

66 *What is your personal branding that makes you special, unique, individual, and memorable?* 99

What you deem as ordinary about yourself may be refreshing and extraordinary to others. Think about it. Batman had his car and Superman had his cape.

What helps people identify your Super Powers? Instead of hiring a personal PR firm to identify and promote your personal brand, ask yourself what strengths you want to be remembered by. Discover what differentiates you—and as Nike so aptly promotes, "Just do it." And you can become the "Pause that Refreshes" like Coca Cola or "Think different" like Apple.

To help get your creative juices flowing, you might look online at lists of the "best taglines ever." Their branding ideas are genius and may be just the catalyst you need to activate your awesome!

Building Personal Brand Awareness

- Intentionally think of yourself as a brand (The American Marketing Association defines a brand as "A name, term, design, symbol, or any other feature that identifies one seller's goods or services as distinct from those of other sellers. The legal term for a brand is trademark.)

- Take a searching inventory of your speech, habits, behaviors, appearance, hobbies, preferences, talents, and products. The key is what makes you distinct and unlike others.
- Ask friends what they think of when they think of you. List for future reference.
- Audit your online presence (Facebook, Twitter, Pinterest, Website, LinkedIn, Email Signature & Language, etc.)
- Ask yourself whether you are happy with what you're giving and receiving, or if you need to make some changes. Be you; stick to your priorities.
- What do you want to be known for? That's your brand.
- What would you like to STOP, START or CHANGE?

10 Strategies to ROCK Your Personal Brand

1. Redesign, renew, and recharge your brand.
2. Decide what value you bring to others and give it.
3. Share your expertise, experience, and education.
4. Refresh your appearance for fashion and flair.
5. Use your signature color and/or accessories.
6. Intertwine others' needs with your offerings.
7. Optimize a physical characteristic that identifies you.
8. Rewrite your story to serve your desired outcomes.
9. Create a website and a business card that stand apart.
10. Remember. . . Be yourself because everyone else is taken!

"Define what your brand stands for, its core values and tone of voice,
and then communicate consistently in those terms."

—Simon Mainwaring

5. DRESS TO IMPRESS

"Your appearance is your expression to others about how you are and what you stand for. The way you look reflects your self-image, attitude, confidence, and state of mind. A strong, purposeful presence is the hallmark of an effective image."
—Natalie Jobity

A picture is truly worth a thousand words and how you dress is the "picture" you provide for all the world to see. The first thing others see is YOU—not your resume, background, or credentials. Like it or not, how we each present ourselves to the world, by way of our appearance, attire, and speech, all send a message.

ASK YOURSELF: Is your appearance representing you well and helping you achieve the results you desire or could you use a style makeover?

People will form impressions, assumptions, opinions, and judgments all within a few short seconds. To make a favorable first impression and make these seconds count, enhance your image by choosing clean, crisp, appropriate attire that reflects confidence and professionalism. When trying to make an excellent first impression in business but in doubt of what to wear, dress one level up from what is expected—if it's casual, dress in business casual, etc.

As your intentioned focus turns to putting your best foot forward, start by asking yourself a few questions:

- Do you care about your appearance? (If not, you may go ahead and close this book and give it away to a friend who does, because there is nothing I could say that would matter!)
- Does your appearance accurately convey the message of who you are that you are trying to get across?
- Do your clothes make you feel happy, beautiful, comfortable in your skin, handsome, confident, or powerful?

- Which outfits do you get the most compliments on when you are wearing them?
- What colors make you feel healthy, vibrant, and alive?

Making a great first impression is not an accident, and with a little planning, experimentation, and application, you can transform your style, substance, and impact.

"There is no question that we are initially judged by our outward appearance and dealt with accordingly. Our clothing is as much a part of the first impression we make as our demeanor is and we might as well take advantage of that fact."
—Leah Feldon, Dressing Rich

Dress to Impress

My brilliant sister Jane Cullison Vosser is an ASID (American Society of Interior Designers) Interior Designer who earned her Bachelor's Degree in Fashion Design and her Master's Degree in Interior Design. Yes, she was a great resource for this chapter!

Jane and her handsome English husband, Peter, have a home in England. One winter night, they decided to get dressed up to attend the Christmas Eve service at St. Paul's Cathedral in London. With throngs of people hoping to get inside, tickets were given away until they ran out. Jane and Peter were fortunate to be two of the lucky ticket recipients. As they vied for a place to sit, they found two seats in the back of the cathedral, far removed from the musical festivities. They were so grateful to have made the cut, it didn't matter that the columns were blocking their view.

Jane was dressed in a velvet dress, a cashmere coat with a fur collar, complemented by her jewelry and finery. Peter was wearing an elegant suit with a cashmere overcoat. Their elegance demonstrated respect and reverence for their special night. As they looked around, they found themselves surrounded by casual spectators who were wearing jeans and sneakers who did not make any effort to dress for the occasion.

An usher soon approached and invited them to move to the front of the cathedral to sit next to the choir under the dome. Apparently, a few VIPs had not arrived and since the evening was being televised, it was important to fill all chairs. Dressing and accessorizing in a mode befitting the occasion provided them with a special opportunity and a lifetime memory.

Professionalism

"You cannot climb the ladder of success dressed in the costume of failure."
—Zig Ziglar

Few places are more important for dressing appropriately than the workplace, where a professional appearance is crucial.

Your profession will typically mandate the expectations, standards, and limitations. Jane shared, "As a designer, I dress stylishly—pulled together and creatively accessorized. Presenting myself as polished, fashionable, and detail-oriented instills the confidence in my clients that I have the creativity and training to produce what they need, to exceed their expectations, and provide an incredible experience."

Think of how dress illustrates professions. If you are an attorney, your dress would typically be formal business attire—a suit, neatly pressed shirt, and leather accessories. Artists may dress Bohemian, whereby the more far out they are, the more creative and artistic they appear. However, if a doctor dressed in that manner, she would not be taken seriously.

Look the part. Even if it is your first job, walk in looking confident and dressed for the position. You will appear to already know what you are doing. The confidence that comes from within blends perfectly with your wardrobe and your shoes to make a sensational impression.

Accessorizing

"To me, accessorizing is like painting. Your clothes become the frame and the accessories you add become the artwork."

—Betty Halbreich, Secrets of a Fashion Therapist

Once you are dressed there may be still more you can do to enhance, complement, or complete your look. How you accessorize your wardrobe can transform the plainest outfit into a dazzling, unforgettable impression. It can be the mark of your own unique style, an extra splash of fashion, or an expression of your mood. Style icon, fashionista, and interior designer Iris Apfel says, "I get more compliments on accessories than anything else. I think they're kind of like herbs and spices. They give zest and zing to an outfit."

Simply changing your accessories will change your entire impression. Start with a simple black dress. Now add a floppy wide-brim hat, sunglasses, big earrings, and sandals and you are ready for a lunch at the beach. Take the same black dress and add a strand of pearls, hose, and high heels and you can attend the opera with confidence and elegance. Same dress, different accessories.

Women are not the only ones who can have fun. A well-dressed man has the same ability. Begin to acquire and play with elements and accessories that can take your style to new heights . . .

- Hats
- Jewelry & Watches
- Scarves & Ties
- Handbags
- Belts
- Shoes & Socks
- Eyeglasses
- Sunglasses
- Jackets
- Vests

Shoe Shine

"If your hair is done and you're wearing good shoes, you can get away with anything."

—Iris Apfel, Style Icon

I had a doctor friend once tell me that he can tell a lot about his patients by the shoes they wear. Interesting!

Do your shoes reflect your personality, style, and credibility? You can be dressed to the nines and have it all going on, but if you don't have shoes to support your look, they can be your undoing. Your shoes should be appropriate, clean, polished, and maintained if you want to make a great impression and fortify your credibility. If your shoes are scuffed, dirty, or worn, clients may wonder what other details you've neglected to attend to.

It is not only about your shoes—care of your feet also counts. Last summer, I saw a lady dressed in a lovely sundress who looked happy and fresh. However, when I saw her feet, I was taken aback. Her toenails were stained and unkempt, and her calloused heels were dry and cracked. Her dress was lovely, but the condition of her feet ruined her whole look.

Research shows that you can correctly judge a person by simply looking at their shoes. Omri Gillath from the University of Kansas has found that by simply examining the condition, cost, style, and color of the shoe, you can guess approximately ninety percent of the owner's personal characteristics such as age, income, gender, and even political affiliation. What are your shoes saying about you? Better take note; it might sway your medical diagnosis.

Looking Like a Million Bucks on a Budget

When my friend Marnie Tate began her financial planning business, she was a single mom with limited resources. She knew very well, though, that to be a consummate professional, she had to dress the part of an expert. She once shared with me, "I only had two suits to meet and greet clients. For six months, I wore one of those two suits every single day. But I wore them right, accessorized them well, and looked like a million bucks. I used to teach classes on 'Dress for Success' and taught that even if you don't have much, dress well.

You reveal a lot about yourself in the first three seconds of meeting someone, so dress for success!"

Proven professionals know that by focusing on quality, you can't lose with the classics and your clothes will last longer. It's not about having expensive clothes, it is about having style.

Appropriateness

An important part of dressing for success is not only wearing something well, but making sure it is appropriate for the occasion or the environment.

---

66 Dressing appropriately in one venue may be highly inappropriate in another. 99

Yet every day we see a lack of modesty and taste, regardless of how uncomfortable it makes others feel.

At a recent networking breakfast, a beautiful young woman sat down beside me. She had chosen to wear a very low cut blouse with her cleavage spilling over. No one at the table remembered her name, her business, or what she had to say because her breasts dominated every one's impression. Her appearance diminished her credibility, reputation, contribution, and perceived intelligence. It was very inappropriate and unprofessional. While it might have been suitable for a cocktail party, her inappropriateness spoiled any possibility for a professional impression.

Seriously, ladies, wearing a low-cut cocktail party dress and heavy make-up for a job interview are simply poor taste. It can almost guarantee you will not get the job, unless of course, it's in a bar. Not only can inappropriate clothing be distracting, but people will make endless judgments about you, whether true or not.

Due to today's relaxed styles and extremes of political correctness, people may wear most anything in the workplace (or elsewhere)—even at the cost of making co-workers and customers uncomfortable. I encourage you to give thought to your own appropriate attire.

"Nothing can put more of a damper on a social or work situation than feeling overdressed, underdressed, or just plain badly dressed."
—Leah Feldon, Dressing Rich

As you consider your own personal style and wardrobe elements, not everything may be suitable for every occasion. Consider how you might need to adapt your choices based on:

- Your age
- Venue
- Culture
- Location
- Demographics

- Tradition
- Environment
- Indoor/Outdoor
- Geography/Climate
- Activities

Differences Can Create Barriers

When my niece was married in South Carolina, our family and friends gathered together for her rehearsal dinner. As young twenty-somethings, her friends arrived dressed in the Goth style, wearing black clothes, chains, black nail polish, heavy mascara, body piercings, and tattoos.

They were quite a contrast to the rest of our family who were conservatively dressed in more traditional styles. Her bridesmaids and groomsmen stood apart from the rest of the family, socially and physically. They congregated together away from the rest of us. I observed awkwardness from both directions which prevented healthy interactions.

The next morning everyone showed up for the wedding wearing tuxedos and bridesmaid's dresses looking beautiful, along with the rest of the family who were also all dressed up. It was as if they were all new-found friends. Everyone got along great and it was a fabulous wedding. People were laughing and connecting and dancing. It was wonderful. Simply the way people were dressed the night before had created an unfortunate barrier and awkward separation.

How often do we see this happen in our country, where people are divided by class, culture, education, age, and more? The differences can divide us simply because of the clothes we wear. It may sound simple and shallow; however, it happens every day.

Modern Day Casualness

The times, they are a-changing! What was once defined by tradition, respect, and custom has evolved into a relaxed and casual society. What is acceptable and normal today would never have been permitted in the past.

One of my friends recently commented that she was amazed how people will attend church in blue jeans and not think twice. No more Sunday best. Having lived by the beach for seventeen years, I became used to people in casual shorts and flip-flops at church. I miss the reverence, but at least they are there.

Beyond casual extends to college classrooms. Students arrive to class in their pajama bottoms, slippers, and t-shirts without anyone giving it a second thought. There is a space and place for everything, isn't there? The key is to ask what is appropriate to wear—where?

Don't even get me started with major news networks. They seem to be mandating female reporters wear false eyelashes, heavy make-up, deep cleavage, bare legs, and spike heels. Respectful journalism has morphed into show business to increase ratings and sell advertising. In my opinion, the modern-day shift in business attire compromises the reverence for journalistic integrity; it's a parade of pretty fashionistas. That's another discussion for another book.

Adaptation & Flexibility

"I love dressing up in superhero outfits and in fact, when I dress up
as Wonder Woman, I actually think that I'm more powerful."

—Olivia Munn

My friend Susanne Gaddis and I attended the "First World Congress on Positive Psychology" in Philadelphia several years ago. This extraordinary event was significant and substantial, bringing together people from over sixty countries to share, learn, and study how the application of "Positive Psychology" can affect and change our world for the better.

Knowing we would be engaging with a diverse and valuable group of people, I wanted to "dress for success" on steroids. To prepare, I packed the best of everything I owned (suits, dresses, shoes, and accessories) so that I would look and feel like a power player about to make my mark. Ha!

We flew into Philadelphia separately and met at the baggage claim in the airport. But there was a problem—my luggage was not there. We waited for the next flight to arrive. Still no luggage. Accepting the outrageously inconvenient inevitability, we went on to the hotel to check-in and register for the conference.

Not wanting to miss a moment, and with no time for shopping, Susanne invited me to dive into her suitcase to see what she could share for me to wear. Mind you, I am 5'4"; she is 5'8". Being flexible and adaptable, I wore her flowered and silky nightgown for the opening day of the conference! Adding accessories (and makeup) can transform even the simplest of clothing. Dressing for success became a relative issue. I discovered that my confidence was not in my suitcase, but inside my heart and head. My luggage finally arrived . . . a year later!

Understanding Others

Years ago, I attended a leadership workshop where we learned how our beliefs create the reality we experience and how we perceive others. One of our homework assignments was to show up the next morning as our alter-ego and dress completely the opposite of who we really were. A matronly librarian type came as a street walker. A polished corporate executive who lived in business suits and polished shoes arrived as a hapless nerd, complete with the taped black rimmed glasses and pants pulled up to his armpits.

This experiment on impressions and comfort zones worked in multiple directions. First, stretching us out of our comfort zones was liberating and we got to experience not only how other people feel, but how differently people treated us based on how we were dressed. Secondly, it revealed that when the first impression we had of each other was turned upside down, how we perceived and felt about each other completely shifted.

It can be a harsh lesson for the person who chooses to wear inappropriate clothing when it does matter to the person observing or evaluating.

Don't Judge a Book by Its Cover

I moved away from home at the age of eighteen, and I had to work a full-time job to support myself through college. For four years, I worked at Carlyle & Company, a jewelry store in the Tallahassee Mall in Tallahassee, Florida.

Every day I would dress up in a nice dress or skirt, with high heels and hose, to greet customers and look professional so that I could sell diamonds, gold, and beautiful jewelry. One day, a filthy man came into the store wearing overalls, with mud under his fingernails, covered in sweat, and smelling bad. My first reaction was "Whoa, I'm going to go take care of other customers."

My manager, Scott, jumped up to greet him and treated him like royalty. By the time that man left, he had spent over five-thousand dollars on jewelry to surprise his wife. It turns out he owned a huge farm north of town and was very wealthy. In my naiveté, I jumped to a conclusion which cost me a big sale. It taught me early that if I was too quick to judge another person, I might miss unexpected opportunities for business, friendships, and life. And that's the "other side of the coin" I encourage you to remember. Needless to say, I didn't get either side of that coin.

One Christmas I attended a lovely party in a friend's home. Toward the end of the evening, I went into the kitchen and began clearing counters, washing dishes, and placing them in the dishwasher to help the hostess. I was wearing my normal combination of a dress with high heels. Another guest named John came into the kitchen and said, "I am so happy to see you washing dishes. You always appear to be an elegant lady who is too elegant to get her hands dirty."

I started laughing because nothing could be further from the truth. He should see me planting flowers, scrubbing toilets, cleaning out from under the refrigerator, or picking up dog poop. Apparently, he had this one impression of me for ten years, which shifted completely after seeing me wash dishes. In this case, he judged my book by my cover, without opening the book!

Color Your World

Color is one of the most important and distinctive elements in enhancing your image. Wearing the colors which are best matched to your personality, energy, skin tone, hair color, and body type will make you look healthier, more vibrant, confident, successful, and approachable.

Experts agree that color can stimulate emotions which evoke different responses. Research has shown that different colors represent different character qualities and have a powerful psychological effect. According to *Psychology Today,* the colors you wear say a lot about you, and they leave a psychological impact on those you meet.

Blue	wise, stable, sensitive, confident, considerate, calm, sincere, honest, dependable
Black	attentive to detail, confident, powerful, can be viewed as threatening, arrogant, or intimidating
Red	strong, passionate, stimulating, courageous, energetic, proactive, driven, determined, exciting
Green	loyal, nurturing, generous, balanced, natural, healthy, healing, growing, compassionate, adaptable
Grey	sophisticated, elegant, authoritative, confident, patient, elegant, conservative
White	logical, organized simple, fair, immaculate, pure
Purple	wealthy, creative, high quality, fantasy, humanitarian
Turquoise	recharges energy and emotions, inspires self-expression, harmonious, communicative
Yellow	illuminating, uplifting, mental clarity, intelligent

66 *Simply by changing colors, you can change moods, communication, perceptions, energy, and expectations.* 99

Color portrays different meanings in life and in business. Choose the colors that not only make you look and feel great, but inspire the emotions you hope to evoke.

6. Healthy Habits & Hygiene

"We are what we repeatedly do. Excellence then, is not an act, but a habit."
—Aristotle

What laughter is to the soul, soap is to the body. Wash. Brush. Hydrate. Manicure. The importance of healthy habits and hygiene for making a positive first impression should go without saying; however, I would be remiss if I did not include this topic in the book, because surprisingly, many people just don't get it.

John Dryden once wrote, "We first make our habits, and then our habits make us." Are your habits and hygiene hindering your success or making a great first impression on your behalf?

Without a second look, they reflect a lot about you—your thoughts, values, beliefs, priorities, self-esteem, self-respect, confidence, and every other category covered in this book that determines how people perceive you. More importantly, your habits and hygiene show how you perceive yourself. Without saying a word, they speak for you. Only you have the power, ability, and personal choice to instill healthy habits and hygiene into your life.

---

66 *When you resolve to live a healthier life, you will feel better, look better, and make a better impression on everyone you meet.* 99

Before we dive into the healthy and wholesome habits that can transform your life, let's address the deal breakers, impression busters, and offenders that instantly create a negative impression.

3 Major Smells That Repel

The sense of smell is closely linked with memory, probably more so than any of our other senses. It is more powerful than you might imagine. Smell stimulates your olfactory glands which in turn trigger various parts of your brain.

We delight in fragrances such as vanilla, cinnamon, and citrus. The aromas from favorite foods, summer rain, fresh baked cookies, or even fresh cut grass elicit varying degrees of pleasure and positive response. Smells can link your memories and perceptions to opinions and judgments. Realize that this connection is vital to how you remember others and how they remember you.

People will carelessly diminish a good impression by not being mindful of how they smell. Since we usually do not smell ourselves, ask a trusted friend or family member if there is anything which could or should be improved. Following is a list of some of the top offenders.

1. **Bad Breath**

   My delightful and witty friend, Roslyn, once joked, "Halitosis is better than no breath at all!" We all got a good laugh and thought it was funny. However, for people who have it, it is not a laughing matter! A well-loved real estate broker whom I would often see at Chamber of Commerce functions had this problem. I adored her; she was a wonderful person. But she had such terribly bad breath that it was hard to focus on what she was saying during conversations. Whenever conversing with her, I could smell her breath. She did not realize it. Rather than telling her, I minimized our interactions. In retrospect, it would have been a favor had I let her know, but I did not want to embarrass her. Yes, she was kind, well-dressed, engaging, sincere, and all the other wonderful qualities that make a great impression, but her breath, unfortunately, destroyed the possibility of her leaving a positive impression.

2. **Body Odor**

   Each person has his or her own distinct smell, as unique as their fingerprints. What can be blamed for the offense? The gamut runs from sweat, bacteria, and infrequent bathing to hormonal changes, diet, and genetics. Wearing soiled or soured clothing or stinky shoes will deteriorate an impression even further. And sometimes people go far in the opposite extreme; they overdo it and wear too much perfume or fragrance. Body odor can be highly offensive, yet it can be easily resolved with good hygiene, daily bathing, wearing deodorant, taking supplements, wearing freshly laundered clothing, and eating a healthy, well-balanced diet. If these don't help, a visit to the doctor is needed.

3. **Smoking**

   Simply put—smoking stinks. My friends who smoke may not realize that people smell them before they even arrive. These days, the odor is offensive and can be a major turnoff to non-smokers. Is it worth the risk of pushing people away? Discreet and considerate smokers will try to refresh and minimize the odor by washing their hands, using mouthwash, and smoking outside. I understand it is a hard habit to break and I appreciate the people who make the effort. Depending on where you live, smoking is highly regulated. Many cities throughout the United States now prohibit smoking in all public places and all places of employment. Seems reason enough to try to quit.

Habits That Hinder

We are creatures of habit and sometimes the habits we fall into undermine our health, our happiness, and our outcomes. Ironically, we are inevitably the only ones who can change them. Unhealthy habits can ensnare us mentally, physically, behaviorally, and subconsciously. Below are just a few less than helpful habits we fall into:

- Biting nails
- Smacking gum
- Chewing tobacco
- Substance addictions
- Picking your nose
- Emotional shopping
- Overeating
- Not doing our homework
- Lying
- Interrupting others
- Gossiping
- Burping
- Spitting
- Rude phone usage
- Cursing
- Oversharing
- Littering
- Compulsive gambling
- Always being late
- Cheating
- Being rude
- Excessive worrying
- Over reacting
- Breaking promises
- Procrastinating
- Skipping breakfast
- Not returning calls
- Negative self-talk

Healthy Habits & Hygiene for a Happy Life

"A healthy outside starts from the inside."
—Robert Urich

There are several notably healthy habits which you can adopt today if you have not already. Since they will all help you feel great, look great, and improve the quality of your life, isn't it worth your effort to make them a part of your reality? I know that trying to begin a new habit may be uncomfortable, inconvenient, or challenging. However, when the goal is to feel terrific, isn't it worth your consideration?

1. **Exercise.** Exercise's short and long-term effects are undeniable. It can improve your mood, reduce stress, and reduce, or even prevent health issues such as diabetes, obesity, and heart disease.

2. **Eat Healthy.** A healthy breakfast jumpstarts your metabolism for the day to provide sustaining energy. Eat lean proteins, vegetables, fruits, and high fiber, complex carbohydrates.

3. **Practice Dental Hygiene.** Brush your teeth 2-3 times a day, floss once a day, and swish mouth-wash for enhanced hygiene and refreshment.

4. **Get Enough Sleep.** Your mental, emotional, and physical regeneration depend on rest-ful sleep.

5. **Use Good Grooming.** Shower daily, wash your hair, wear deodorant and/or antiperspirant, and wear clean, fresh clothes.

6. **Get Your Hair Done.** There is no reason to be un-brushed, disheveled, or unwashed. Try a professional style and perhaps even a new color that complements your appearance and makes a statement about who you are. We see hair first—before eye contact, the handshake, or the 10-second introduction.

7. **Women.** Be considerate about wearing perfume. Ladies want to smell good, but wearing heavy fragrance can push people away. Shape your eyebrows and wear enough make-up to highlight your attributes.

8. **Men.** Shave, trim your beard, eyebrows, nose and ear hairs!

9. **Ditch Addictions.** Any habit which we indulge in to excess demonstrates that it has a hold on us; it demonstrates that we really are not in control of our impulses. Drinking, smoking, and eating excessively are activities that diminish the impression others have of us.

10. **Nice Nails.** Trimmed and cleaned nails present attentive self-care, especially when you use your hands in your profession. Getting an occasional manicure and pedicure is not only a nice pampering, but it enhances your presentation greatly.

11. **Positive Thinking & Optimism.** Yes, your attitude is the result of your habitual thought patterns. First and foremost, do this for *you.*

These healthy habits and good hygiene practices deserve your attention. If you do not adopt healthy habits and hygiene, the neglect may nullify everything else that you're doing well. Poor habits can invalidate your credibility and undermine your success in all areas.

From a Gentleman's Perspective

Daniel served on the Board of Advisors for *Shape Magazine* for over 15 years and won the Wisconsin State Body Building Championship's Master's Division at age 59. Yes, he knows a thing or two about healthy habits. He makes an intentional effort daily to work out, eat right, care for himself, and live a clean lifestyle. He is one of the finest examples I've seen for someone who exemplifies healthy habits and hygiene. When writing this chapter, I asked him to share his perspective.

He shared, "Healthy habits and hygiene mean everything to me, for both myself and others. I never go to work without shaving. My hair is always washed and styled. I may wear clothes that are not tie worthy, but I select clothing that complements my physique. I am close to people all day long and want to make sure of three things: Since I have a physical job, I make sure I use deodorant, a high-quality cologne, and mouthwash. I make sure that I always have fresh breath. It gives me confidence for being face to face with people.

Since I make such a diligent effort, I am impressed by individuals who do the same. It says a lot about their own levels of self-esteem, self-respect, and personal care, all of which leave a more favorable impression."

Understanding the 3-Step Habit Process

In his best-selling book, *The Power of Habit: Why We Do What We Do in Life and Business*, Charles Duhiggs shares his three-step habit formation process to illustrate how habits are made and how they can be de-constructed.

1. **Reminder**—The reminder which elicits the behavior; the cue or trigger which initiates the habit.
2. **Routine**—Your actual behavior; the action you take and the habit itself.
3. **Reward**—The benefit gained or perceived payoff you experience from doing the behavior or exercising your habit.

As you review the elements in this model, consider the habits you have developed in your life from the inside out. Make an intentional shift away from the less desirable habits to create more beneficial ones so that you can achieve more favorable outcomes.

7. $\mathcal{P}$UNCTUALITY $\mathcal{P}$LUS

"The habit of being prompt, once formed, extends to everything—meeting friends, paying debts, going to church, reaching and leaving a place of business, keeping promises, retiring at night and rising in the morning, and, indeed, to every relation and act, however trivial it may seem to observers."
—William Makepeace Thayer, Tact and Grit, 1882

Punctuality

Punctuality has been called a "homely, but solid virtue." Although it is not fancy, it is a strong reflection of a person's character. Arriving on time for your engagements demonstrates preparation, respect, integrity, and enthusiasm, all of which serve to make a positive impression on the people whom you are meeting, especially when they are depending on you—or paying you!

When you have scheduled an appointment, or have made a commitment, you have essentially made a promise. Being punctual demonstrates your consideration for others and that you can be depended upon.

Lombardi Time

"Punctuality is the Politeness of Kings."
—King Louis XVII of France

Legendary football Coach Vince Lombardi is well remembered for his unwavering requirement for his players and coaches to not only arrive on time, but to be fifteen minutes early. If he told you to be somewhere and you arrived exactly on time, you were already late!

For those important meetings, try to know the expectations of the person with whom you are meeting—arriving on time with a little extra preparation is sure to impress.

I recently met a lady for lunch who was the creator of a personality profile assessment tool which she markets to companies to help improve their productivity, performance, and profitability. Prior to our appointment, she emailed me the link to take her assessment so that she would have a "clear" picture of my strengths and personality when we met.

When I arrived promptly on time, she was already waiting for me at the door. She proceeded to inquire, "When you have appointments, do you typically arrive early, at the exact time, or late?" Knowing her expertise, I knew that regardless of my answer, it would reveal clues to my personality. I said, "Today, I did the first two. Although I walked in on the dot, I have been sitting in my car in the parking lot for fifteen minutes." I may have confused her theory! It's sometimes fun to keep people guessing.

Arriving Early

"Better three hours too soon than a minute too late."
—William Shakespeare

In business, developing this habit is an excellent way to make a great first impression. The extra minutes will allow you to catch your breath, collect your thoughts, and prepare for your meeting or speaking engagement. It will also provide you with the flexibility and buffer for possible delays in traffic, getting lost, or taking a wrong turn. You can learn a great deal about people by simply observing how they manage their time.

As a professional speaker, it is critical that I arrive early to make sure that everything is ready before my audience arrives. Not only does arriving early give me a chance to make sure the room is set up and my technology is working, but it provides a few minutes for me to breathe, focus, and shift my mindset before I go on stage to rock my talk! It also empowers me with an air of relaxed confidence so that as people arrive, I can meet and greet them like a hostess at a party.

It is especially wonderful when I can connect, shake hands, and learn names before my program begins so that the entire event is more personal, intimate, and engaging. When we get to know each other before I ever step on that stage, everyone feels more valued and important. Additionally, it creates a comfortable familiarity which removes tension like magic.

I'm late! I'm late! For a Very Important Date!

"I could never think well of a man's intellectual or moral character if he was habitually unfaithful to his appointments."

—Emmons

If you tend to always be late, you're harming your reputation. When you are meeting someone for the first time, they are not interested in your "good excuse" for running late. Rather, what it tells them about you is that . . .

- You do not keep your word.
- You cannot be depended upon.
- You are an incompetent time manager.
- You don't value their feelings, schedules, or opinions.
- You leave the impression of being self-important.

All of this is completely preventable by your making punctuality and promptness a true priority in your life, personally and professionally.

We have multi-tasking mania. In our society, it has become common and predictable for people to stay nonstop busy, juggle priorities, and overextend. If you schedule things back to back and being late becomes the norm, it is one habit that is best to break.

Respecting Other People's Time

Tina is a biochemist who worked in the medical research field until she launched her speaking and training business in Positive Psychology.

She shared with me, "When I think about the leaders and managers that I've worked for over the years, there is a distinguishing factor between the ones who respect their employees' time and the ones who don't. Leaders who are busy *and caring* demonstrate greater respect and consideration.

Then there are the ones who act like their time is all that matters, don't give a second thought to imposing on people's schedules, and make people wait, or let meetings drag on and waste people's time. This one difference can make or break how people feel about the person and their ability to lead."

Thankfully, I have been very healthy throughout my life. Typically, I have only one doctor's appointment each year for my annual checkup. Even though the appointment is made months in advance, I would always end up waiting to see the doctor for 1-2 hours in the lobby. I began to feel that the consistent tardiness was disrespectful, rude, and tiring. After this happened multiple times, I became so irritated by the lack of consideration that I simply found another doctor. It's no longer my problem.

Timely Tips for Making a Great Impression

- Be on time!
- If you have a 15-minute appointment—keep it at fifteen minutes unless there is mutual agreement to continue.
- When beginning a conversation, ask the other person, "Do you have time to speak right now?" If they say no, you can say, "I have some valuable information to share with you. What time would work best for you?"
- Start and end your meetings on time and stick to the agenda.

8. $\mathcal{E}$XPERTISE, $\mathcal{E}$XPERIENCE & $\mathcal{E}$DUCATION

"There aren't shortcuts. Merely direct paths. Most people don't take them, because they frighten us. Things that look like shortcuts are usually detours disguised as less work."

—Seth Godin

Expertise

Your expertise elevates the impressions you make to an entirely new realm. When you have paid the price, earned the right, and done the homework to be called an expert, people perceive you differently.

In the speaking and training industry, companies rarely want to hire just "a speaker." They want to hire an expert. It is that level of expertise that earns the higher dollars because clients believe an expert will bring higher value in teaching, training, and takeaways.

> 66 *Becoming an expert will make you more valuable and more interesting in your field of endeavor.* 99

Whether you become an expert in scuba diving, positive psychology, veterinary medicine, or cake baking, the extra knowledge and experience changes how people perceive and receive you. If your field of endeavor no longer lights your fire or drives your passion, ask yourself what else you are interested in—then work hard, study up, and learn everything you can to develop your expertise.

I have been a student of Brendon Burchard for several years. He says, "No matter how small you start, start something that matters."

He is a world changer indeed, and has devoted his professional career to teaching people how to package and position their knowledge, experience, and passions to build their expert empire.

Last year, I ventured out to California with my friend Tina to attend his life-changing Experts Academy. He did not disappoint, and he inspired us all with brilliant tools to make a difference in the world. He contends that everyone has something of value that is uniquely their own. By developing your passion, interest, and experience, you too can become an expert.

According to thought leader and *Outliers* author Malcolm Gladwell, it takes about ten thousand hours of practice to achieve mastery in a particular field. While there may be a shorter path to positioning yourself as an expert, it still requires focus, learning, and the belief that you can do it—followed with dedicated action.

7 Great Ways to Become an Expert

1. **Learn everything you can about the subject**
   Develop your knowledge: read books, attend classes, listen to your market, get training, attend seminars, find a mentor, join a master-mind group of like-minded individuals, watch videos, and study.

2. **Put in the time**
   Practice, apply, experiment, volunteer, and work within your area of knowledge to deepen your own understanding as you build real-life experience.

3. **Share with others**
   Deliver presentations and teach others on your topic. Look what TED Talks have done for normal people who simply presented their passion and thereby launched careers, fame, and fortune. Interact with your target market. Maximize use of the Internet and SEO.

4. **Get published**

   Create content, write a book, build a blog, post on social media, and write articles for professional publications and news sites to build your intellectual portfolio of expertise. Repurpose content in a variety of ways.

5. **Keep stretching**

   Become a thought leader by taking an idea, belief, or process and turning it inside-out and upside-down. Bust beyond the box and shatter a few ceilings to go where no one has gone before. Make your mark by becoming a pioneer in your pursuits.

6. **Get interviewed**

   Oprah launched many a career by simply interviewing new authors. Find ways to be interviewed on radio, podcasts, Internet radio, and television.

7. **SEO (Search Engine Optimization)**

   By establishing a strategic online presence through your website, social media, keywords, meta tags, and Google AdWords, the world may discover your expertise and "beat a path to your door."

Becoming an expert not only establishes you as a leader in your field, it will make you a trusted resource that people can rely on for new and innovative ideas. In addition to raising the stakes and helping you increase your income, your expertise will serve to make a powerful first impression, which will truly help you shine and stand apart from the crowd. Having fun and meeting interesting, incredible people along the way is an added bonus!

Experience

> *"I offer my expertise and experience for hire in order to help a group of people reach the summit."*
>
> —Anatoli Boukreev

"Been there, done that!" Life is said to be your greatest teacher so don't let school get in the way of your education. Simply by living life you will gain new experiences that are uniquely your own. Your vantage points along your journey will help you form your perceptions, grow your influence, and ground you in a wisdom which can only be gained from having been there and having done it.

Building Professional Credibility

"Trust is built on credibility and credibility comes from acting in others' interests before your own."
—Stephen Denny, Killing Giants

Your professional experience can strengthen your resume, increase your earning potential, prove dependability, instill trust, and open new doors of opportunity which would remain closed otherwise.

If you were to spend your own time and money to hire a consultant, coach, or trainer, wouldn't it give you more confidence knowing that they have "walked the talk" and have vast experience with what they are teaching?

---

66 *Take your place among experienced professionals by focusing on ways to learn, grow, and succeed.* 99

A serious challenge facing corporate America today is that the Baby Boomer generation is beginning to retire. And as they are leaving the workforce, they are taking their intellectual capital with them.

Companies that do not have a succession plan in place in which their seasoned professionals are teaching the younger, less experienced generations risk losing far more than talent. The depth of their experience is a valuable commodity and resource.

This trend has birthed wildly successful consulting firms that hire or subcontract with experts who have the experience companies need to be successful. Regardless of whether the professional had experience as a CEO, CFO, COO, Marketing Director, HR Manager, or Sales VP, their knowledge, know-how, and expertise can command a premium.

10 Lessons Learned from Experience

"The difference between school and life? In school, you're taught a lesson and then given a test. In life, you're given a test that teaches you a lesson."

—Tom Bodett

Experience helps you to . . .

1. Learn what works and what doesn't.
2. Discover what to do and what not to do.
3. Gain and retain information longer.
4. Build your confidence and expertise.
5. Grow your emotional intelligence.
6. Expand your awareness and understanding.
7. Establish credibility and know-how.
8. Learn the value of patience, persistence, and timing.
9. Receive a priceless education if you choose to learn from it and apply the lessons.
10. Look back on your life with the fulfillment and satisfaction of knowing that you used your time well.

Ernestine Shepherd is a beautiful, soulful, and disciplined young lady who began body building in her mid-50s. Having never belonged to a gym, she began her journey with her sister to look and feel better. Now, at eighty, she has earned the title of, "World's Oldest Female Body Builder," and has won numerous championships and competitions. Her special experience and unique story have inspired millions to take better care of their health by eating right and exercising, regardless of their age. Her experience and expertise impress everyone who hears her story.

Experience is Diverse

When my friend Amy Tolbert (ECCOInternational.com) was interviewing people to hire a new business development director for her global training and communications company, an attorney submitted his resume. At first glance, she wondered why he would be interested because he didn't have any training and development experience. What he did have, however, was business experience in networking, marketing, and relationship building—which equals a master's degree in development. She decided to hire him and was impressed that he was able to hit the ground running. He secured business faster and more successfully than most could have. My advice; keep an open mind when reading those resumes!

Education

"An education is an esteemed commodity in our society. Rightfully so, school will teach you the history of humankind, make you a master of your field, and qualify you for work in the real world. Without a proper education, one often finds their success impeded and opportunities lacking."

—Carmen Harra, Ph.D.

Getting an education is not only a matter of checking the boxes as your life progresses; it is a gift which can enrich every aspect of your world. A quality education prepares you to make a living, make better choices, and have more doors open as you build a life. Your education can be the 'make or break' difference when a hiring manger reads your resume or invites you in for an interview. In our competitive world, today a Master's Degree has become the new differentiator that a Bachelor's Degree once was.

Your education is something no one can ever take away from you. I was intrigued to meet a lady with two sons who are both fighter pilots in the U.S. Marines. I asked what they had earned their degrees in—her answer, American History and Fine Art. Isn't it interesting that a prerequisite for flight school was simply to have a college degree, regardless of the area of study? It is a calling card that will unlock more doors than you can imagine.

Your level of education speaks on your behalf. It demonstrates your ability to establish a clear vision, prioritize your goals, and honor your commitments. Oh yeah, did I mention it also makes you smarter?

You Are Never Too Old to Learn

Throughout my life, I was a "B–average" student. Sometimes I would only do whatever it took to simply pass the class. I never saw myself as being especially smart or academically gifted. I was more motivated by not disappointing my parents or grandparents than I was in gaining knowledge.

Getting a college education was an expectation and a significant part of developing my self-confidence and self-esteem. Graduating with an Associate's Degree from Tallahassee Community College and a Bachelor's Degree in Marketing from Florida State University's Business School laid a wonderful foundation as I ventured into the world to create various career experiences.

It wasn't until my mid-forties when I earned my Master's Degree from the University of West Florida in Human Performance Technology that I ever made straight A's. Excelling in and attaining my Master's Degree has changed my world professionally. It has enriched every offering, program, and concept I deliver as a speaker, author, and trainer.

What would you like to learn? Is there a topic or talent that sparks your interest? Would learning something new enhance your life for the better?

My childhood friend Marc Seals was speaking to his grandmother, Mary Seals, about whether he should pursue a Ph.D. He said, "Gammy, I would be thirty-five years old before I would graduate!" She lovingly replied, "You're going to be thirty-five years old anyway. Wouldn't you rather be thirty-five years old with a Ph.D. than without one?" I am happy to report that Mark not only received his Ph.D., but he went on to become a successful professor with a major university.

Learning from Life's Hard Knocks

- Rather than allowing your failures to define you, learn from your experience to do better next time.
- Rather than staying stuck in stress, unhappiness, or grief, use your experience to find gifts in the pain and grow.

Share Your Stories

"The best brands are built on great stories."
—Ian Rowden, Chief Marketing Officer, Virgin Group

You have a lifetime full of stories—from the lessons you have learned to the adventures you have experienced. They are golden and can be used in creative ways to share your wisdom and demonstrate your unique expertise. Especially in business.

Amy uses stories to illustrate her professional track record. When a client asked her how she would design a two-day conference for three hundred people, she did not answer their question directly. Instead, she shared a story of a similar event by saying, "When I facilitated a three-and-a-half-day conference for five hundred people, the design was very intense. And this is what we did . . ." By answering their question with a story, it made her qualifications all the more credible.

Storytelling has also become an integral part of strategic brand marketing—and gives customers something they can care about and buy into. By connecting stories and emotions to their brands, companies are better able to distinguish themselves from their competition. And you can do the same. Stories help people connect with you from their hearts rather than just their heads. Everyone loves a great story so learn to tell yours well.

8 WAYS TO **MASTER**
The Art of **PREPARATION**

1. *Mastering Your Mindset.* Be and Do what it takes to Have superb results. Nurture a mindset that works for you, rather than against you. Your inner thoughts determine your outer world.

2. *Emotional Intelligence.* Developing your EI will allow you to explore new depths of understanding in yourself and others. It will give you insight as to why people behave as they do and assist you in areas you may wish to improve.

3. *Prepare for Success.* Feel the satisfaction and power of having your act together! Get organized beforehand to get better results. Prior Planning Prevents Poor Performance.

4. *Your Personal Brand.* Create your own personal brand to stand apart from the crowd. Package your unique talents, style, personality, and products. Show and tell who you are and what you do—to the world.

5. *Dress to Impress.* Making a great first impression is not an accident, and with a little planning, experimentation, and application, you can transform your dress, style, substance, and impact to leave a positive long-lasting effect.

6. *Healthy Habits & Hygiene.* Make the personal choice to instill healthy habits and hygiene into your life. When you resolve to live a healthier life, you will feel better, look better, enjoy improved well-being and make a better impression.

7. *Punctuality Plus.* When you have scheduled an appointment, or have made a commitment, you have essentially made a promise. Being punctual demonstrates your consideration for others and that you can be depended upon.

8. *Expertise, Experience & Education.* Your expertise elevates your impressions to an entirely new realm. When you have paid the price, earned the right, and done the homework to be called an expert, people will be impressed.

3

The Art *of*

BODY LANGUAGE

8 WAYS TO OPTIMIZE
NON-VERBAL COMMUNICATION
FOR POSITIVE IMPACT

The *Art* of BODY LANGUAGE

Your body language is your primary language—and one that every person understands! Although it is non-verbal, evidence suggests that our body language and tone of voice can have a bigger impact and account for more of our communication than the words we speak. Your body language continuously communicates for you, whether you are aware of it or not. Are your intended messages being well conveyed?

One of the most compelling things about you is the energy you put forth—whether it is positive, negative, or neutral. And that is only the beginning. The way you walk, talk, stand, and carry yourself sends messages to others that can attract or repel, encourage or discourage, and impress or depress. Using your body language to your advantage can not only improve how others perceive you, but can raise your own levels of confidence, competence, and self-esteem.

Given its significance, it is wise to learn, explore, and apply *The Art of Body Language*. Being mindful of your body movement, facial expressions, voice tone, gestures, orientation, postures, and touch will help you project personal excellence for transforming your communications with others.

1. *Energy & Aura*
2. *Approachability*
3. *Mirror, Mirror*
4. *Eye Contact*
5. *Smiling & Expressions of Emotion*
6. *Poise, Postures & Gestures*
7. *Orientation & Proximity*
8. *Handshakes, Hugs & Other Touching*

1. $\mathscr{E}$NERGY & $\mathscr{A}$URA

"We are all energy, radiating our own unique energy signature. Feelings, thoughts, and emotions play a vital role and quantum physics help us to see the significance of how we all feel. If all of us are in a peaceful, loving state inside, it will no doubt impact the external world around us and influence how others feel as well."

—Arjun Walia

We live in a universe made up of energy. The energy that binds, as it whirls and swirls physical atoms, exists at varying levels of vibration and frequency. Science proves that what appears to be solid is simply moving at a slower rate. Whereas, what is moving, grooving, and flowing, has a higher rate of vibration. We as humans work the same way.

Like everything else in our world, we too are energy. Each one of us is an energy being releasing our own distinctive energy signature that is perceptible to others by way of our choices, perceptions, behaviors, attitudes, and physical cues.

You know when you feel good and you know when you feel bad. As a result, you are experiencing and displaying a wide range of energies, aren't you? Some bring you up, while some bring you down. Start paying attention to your unique energy. In this chapter, you will learn how to feel, feed, and harness the energy of your intentional choosing.

Your energy naturally produces a **physical presence**. I can see a person from across a crowded room and feel her energy. Before I've ever met her or shared the same space, I will pick up her vibe to know if she is someone I would like to know or if she is better to avoid.

At networking events, I am a heat-seeking missile for happy, vibrant people. With experience and practice, you can develop a sixth sense about whom to approach and of whom to be wary. I'm drawn to people with positive energy. I would rather be lifted up than pulled down. Wouldn't you?

Energetic Impact

"With every word and every action, you are either positively affecting or negatively infecting others."
—Susanne Gaddis, Ph.D.

The difference between a positive attitude and a negative attitude can be measured by its level of energy, both inwardly and outwardly.

Imagine how your positive attitude feels when you are enjoying a fabulous day—the sky is blue, the grass is green, the birds are singing—and all is right in your world. You are filled with boundless energy and joyful optimism. Life is great!

And then . . . you cross the path of an energy vampire whose low vibe and toxic energy drains out every bit of yours—pulling you down.

---

66 *Energy is contagious and infectious and whether it is the good kind or the bad kind—other people feel it.* 99

In his book, *Don't Sweat the Small Stuff for Kids,* Richard Carlson has a chapter entitled, "Don't Throw Up on Your Friends." He shares a funny metaphor about energy and attitude. When you are sick, miserable, and contagious, isn't it best to stay home and get better so that you do not go out into the world and infect others with your yuck?

Unfortunately, while people may be considerate with their illness, they often lack the same consideration with their bad attitudes, not thinking twice about spewing their negative energy on everyone around them and making others sick in the process. Talk about making a bad impression, much less setting you up for an unfavorable outcome!

Have you ever had to work with one of these types of draining people? Most likely.

We prefer to be around others who bring out the best in us and make us feel good, don't we? Customers want to do business with people who make them feel valued, appreciated, and happy. Bringing a great attitude with positive energy is one of the best strategies you can have for your personal and professional success. Matching our energy with another person's will help us build rapport and relationships more easily.

Expansion and Contraction

We are all wired with a natural propensity to learn, grow, and expand. Think of the positive things that make you happy, bring you joy, deepen your understanding, and make you feel wonderful. These things enlarge and grow with positive energy, don't they? The opposite is true as well; negative things make us feel stressed, sad, angry, or overwhelmed. They leave us feeling depleted and contracted.

ASK YOURSELF: Who are the people you are drawn to who bring out the best in you? How do they make you feel? Is your positive energy doing the same thing for others?

Upbeat people make us feel appreciated, important, and fantastic. These are the folks who expand and warm us with their positive energy. The Broaden-and-Build Theory in Positive Psychology suggests that positive emotions initiate upward spirals of positivity which contribute to our optimal well-being. It is no wonder positive people are more likely to make a positive impact!

However, people who cast a negative energy can make us feel doubtful, devalued, and disrespected. In response, we contract and are left cold as our awesome energy evaporates in their shadow. Downward emotional spirals ensue.

How we feel with someone—if they improve our mood or cause our heart to sink—can determine the health of the relationship. *How do you feel* around them? It's a simple measurement tool.

A light-hearted point to consider: Do you know the number one reason a man **falls in love** with a woman? Because of *how she makes* *him feel* about himself. Do you know the number one reason a man **falls out of love** with a woman? Because of *how she makes him feel* about himself! It is the same reason! When you inspire and motivate another person through your positive energy, they want you to stick around!

Soul Mates and Kindred Spirits

Throughout your life you will meet thousands of people, but every once in a while, you feel instant chemistry with a person and connect immediately. It is like meeting an old friend or returning home again. Your relationship enjoys easy compatibility and commonality. Not only can you sometimes finish each other's sentences, but regardless of how much time may pass, you can reunite and start up wherever you left off.

My friend Shelby Deering (ShelbyDeering.com) is a prolific free-lance writer. She shared with me that she and her best friend, Diana, felt like kindred spirits from the moment they met. They instantly felt a shared energy which has only continued to deepen and bond them with time. Shelby and Diana feed off each other's energy and understand one another in profound ways. She shared, "It's not about soul mates having to be a romantic partner as much as it is about building friendships with people whose energy matches your own." Recognizing the importance of positive energy, Shelby continued, "When I'm having low energy and feeling tired, bored, or defeated, I crave being around a person with a higher energy to bring me back up."

Chemistry

Instant chemistry feels great! It is a raw, organic emotion. The art and science behind relationship chemistry is still a mystery to me, but it is always a delight when it happens. You certainly know when you feel it, and that sizzle begins many a new relationship.

Ask anyone who has ever fallen in love at first sight and they will tell you—their mutual chemistry created an instant attraction. We have all known friends who went on a first date and knew instantly that they would spend the rest of their life with that person. Or, they knew instantly there was no chance because there was no chemistry at all.

Is chemistry a biological reaction which supports the propagation of our species? Or is it simply about being excited to find someone with mutually shared values, passions, interests, or experiences? Or is it because you have the same energy, vibrate at the same frequency, or share the same attitude? Regardless of how it happens, a robust and healthy chemistry is always a nice surprise and something to be celebrated.

Magnetism & the Attractor Factor

"Your vibe attracts your tribe."
—Unknown

It's a fact. We are magnets who attract whatever we are being. When we emit positive energy, thoughts, feelings, and vibrations, we attract more positives to us. When we emit negative energy, thoughts, feelings, and vibrations, we attract more negatives.

The "Law of Attraction" simply states: "What you think about, you bring about." Whatever you focus on will expand and attract more of the same. Whatever you are putting out there is usually what you are getting back. **So, if you don't like what you're getting, you've got to change what you are giving.**

You give a smile . . . you get a smile back. If you point fingers with anger, you will get anger in return. If you are obsessing about scarcity, you will continue to live in lack. If you focus on nurturing friends, you will enjoy more enriching relationships.

Without even realizing it, we magnetize people, opportunities, and outcomes. Many people continue to attract dysfunctional folks who bring trauma, drama, crisis, and negativity and then wonder why they are so miserable. Be cognizant of how you're *being* because it is most certainly attracting what you're *receiving*.

Cheri Davis is a fun, energetic, positive, and beautiful friend. We both share a vibrant and positive energy which is a rare and wonderful quality. No matter what is going on in the world, we have a magic ability to energize each other and make the day better simply by speaking. She once said to me, "Susan, our low is most people's high." Indeed. We will not always match the energies of others, and when theirs is lower than ours, that can be a very good thing!

Emotion is energy in motion; therefore, different states of mind, perceptions, and feelings can all result in different electromagnetic frequencies. How can you elevate your enthusiasm and energize your life?

15 Ways to Improve Your Energy & Raise Your Vibration

1. Take care of yourself—mind, body, emotions, and spirit.
2. Eat and drink nutritious, energy-giving food.
3. Exercise and engage your endorphins.
4. Meditate to reset, renew, and recharge.
5. Listen to music.
6. Perform random acts of kindness.
7. Get a good night's rest.
8. Plan down-time to rejuvenate.
9. Use positive affirmations to shift your mindset and re-train your brain for positivity.
10. Be fully present and engaged.
11. Be in the Now Moment—don't squander your energy on a past you can't change or a future which has not yet happened.
12. Connect with loved ones.
13. Find humor, fun, and laughter! Pump up your endorphins.

14. Access your joy within; feel and focus on it, allowing it to expand to fill your entire being.
15. Guard your energy by setting boundaries, just saying 'no," and limiting your interactions with people who drain you. The measure—how do they make you feel?

UN-impressives

What saps your energy and drains your strength? If it makes you feel bad on the inside, it will make those around you feel bad too! Don't be the energy vampire whom people want to avoid. Ask yourself and become more aware—are you . . .

- Speaking poorly of others in judgment, gossip, and intolerance?
- Looking for, dwelling on, and obsessing over the negative?
- Being grumpy, negative, and infecting others with your bad attitude or victim mentality?

My friend Deborah SuZan was taught at an early age to sing a love song to God every morning. It taught her to value the circle of love— for when you give love, you get love in return. Living the principles of positive energy and activating the law of attraction, Deborah shares, "You have to have something that raises your vibration every day. Whether it be listening to music, setting your intention for the day, praying, or surrounding yourself with positive people."

Years ago, Deborah worked with a dynamic real estate sales team. She remembers well how their accountability coach would get them fired up with cheering and jumping up and down to raise their vibrational energy before making sales calls. Practices like this can bring out the kids in people; it certainly worked well for them. This higher energy empowered their presentations, creating better results. Discover innovative ways to bring up your energy too!

2. APPROACHABILITY

"Being at ease with ourselves helps others be at ease with us.
We can give no greater gift to others than putting them at ease."

—John Maxwell

What makes one person approachable and another one not? That simple difference alone can make or break your success in your life, in your relationships, and in your career. It is a crucial way of being that empowers you with an extraordinary edge to make a great first impression, invite interaction, build rapport, and win friends.

Be Warm & Inviting

Don't you love meeting an approachable person? They roll out the proverbial "welcome mat." Their energy and engaging openness make us feel safe. They project the messages, "I'm so glad to meet you. I like you. Tell me more about you. I'm so glad that you're here," without even saying a word.

"We'll Leave the Light on for You!" This Motel 6 slogan has been a successful marketing strategy for years because of its warm invitation and friendly welcome. They know that the comforts of home appeal to us all.

We are comforted when a person, place, or business is warm and inviting. Making us feel this way increases the likelihood that we will want to learn more, do business with them, or pursue a meaningful interaction.

Consider how others may feel about you before, during, and after talking. Are you projecting an attitude that results in others feeling accepted and welcome? Are you encouraging people to speak and engage with you through your approachability?

Expect good things from people; they feel it. You never know who you are going to meet, and projecting approachability will open doors of opportunity for you that you may not have discovered otherwise.

Consistency of Comfort & Caring

"Comfort is absolutely essential to approachability. From remembering names to open body language to appropriate topics of discussion, comfort is king. And if you want to assure that co-workers, clients, friends, family—even strangers—can approach you AND be approached by you, they have to be comfortable. And so do you."

—Lee Hopkins

Approachable people are "straight-up." It is comforting to know exactly what to expect when you see them. What you see is what you get! The consistency of their moods and emotions creates a predictable and consistent outcome that can be reassuring in our turbulent times. You know you can depend on them to be well balanced, accepting, and empathetic to the needs and feelings of others.

Create Emotional Safety

Having moved from Florida to Wisconsin, it has been an interesting exercise for me to attend networking events where I did not know a soul. I would silently scan the room to see who was approachable and who was not. It was those individuals who put out the approachable vibes whom I would be magnetized toward to engage in conversation.

Being a keen observer, I would think to myself, *who is approachable? Who is someone I'd like to know? Who is putting out welcoming vibes?*

❝ *The approachable individuals are the first ones that I introduce myself to because they make me feel emotionally safe.* ❞

I attended such an event when the Middleton Chamber of Commerce held its annual holiday party. Yes, I went alone. However, once inside, I noticed a lovely blonde lady wearing a bright red dress, a smile on her face, and her heart on her sleeve. Her dazzling approachability opened the door for the two of us to create a new and wonderful friendship. Today, I count Deborah SuZan among my closest friends and it was her approachability with her noticeable friendliness that made it possible.

Are you being approachable when you are around new people? Ever not know what to say? Simply smile when you make eye contact. This is a subliminal invitation to help others feel safe—allowing conversation to follow naturally.

As humans, we are all insecure to a certain degree, and we don't want to risk looking stupid, being rejected, or feeling awkward. An approachable person intuitively knows how to set new acquaintances at ease and create a safety net for them to be vulnerable and authentic.

An Open-Door Policy

"A leader that is visible and receptive will often hear of ideas, issues, problems, and circumstances that would never come to light otherwise."

—Tim Cummuta

"Welcome" is a word to use often! Leaders who maintain an open-door policy inspire trust, teamwork, and healthier communication. They are more likely to earn respect, gain buy-in, and foster collaboration.

When individuals feel comfortable approaching their leaders, their confidence to share ideas, discuss problems, and offer suggestions is strengthened. It emboldens them to take personal ownership and perform at higher levels within the organization.

Unfortunately, unapproachable leaders create a tense environment that may prevent their people from bringing their best strengths and talents or challenges and solutions forward.

In her book, *The Approachability Factor,* my friend Laura Stack (theproductivitypro.com) writes, "Being personable is a leadership strength, while being unapproachable, prickly or guarded shuts people up and shuts them down, cutting off information flow and collaboration vital for a team to do its best work."

UN-Approachable and UN-Impressive

"That's why I don't understand why actors become arrogant and are completely unapproachable—because as an actor, the most valuable thing you can do is talk to people and hear their stories, because it'll all come in handy."

—Daniel Radcliffe

Trying to engage with an unapproachable person can lead to embarrassment, alienation, and resistance. Why would we set ourselves up for that kind of pain and failure? It's no wonder that people may avoid them—the risk of rejection is too great. Unapproachable behaviors include a person who is . . .

- Tense and prickly.
- Remote and preoccupied.
- Cold and distant.
- Withholding of acknowledgement or response.
- Apathetic and disconnected.
- Preoccupied and distracted.
- Intimidating.
- Snobbish or cliquish.

12 Ways to Maximize Your Approachability

There are new habits you can adopt starting NOW that make you approachable and encourage other people to engage with you. Approachable people . . .

1. Use body language to their advantage.
2. Are open-minded to new people and new experiences.
3. Encourage others to feel better about themselves.
4. Are willing to be told not what they want to hear, but what they need to hear.
5. Provide an inviting aura that is warm and comforting.
6. Realize that authenticity and transparency earn trust.
7. Intuitively tune into the feelings and needs of others.
8. Are emotionally steady and respond appropriately when they sense awkwardness or discomfort in others.
9. Radiate happiness and curbs cynicism.
10. Provide a safe environment for others to express themselves.
11. Make others feel valued and appreciated.
12. Listen and consider other people's viewpoints and opinions.

In his book, *The Power of Approachability*, approachability expert and speaker Scott Ginsberg (hellomynameisscott.com) encourages readers to think of their communication interactions in terms of approachability. He shares that approachability is a two-way street with inbound and outbound channels. **Inbound**, or reactive approachability, is akin to welcoming others onto your front porch by being open, available, and accessible. **Outbound**, or proactive approachability, is about taking the initiative to step on someone else's porch and being bold enough to break the silence. Being aware of this duality will help you maximize your communication opportunities with confidence and comfort.

> *"Your initial impression goes beyond how stylishly you're dressed or if your hair looks great that day. Do you portray confidence, trust, and approachability?"*
> —Linda Swindling, Author of *Ask Outrageously!*

3. $\mathcal{M}$IRROR, $\mathcal{M}$IRROR

"There are two ways of spreading light; to be the
candle or the mirror that reflects it."

—Edith Wharton

irroring is a powerful neuro-linguistic programming technique that can be used to bond with others, build rapport, and reach mutual understanding more quickly. You may already be using it instinctively without even being aware. It is simply the process of discreetly matching and mirroring the subtle behaviors and qualities of the person with whom you are connecting. It's a form of behavioral reflection that unconsciously reveals, "We're more alike than we are different."

It is especially helpful when our differences may divide. Think of the times when you have made a diligent effort to speak in another person's native language to communicate and connect with comfort. By doing this, you are extending a considerate courtesy to meet them where they are, thus removing barriers and improving engagement.

Coordinating your gestures with someone's subtle behaviors, can help you gain understanding, realize comfortable compatibility, and develop mutual trust.

Why Does Mirroring Work?

Scientific research suggests that this technique works because of the **mirror-neurons** which are fired in our brains when we both perceive and take action. When we observe someone doing something, we may feel as if we are having the same experience.

ASK YOURSELF: When you see someone smile, does it naturally make you want to smile back? When you are irritable, do you find that people mirror your irritability? When someone yawns around you, do automatically do the same?When you hear someone celebrating, do you feel inclined to join in and celebrate too?

Your responses are not forced, but instinctual and empathetic. Mirroring provides social cues through body language and behavior which enable us to develop more empathy and understanding for others.

Why Do We Like Whom We Like?

Who are we the most comfortable with? People who are the most like us! The "Similarity-Attraction Hypothesis" (Newcomb, 1956) found that similar (real or perceived) personalities are a major determinant of our likability and friendship choices. It is simply human to gravitate toward people like us. This tribal inclination runs the gamut across demographics of age, ethnicity, culture, education, religion, and even personality style. Mirroring will enable you to find ways to **create the comfort of familiarity through similarity.**

Matching and Mirroring in Business

Since we know people like to do business with people who are most like themselves, consider this: Excellent sales people understand that "matching and mirroring" another person's body language is a powerful technique and subliminal way to develop trust, build rapport, and make their clients more comfortable and engaging. Subtly mirroring the postures, gestures, and body language of your client inspires a kinship of commonality.

Early in my sales career, various sales trainers taught our teams how to use matching and mirroring to build rapport and earn trust with our clients. When done well, it would inevitably help us improve customer service and closing ratios. It was not encouraged as a deceptive sales practice to manipulate, but rather a subtle way to make a great first impression and connect on a meaningful level.

By mirroring, speaking, and moving in tandem with my clients, I provided them with a sense of familiar comfort and ease which helped us work well together. When they leaned forward, I would lean forward. When they crossed their arms, I would cross my arms. When they began speaking slowly and quietly, I would do the same. These subtle actions help to us to communicate more effectively.

The Attractor Factor for Shifting Others

Becoming aware of what you are doing and how others perceive you will provide you with instant insight for making changes where necessary. Whatever you are putting out into the universe is going to be returned unto you and have a direct correlation to what you are getting back. In many ways, you are a magnet and manifest accordingly.

Think of your personal and professional life—are you attracting what you want? Are you attracting the kind of people you like? Do you feel that life is working for you or against you? How have others been treating you? Are you pleased with your results?

You can shift other people's attitudes by shifting your own. When people project rudeness, impatience, and intolerance they attract the same in return. If someone looks like they are having a difficult day, you can shift their world by simply sharing a kind word.

Modeling for others a sincerely positive and encouraging countenance will not only enrich their lives, it can foster trust and appreciation for you. This subtle technique of mirroring can help others feel compatibility with you and lead them to feel better about themselves. A win for everybody!

4 Tips for Mirroring Others

1. **Body language.** When they smile, you smile. When they lean back in their chair, you lean back in your chair. When they cross their legs, or fold their arms, you do the same.
2. **Vocabulary or specific words.** Notice their language and the words they choose and use—their keywords, expressions, expletives, or phrases.

3. **Communication style.** People receive, process, and deliver information in different ways. Notice whether someone is results driven or relaxed, emotional or pragmatic, talkative or observant. Recognizing their style will enable you to adapt your style to theirs to build rapport and improve communication.

4. **Vocal style.**

   a. **Speech rate**—If they are talking fast, you talk fast. If they are talking slowly, you talk slowly. Consider rhythm, pace, and tempo.

   b. **Volume**—If they are speaking quietly and softly, match their volume.

   c. **Tone**—Mirror their emotion, tone, and pitch. You can even seek to mirror their grammar and dialect, as long as it is discreet and respectful.

Mirroring and matching works at the sub-conscious level and serves to make the other person feel more "comfortable" and connected to you. These subliminal actions can create a subconscious feeling of unison and connection that demonstrate how much you have in common.

4. $\mathcal{E}$YE $\mathcal{C}$ONTACT

"There is a saying, 'Eyes are the windows to the soul.' It means, mostly, people can see through someone else by eye contact in seven seconds. I have a habit that if I meet someone I don't know, I'd like to look at her or his eyes on purpose. When my eyes lay on them, I can immediately see their true color."

—Peng Liyuan

"Your eyes are the windows to your soul" indeed. It is a cliché for a good reason—it is a timeless truth with universal application. Your direct eye contact is one of the best compliments you can give another human being. You are subliminally telling them that you are listening, they matter, and that what they have to say is important. Meaningful eye contact has the power to transcend time and space to connect us with others and can be one of the most gracious and important ways to demonstrate attention and respect.

Your Eyes Have It

When you make eye contact with another person, you can send thousands of silent messages without even speaking a word. No wonder eye contact can be both a direct form of communication and an elusive attribute at the same time. One simple glance can convey to your recipient that you are . . .

- Present
- Interested
- Paying attention
- Being respectful
- Listening
- Confident
- Engaged
- Caring
- Dedicated
- Appreciative
- Empathetic
- Focused
- Supportive
- Trustworthy
- Acknowledging
- Excited

This list barely scratches the surface; however, it opens the conversation about how vital your eye contact is for making positive first impressions. Whether it is in a sales situation, love at first sight, a husband and wife having an important conversation, a parent disciplining a child, or a teacher instructing her students, eye contact is a powerful body language for enriching engagement, focus, and communication.

Cultural Exceptions and Awareness

As we explore this valuable non-verbal language, please note that these principles do not apply in many cultures around the world. In some cultures, direct eye contact may offend, affront, violate, or threaten.

Being culturally aware and respectful of others' cultures will help you to keep the habit of making eye contact in context. As a matter of fact, in some parts of the world making eye contact can be construed as being exactly the opposite of what I am sharing in these pages. Making a great first impression is always about the specific environment and circumstance, isn't it?

Eye Contact Can Reveal if a Person is . . .

- Shy or gregarious
- Honest or deceitful
- Confident or terrified
- Interested or bored
- Patient or irritated
- Sincere or inauthentic
- Organized or Unprepared
- Attentive or distracted

We've all been in the middle of a conversation and the person with whom we are speaking breaks eye contact, appears distracted, glazes over, or looks elsewhere. Their simple eye movement can quickly break down communications by making us feel ignored, dismissed, or rejected. For some, it may be accidental and unintentional, while for others, avoiding eye contact is on purpose.

12 Reasons Why People Avoid Eye Contact

1.   They do not want to reveal their feelings.
2.   They are not being honest and truthful.
3.   It makes them feel vulnerable and exposed.
4.   They are being rude or indifferent.
5.   They are ashamed or embarrassed to talk about something.
6.   They are nervous or lacking confidence.
7.   It makes them feel very uncomfortable.
8.   They are arrogant, snobby, and pretentious.
9.   They are afraid of saying the wrong thing or looking stupid.
10. They are shy or introverted.
11. They are accessing internal thoughts or emotions to process and contemplate information.
12. Or as mentioned before, and important to remember, it may simply be a cultural value or behavior.

Too Much of a Good Thing

There are times when eye contact can move to the dark side and become creepy, hostile, rude, or condescending. When it is overused or made for the wrong reasons, eye contact can make others feel uncomfortable and leave a terrible impression . . .

- obsessive staring
- mocking
- too much intensity
- inappropriate focus
- averting eyes
- obvious contempt
- gawking, ogling
- casting the "evil eye"
- over-watching
- intimidating
- unwelcome looks
- rolling the eyes

As with most things in life, a healthy balance will keep us on the right path. To avoid too much eye contact or too little, seek to create a comfortable mix. It is generally encouraged to use more eye contact when you are listening and less when you are speaking.

LISTEN!

My friend Julie McCarthy told me how she wanted to impress upon her children how important it was to make eye contact to succeed in life. So, she created the memorable acronym "LISTEN" to help them remember. One day her son's football coach complimented her on how attentive and engaged he was in practice. The coach continued to share how he appreciated that her son would hold eye contact whenever he was speaking. When she later spoke to her son about this he responded, "Mom, that is what you always taught me!" Using Julie's method, when you actively **LISTEN** you will make a great impression:

Look In Side Their Eyes Now

Connecting with Your Audience

"As any speaker will tell you, when you address a large number of people from a stage, you try to make eye contact with people in the audience to communicate that you're accessible and interested in them."

—Simon Mainwaring

When speakers make eye contact with an audience, they will be perceived as being more prepared, more competent, confident, and trustworthy. Eye contact helps to relax the speaker and reminds them that their audience is made up of separate individuals who perceive things differently. Audience response is clearly seen in the expressions of their eyes.

Chris Clarke-Epstein, CSP (change101.com) is a recognized and award-winning change expert who is a national speaker and trainer.

Although she is an introvert, she told me: "I try to make eye contact while I am speaking to make a specific point. It is a very powerful way to connect with my audience." Chris will walk around the room and pause when she is saying something, while looking directly at each person. She continues, "The beauty of speaking with small groups is that I am able to make eye contact with everyone there."

7 Ways to Improve Eye Contact at any Time

1. Relax into the moment by smiling.
2. Practice making eye contact with people you trust, so that when you are with strangers, it is easier to form a connection.
3. When you feel uncomfortable, begin by looking at their mouth or forehead.
4. Lean in and show that you are interested and attentive.
5. Put a little space between you and the other person.
6. Remember that the other person may be feeling just as awkward.
7. Don't give them a blank stare throughout a conversation. Rather, practice gazing down or to the side every few moments so that you appear relaxed.

5. Smiling & Expressions of Emotion

"Smiling people are better rewarded socially—they have more friends and receive more cooperation, help, and support."

—Dr. T.P. Chia

Have you heard that a smile is the shortest distance between people? *I love that!* There is nothing like a genuine smile to create a first impression with positive impact. A genuine smile is inviting, contagious, encouraging, and brings joy into the world. It instantly tells others that you are glad to see them, that they are important and you are approachable. Accompanied with good eye contact, a smile serves as an immediate icebreaker to warm up relations and turn a stranger into a friend. You can transform your entire physical appearance, personal experience, energy, and social success simply by smiling. And it is also good to do just for you!

A Gift

"A smile cannot be bought, begged, borrowed, or stolen and it is of no value unless given away."

—Dale Carnegie

Smiling is truly one of the most generous gifts you can give to another. You never know when your smile may inspire the sad, encourage the hopeless, heal a heart, or change someone's world for the better. You would be surprised how even the simplest of smiles can ease a social situation, encourage another, remove barriers, and dissolve differences. It is not only a gift to the recipient, but you will receive affirming returns on your investment.

For the Health of It

Research has shown that smiling releases endorphins—the **happy hormones** that shift your physiology for improved well-being. When you smile and your eyes crinkle, your body releases chemicals that change the chemistry of your brain, lifting spirits, and reducing pain. Even when it is hard to smile and you are forcing it, positive changes take place in your physiology.

Smiling reduces blood pressure by lowering the stress-inducing hormones, such as adrenaline and cortisol. As my mother, who is now in her eighties, navigates the challenges of aging, her mantra has become, "Keep moving and keep smiling." She has observed the rapid decline of her friends who haven't. She is striving to stay strong, happy, and vital; her desire to smile is helping her to live a healthier, more satisfying, and longer life.

Universal Body Language

"A warm smile is the universal language of kindness."
—William Arthur

As the saying goes, "Smile and the world smiles with you, cry and you cry alone." Smiling is a universal symbol of happiness that transcends language and communication challenges. A smile is one of the most powerful and important body language cues we share with others—and as such a heartfelt emotion, it's impossible to express its effect on others in words.

Your smile is a magnet for goodwill and positivity. In unison with your attitude, people gravitate to happy people! Your smile is a kind hello and a sincere invitation that opens the gateway to engage others and begin conversations. Your smile draws people to you as it simultaneously brings out the best in you both.

Improves Appearance

A genuine smile is your best fashion accessory and the most important thing you can wear. No matter your age, a smile makes you look and feel better. People spend billions of dollars every year to get pumped, pulled, tucked, and tweaked in hopes of being more beautiful. But there is nothing like a genuine smile to transform your appearance and provide an instant facelift. I told my life-mate, Daniel, that his smile is the sexiest thing about him! The biggest wrinkles on my face are my smile lines. There is no need for Botox or fillers to erase the years of joy that I have known through life.

Reciprocity

"Too often we underestimate the power of a touch, a smile, a kind word, a listening ear, an honest compliment or the smallest act of caring, all of which have the potential to turn a life around."
—Leo Buscaglia

When you see people smiling, does it give you a sense of connection with them? The law of reciprocity illustrates it is hard to not smile back when someone smiles at you. A friend recently shared that even if he is in a rough mood, when someone smiles at him it enhances his kindness and encourages him to project a better attitude.

I attended a symposium to hear Shilagh Mirgain, Ph.D. speak on mindful leadership. Throughout her program, I made sure to make eye contact and smile to support, affirm, and engage with her presentation. When audience members do this for me, it adds an extra punch of dynamic energy that enriches my presentations and improves my performance.

Service with a Smile

One of the speaking programs I deliver is entitled, "Service with a Smile . . . How to Create a Sensational Customer Experience." Smiling is at the heart of my teaching because when employees smile while delivering service, it tells the guest/client/customer . . .

- You matter.
- You are important.
- We are glad you are here.
- We appreciate your business.

Whether you smile to make a great first impression for customer service, building rapport, communicating your intentions, networking, sharing your happiness, closing deals, or demonstrating you are fully present and engaged, smiling is the key to your success.

Make Smiling Your Super Power

"A smile is the light in your window that tells others that there is a caring, sharing person inside."
—Denis Waitley

As the youngest of five daughters, I was the last to start high school. The night before my first day of ninth grade, I was filled with fearful anticipation and anxiety. In hopes of finding solace, I asked my sister, Farrell, who was a mature and powerful junior, "How am I going to survive? How am I going to make friends? How am I going to fit in?"

In her infinite 16-year-old wisdom, she gave me some of the best advice of my life. Her words of wisdom have helped me succeed in networking, relationships, and business ever since. She said, "All you have to do is smile."

"Okay, but I know it can't be that easy," I responded. "I can do that. But how am I going to fit in and make friends?" With a hint of impatience, she said, "Susan, chill out! Just smile!"

Being driven by an upperclassman the next morning at least saved me from the agony of riding a school bus. As she pulled into the parking lot, my first day of high school had begun. Leon High School in Tallahassee, Florida sits on a high hill overlooking the track and ball fields. Since we parked all the way down by the track, the three-story red brick building was an intimidating sight as we scaled the steep hill.

After climbing three sets of steps, I finally arrived at the front double doors of the school—just like one sees in the movies! As I entered the lobby, what I saw inside was bone chilling. Groups of kids were already in cliques, standing in circles talking, like pools of sharks. I felt that if I didn't say the right thing, act the right way, or do the right thing I was going to get eaten alive.

Pushing fear aside, I remembered what my sister had said. So, I smiled to mask my self-doubt, lack of confidence, and fear. What happened over the next weeks and months was astounding. I learned the secret to surviving high school. When you smile at others—they will smile back!

It became a life-changing experiment in making friends and building confidence. What I didn't realize at the time was that almost everyone else was just as scared as I was. When I gave them a smile, it gave them emotional safety and comfort. By the end of my freshman year, I was Class President, Class Queen, in student government, and a bat girl on the baseball team. None of it would have been possible if I had not learned early on that smiling was my super power. It can be yours, too!

Smiling Bloopers

- Insincere smiling can backfire! (Different from a shy smile that just beckons a friendly "hello.")
- Transitioning from a smile to a straight face, too quickly, may give others the impression that you are fake or do not like them.
- Going overboard and smiling all the time, especially when it is inappropriate, will make you appear insincere.

- If your mouth smiles, but your eyes don't, there is a disconnect that can make you appear less authentic and trustworthy.

Simply Smile and Nod

"Smiles are probably the most underrated facial expressions, much more complicated than most people realize. There are dozens of smiles, each differing in appearance and in the message expressed."

—Paul Ekman

Have you decided to simply smile and nod to avoid a confrontation with someone who was being a jerk? Have you ever feigned agreement with your face to get along with others, even when you disagreed with their position? We all have. Your expressions of emotion can protect you at times in awkward situations, and when used with integrity. Test the waters by responding with an expression of curiosity or bewilderment when someone is acting inappropriately.

Expressions of Emotion

"The face is a picture of the mind with the eyes as its interpreter."
—Marcus Tullius Cicero

While smiling is a powerful facial gesture, there are other expressions on your face which reveal an extraordinary number of emotions. A body language of its own, people will read your facial messages and form opinions about you before you've even said a word. It is one of your most powerful non-verbal behaviors. People do read a book by its cover and these expressions provide glimpses into what they will find inside.

What are you projecting? How are you showing up? Are you aware of how your expressions are impacting your communication with others? At any moment, you can use your face to open doors of opportunity if it demonstrates interest, enthusiasm, respect, understanding, delight, agreement, and more.

Look at the single words below; wear these emotions on your face for just a moment. Try them on for size and note how they make you feel:

ASK YOURSELF: Happiness. Fear. Anger. Sadness. Contempt. Surprise. Disgust.

These are the basic human emotions which communicate with clear understanding across cultures, languages, and countries. In other words, a smile naturally conveys happiness and a frown naturally conveys sadness, no matter where you may be using your passport.

According to the "universality studies" conducted by psychologists Paul Ekman, Carroll Izard, and Friesen (1969-1972), the words above describe the natural expressions of emotion shared by the *entire* human race.

Beyond these universal ones, there are hundreds of variations which are often a matter of choice, whether consciously or sub-consciously. Most every facial movement is connected to an emotion that conveys your state of being and your attitude.

It is through these facial expressions that we write and feel our life story, create lifelong social habits—through which we are received and perceived by a multitude of others. **When you want to make a positive first impression, let your face know!**

Seeing Your Expressions Through the Eyes of Others

Take the initiative to stand in front of a mirror and practice a wide range of emotions so that you can see what other people are seeing. Video tape yourself and watch your movements and your expressions. You can pick up on clues to what you need to fix and where you could improve your presentation.

My friend Julie was cooking dinner in her kitchen one night. Her expression was blank as she stood alone working by herself. Her daughter walked in and gasped, "Mom! What's wrong?" She said "Nothing. I'm fine." In response, her daughter added, "Then tell your face! You scared me!" Emotional expressions can easily be misinterpreted when we are not aware of what people are seeing. Being deep in thought can look that way.

Behind the Poker Face

Obviously, I've never had a good poker face my entire life! The old-fashioned term "poker face" connotes that a person is expressionless, leaving the people around them clueless as to what is going on in one's heart and head. The poker face conceals his thoughts and feelings to such a degree that it is difficult to interpret his emotions. Believe me, there have been times when I wish I could have carried this off.

When my son was a teenager, he would use this tactic when I was lecturing, nagging, or suggesting. As a parent, it was maddening because I could not read his reactions! His stoicism would sometimes deflate my efforts or make me surrender in laughter, changing the subject all together.

Be aware, putting on a poker face can backfire during your first impressions because it can make people uncomfortable and make you more difficult to read and harder to get to know.

Well Hello Halo!

It is human nature for us to make generalized judgments about a person using only a couple of traits. The "Expressivity Halo" theory explains how we connect various personalities to specific facial expressions and assign assumptions about that person.

For instance, we are more likely to trust a person who is easier to read; they're easier to believe. Or we tend to think that an energetic and happy person will be more productive. Even traits such as competence, dominance, and courage can be conveyed by certain facial expressions and will stimulate unconscious bias.

ASK YOURSELF: Are your facial expressions in alignment with your true personality? Are they working on your behalf to project the best impression possible?

It's Showtime!

As a professional speaker, my facial expressions are essential for effectively telling stories, engaging audiences, fostering involvement, and connecting on a personal level. One day I decided to get Botox in my forehead to erase a few wrinkles and signs of aging. Much to my surprise and disappointment, I could no longer raise my eyebrows. My face was stuck in a heavy-browed expression, which is the polar-opposite of my joyful spirit and enthusiastic nature. It makes a funny story, but it taught me that authenticity wins over vanity any day!

6. Poise, Postures, & Gestures

"Remember that poise and power are inseparably associated.
The calm and balanced mind is the strong and great mind;
the hurried and agitated mind is the weak one."

—Wallace D. Walters

- **Poise:** a graceful and elegant bearing in person; a composure of dignity and manner.
- **Postures:** the position of a person's body when standing, sitting, or walking; carriage, bearing, and stance.
- **Gestures:** moving parts of your body to express an idea, opinion, emotion, or meaning.

Nonverbal Body Language

Poise confirms purpose. Postures portray personality. Gestures express emotions. Your **poise, postures,** and **gestures** make a powerful statement about who you are and how you feel about yourself. This dynamic trio speaks volumes about you.

Since non-verbal signals have five times the impact of verbal signals, paying attention to the image you are projecting is crucial to your first impressions.

ASK YOURSELF: Do you appear self-confident or unsure? Do you project a calm demeanor or scream instability? Do you come across as a leader or try to stay invisible? Do you walk with purpose and intention or doubt and trepidation? Do you look vibrant and energetic, or stressed and overwhelmed?

I hope you took the time to answer those questions. Because your poise, postures, and gestures are the physical manifestations of your attitudes, perceptions, belief systems, self-esteem, feelings, and engagement. Be sure to know if they are working well or hindering the actualization of your potential. Being the architect for your habitual patterns of non-verbal language, you have the power to change any of it at any time.

Making an Entrance

How do you enter a room? How do you walk into a job interview? How do you approach a sales prospect for the first time? Accomplished leaders know that the way they make an entrance can project their confidence and set the tone for their interaction with others. Use your poise, postures, and gestures to make it grand.

Poise

"For beautiful eyes, look for the good in others; for beautiful lips, speak only words of kindness; and for poise, walk with the knowledge that you are never alone."
—Audrey Hepburn

It has been said that poise is our highest state of consciousness. It reflects your presence, composure, balance, gratitude, discretion, and self-respect. Whether a man or a woman, a poised person carries within themselves an elegant air of dignity and grace. Their personal brand is polished and purposeful.

Poised Positioning

"Poise is an unseen power and this unseen power is always ready to come to the aid of the outer action.
—Sri Chinmoy

- Be mindful of how you use your body to communicate.
- Be fully present in the moment.
- Be thoughtful and gracious in your actions.
- Be fluid and elegant in your movements.

- Express flow—walk in freedom and spontaneity.
- Develop an unshakeable sense of authentic inner confidence and certainty.
- Develop a deep respect for others.
- Move slower and more deliberately.
- Walk in integrity, class, and modesty.
- Smile kindly and laugh softly.
- Become a student of manners and etiquette.

Social Graces

In years gone by, particularly in the East and the South, ladies would attend charm school to learn how to elegantly stand, sit, dance, and walk. Even today, there are "Cotillion" classes for young people to learn how to carry themselves with dignity and use proper social graces. I don't mind sounding old-fashioned because these culturally rich rituals lay a firm foundation for the appropriate behaviors and excellent manners necessary for a positive impression. Embracing a tried and true tradition can *sometimes* be beneficial. Let's avoid the awkward, embarrassing, and unsophisticated ways we see all too often.

Postures

"Elegance is usually confused with superficiality, fashion, lack of depth. This is a serious mistake: human beings need to have elegance in their actions and in their posture because this word is synonymous with good taste, amiability, equilibrium and harmony."

—Paulo Coelho

9 Reasons Why Improving Your Posture is Important

By projecting strength and excellence in your physical presence, you will . . .

1. Look better and feel better.
2. Appear, *and be,* more fit and healthy.
3. Powerfully influence your mindset.
4. Appear more confident, self-assured, and competent.
5. Carry yourself with more purpose and intention.
6. Breathe deeper and get more oxygen in your body, which will improve your energy and health.
7. Reduce or prevent back pain and muscle tension.
8. Improve productivity by energizing your physiology.
9. Make a significantly more positive impression.

Proper posture conveys that you are ready to take command and master new situations. When you project this level of confidence, you will instill confidence in others.

12 Ways to Improve & Project Confident Posture

1. **Go people watching.** Note how you interpret the different postures you observe. This will expand your awareness of how posture impacts first impressions and will help you become more aware of yours.
2. **Stand in front of a mirror** to see what other people are seeing. Are your shoulders level? Are your hips level? Do you appear aligned? Are you projecting confidence or timidity?
3. **Take posture pictures** to provide you with points of reference and a baseline over time. Look at past photos of yourself.
4. **Stand with your back against a wall and align your spine.**
5. **Evenly balance on both feet, spaced hip-width apart.**
6. **Take yoga or Pilates** classes to strengthen your core muscles, improve flexibility, and balance, all which support your posture.
7. **Consciously pull your shoulders back,** stand erect with chin held high.

8. **Practice** tucking in your stomach, pulling your shoulders back, raising your chin, and looking straight ahead.
9. **Sit up straight** without being rigid.
10. **Enter a room** like you belong there or own it.
11. **Stand with an open stance** to be welcoming and approachable.
12. **Angle your body** towards the person to whom you are speaking. Angling your body away may signify that you are indifferent, fearful, putting up a barrier, or trying to get away from them.

"Good posture is not just "sitting or standing up straight." It is about moving in a fluid manner that evenly lubricates your joints and uses your muscles in a balanced way. The definition of good posture considers the alignment and positioning of the body with respect to gravity."
—Helen Potter FACP, Specialist Musculoskeletal Physiotherapist

What Does Poor Posture Look Like?

- Stiff & rigid
- Slumping
- Slouching
- Hunched over
- Rounded shoulders
- Overly arched back
- Stumbling
- Head forward

In sensitivity, we must be aware that many people suffer from poor posture because of physical disability, injury, health issues, heredity, obesity, or musculoskeletal construction. These descriptions are not meant to offend or judge people who are *unable* to change their posture.

Poor Posture Promotes . . .

In addition to sabotaging people's perceptions and impressions of you, poor posture can cause uncomfortable health issues:

- Fatigue
- Discomfort
- Neck and back pain
- Muscle imbalance
- Headaches and body aches
- Structural changes to your body

Power Posing

Harvard professor, Amy Cuddy, delivered a dynamic and ground-breaking Ted Talk entitled, *Your Body Language Shapes Who You Are.* As a sociology professor at Harvard, she conducted research to ascertain how our body language impacts others and how we feel about ourselves. Her research revealed that when people use expansive positions and "high-power" poses, it literally powers them up!

Her research suggests that by assuming these power poses for only two minutes, it may increase a person's testosterone and decrease their cortisol. Although her conclusions are still being tested, I have found her results to apply in my life. Try it for yourself to see how it makes you feel!

Stand for two minutes with legs apart, and with your hands on your hips, or stretch your arms wide open overhead. Another power pose is to lean back in your chair with your feet propped up and your hands behind the head. When in these expansive positions, you take up more space, breathe in more confidence, and appear larger than life.

The next time you have a high-stakes meeting, a presentation, or an important social engagement, practice power posing beforehand to potently and powerfully impact your confidence.

Gesturing with Your Hands

Ask any person trained in sign language and they will confirm the fact that you can talk with your hands. Your hand gestures communicate for you and are an integral part of your language. While some people may come by hand gestures naturally, you can learn to be even more expressive to get your points across—and to be memorable. Simply by reading the hand gestures below and mimicking them, you will quickly see how each conjures a different interpretation.

- Clapping
- Finger pointing
- Counting
- Start
- Stop
- Held out & open
- Middle finger
- Fingers crossed
- Okay
- Peace sign
- "No-no" finger shake
- Gesturing to self
- Hands facing up
- A tiny pinch
- Cupped together
- Wipe the slate clean
- Clenched fist
- Praying hands
- Shhh . . . (finger over mouth)
- Inviting together

A smart way of using your hands to make you look more interesting, thoughtful, and self-assured is to steeple your hands and fingers. Try using it strategically in formal environments or workplaces to show confidence and consideration.

We must remember that some hand gestures which are commonly used and widely accepted in the U.S. might be considered rude or offensive in other countries. As always, I encourage you to be mindful of how and where you use certain gestures to assure you maintain your professionalism and positive impressions.

Gestures and the Signals They Send

- Rubbing your face, palms, and neck may signify anxiety and stress.

- Arms crossed with clenched fists may signify hostility, anger, and impatience.
- Arms crossed with each hand gripping other arm may signify insecurity and self-doubt.
- Arms crossed with thumbs up may signify interest and engagement.
- Or my favorite—arms crossed may signify that you are simply cold!
- Fidgeting and squirming may signify that you are lying, afraid of being found out, insecure, or uncomfortable.
- Standing with your hands behind your back may signify power and superiority.

Kinesthetic Responsiveness

In his book, *How to Win Friends & Influence People,* Dale Carnegie encourages you to greet people with "animation and enthusiasm." This form of kinesthetic responsiveness provides a splendid example of how impactful your gestures can be while responding to others. Whether it be running up to an old friend you have not seen in a while or standing up to greet a business associate when he approaches your table, being kinesthetically responsive is an impactful way to gesture your level of interest, engagement, and enthusiasm.

Exaggerating Your Gestures

Have you ever walked through a door and been jumped on by an over-enthusiastic dog with big paws who practically knocked you down? Some people have that effect. Being too flamboyant and over-boisterous can be overkill and push people away. Drama queens and kings have mastered these exaggerations, much to the chagrin of their observers. Remaining intentional in your gestures is a mark of poise, elegance, and maturity.

Projecting Excellence

As a professional speaker, Susanne travels all over the country and practically lives on airplanes. One day as she entered security to board yet another flight, she was struck by the poise, posture, and gestures of the man in front of her in line. As a communications expert, she observed his excellent presentation with appreciation and awe.

The gentleman was dressed impeccably in a crisp white shirt and well-fitted suit and he sported a new haircut. She watched him as he removed his flawless leather belt, his gold money clip, and well-polished shoes. (And of course, he had Listerine in a baggie to ensure fresh breath!) The care with which he dismantled was impressive. His poised and fluid movements were deliberate and respectful of his personal possessions. As he regrouped and proceeded down the concourse, she was struck by how his stance and carriage intrigued and impressed her. His projection of elegance created a presence of pride and dignity. He left a remarkable impression.

In her book, *Ask Outrageously!,* my friend Linda Swindling suggests to "Mimic the body language of the most powerful people you know. They stand up straight, make appropriate eye contact, and use gestures to convey their points. Look at their feet. Usually they are placed about shoulder-width apart. They have an open stance. They smile and nod when they agree."

Begin paying attention to the poise, postures, and gestures of the people whom you admire and respect the most. How do they carry themselves to project excellence? Adapting their behaviors may serve you well to enhance and improve your body language.

7. ORIENTATION & PROXIMITY

Social orientation can be used to your advantage to make a great first impression; however, it can also backfire when we violate the boundaries of someone else's personal space. Awareness of space, orientation, and proximity is a powerful tool for your relationship toolbox.

The Dance of Spatial Orientation

Become aware of the physical distance and spatial orientation that you experience while in the company of others. Being empathetic and sensitive to a person's **physical comfort zone** can have a huge effect on the way in which you are received and perceived.

One of my girlfriends is deaf in her left ear. If I am having a conversation with her on her left side, hearing is difficult and communication can become frustrating for her. However, if I orient myself to her right side, she can hear me clearly and communication is much clearer.

I have a few friends who are confined to wheelchairs for access and mobility. I don't want to always be looking down at them while they are looking up at me. To enjoy a meaningful conversation, I'm quick to kneel beside them or pull up a chair to talk at the same height. Begin to recognize the orientation of other people and align yourself with their body position and physical needs so that you may connect on a more balanced and effective level.

When my son was in kindergarten, he had a wonderful teacher named Debbie Zahl. She was a tall lady by nature and to her five-year-old students she must have seemed like a giant. When she wanted to connect with a student on a personal level, she would lower herself to their height and meet them eye to eye, making communication more effective. Otherwise, she might have left them feeling overpowered and intimidated. Our spatial orientation and proximity have a definite impact on how our message is received.

The Warm Welcome of Hospitality

Walt Disney World is the epitome of world-class customer service. Employees must be hyper-vigilant of spatial orientation to engage, impress, and interact with guests. For simply being near a guest, employees are trained to:

- Make eye contact and smile.
- Greet and welcome each and every guest.
- Seek out guest contact.
- Provide immediate service recovery.
- Always display appropriate body language.
- Preserve the "magical" guest experience.
- Thank each guest and demonstrate that appreciation.

Many hospitality companies follow the "5 and 10 rule," whereby when a customer is within *ten feet* of the employee, they should provide acknowledgement with eye contact and a genuine smile. When the customer is within *five feet,* it is encouraged to provide a warm welcome, sincere greeting, a friendly gesture, and offer to help, or to engage him or her in conversation.

King Arthur's Round Table

In the legend of Camelot, King Arthur gave consideration as to how his knights might be positioned spatially to impart a message of power and status. He decided they would have their meetings at a round table, which meant that they were all considered equal and there was no "head of the table." He built a league based on equality and mutual respect to unify and fortify the power of teamwork.

When you are sitting behind a desk with a person on the other side, there is a barrier between you that becomes a psychological and subliminal message. Some of the best leaders I know have a round table or a circle of chairs in their offices so that when people come in to speak with them, the arrangement lends itself to more engaging interaction. Using a round table in which there is no head fosters collaboration, cooperation, mutual respect, and equal positioning.

When having lunch or dinner at a long rectangular table, I prefer to take a middle chair so that I can turn to my left or to my right to make meaningful conversation with the people in attendance. When I have been seated at the very end, it can prove to be difficult to speak, hear, and connect with everyone there. Think ahead, and whenever possible, put yourself in the middle of the action!

Proxemics

Proxemics is the study of human use of space and the effects that population density has on behavior, social interaction, and communication. Imagine invisible bubbles around every person that provide each of us with comfort zones for social engagement and interaction. In 1966, American anthropologist Edward T. Hall specified four distinct distance zones to describe the perception of physical space around us. Understanding these zones and honoring their invisible boundaries will give you a sixth sense about another person's "space" as well as your own.

- **Intimate Zone** (less than 2') —This zone represents our personal space and is reserved for the most trusted and loved people in our lives. Touching, hugging, standing side by side, and engaging in private conversations is common and encouraged. When an interloper violates this personal space, great discomfort and awkwardness can be created. What to do? Take a step back or sideways.
- **Personal Zone** (2'-4') —This is the distance for interaction with good friends, family, social gatherings, or parties. It's an

easy and relaxed space for talking, shaking hands, gesturing, laughing and making faces.

- **Social Zone** (4'-12') —This zone seems to be an appropriate distance for casual friends, colleagues, and acquaintances to interact. It is the comfortable distance we maintain while interacting or addressing large groups of people.
- **Public Zone** (over 12') —This is the distance we keep from strangers or persons with little acquaintance. It provides the greatest distance between people. This is a safe space that still allows us to experience community and belonging with new people.

As you navigate the various zones with people, a variety of specific physical and psychological responses is elicited from them. Until you know someone, avoid invading his or her personal space. Getting closer gradually demonstrates that you like the other person. This gradual and comfortable approach begins the circle of rapport—he sees that you like him, he likes that you like him, and he reciprocates by liking you back.

As you seek new opportunities to make favorable first impressions, be ever aware of the subtle effect that physical positioning and distance/closeness can have on your interactions with others and use this understanding to your advantage.

8. $\mathcal{H}$ANDSHAKES, $\mathcal{H}$UGS & $\mathcal{O}$THER $\mathcal{T}$OUCHING

"Too often we underestimate the power of a touch, a smile, a kind word,
a listening ear, an honest compliment, or the smallest act of caring,
all of which have the potential to turn a life around."
—Leo Buscaglia

To touch or not to touch . . . that is the question. Handshakes, hugs, and other touching all have their appropriate space and place. The key to success in this area is to know when, where, and how to best put these into action. What is acceptable on a personal level is very different from what is acceptable on a business level. When we utilize touch well, we will elevate our presentation, demonstrate respect, and convey confidence. However, when we use touch poorly, it can be disastrous, personally and professionally.

Handshakes

"In my lifetime, as a younger man, you were assumed to be an honest
person. Your word was your bond, and a handshake was as
good as a contract in business."
—Mark Skousen

A simple handshake is not always a simple handshake. The way it is delivered can take on a million meanings and interpretations. As with every other form of body language and non-verbal communication, you are sending silent messages simply by the way you shake hands.

Your handshake has the power to reveal your strength of character, make a promise, demonstrate your level of respect, exercise your etiquette, and represent your business acumen. Learning how to do it well will take you far in life and in business.

A strong handshake conveys confidence, clarity, strength, and intention. As with everything else in life, if it is overzealous, it may be seen as aggressive, arrogant, or dominating. A bone-crushing vice-grip is just plain obnoxious and one of the fastest ways to make someone angry.

A person who offers a loose handshake, on the other hand (pun intended), may be interpreted as being uninterested, lacking confidence and self-esteem, weak, or being wishy-washy. Whether too strong or too weak, a bad handshake can set you back and close down a potentially rewarding relationship before it ever gets started.

Research by the Income Center for Trade Shows found that people are twice as likely to remember you if you shake hands. According to the American Management Association, it takes only *one-fortieth* of a second to create a human bond. Whether you shake someone's hand, squeeze their arm, or touch their shoulder, make these moments count to be remembered favorably.

What does a solid, comfortable, impressive handshake look and feel like? To deliver a great handshake . . .

- Extend your right hand out vertically at a comfortable waist level toward the person you are meeting.
- Connect hands with web to web contact made between the thumb and index finger.
- Be intentional and appropriate by showing mutual respect and teamwork.
- Gently squeeze firmly enough to be confident, yet lightly enough to be gracious. Shake a few times for good measure.
- Discreetly rotate your wrist so that your hand is slightly on top of theirs when you want to subconsciously convey self-assurance.
- Make eye contact and smile to show sincerity. Throw in an acknowledging head nod for good measure. Avoiding eye

contact may be interpreted that you are not attentive or have
something to hide.

- Introduce yourself and when they share their name, repeat it
back to them to help you remember it. "It is nice to meet you
John."
- When in doubt, mirror their handshake to adapt to what
makes them feel comfortable. Customize accordingly to the
gender, age, position, personality, and culture of the person
you are meeting.

Palm Reading 101

"Touch has a memory."
—John Keats

- **Palm Up**— Conveys openness, service, humility, and
sympathy.
- **Palm Down**—Demonstrates authority, superiority, and
control.
- **Palm Vertical**—Shows you are meeting on equal terms with
a mutually respectful greeting.
- **Palm Wet, Cold, or Clammy**—Ick! The "dead fish" is creepy.
Make your hands warm and dry before reaching out to touch
someone, please! It can also be conveyed as being nervous
or over-excited.
- **Palm Perfect**—This is my favorite. Better known as the
"hand hug." While you are shaking hands with your right
hand, place your left hand on top, wrapping both people
in warmth and trust. This two-handed shake illustrates
affection, caring, or concern, especially when you then reach
up to grasp their arm or shoulder.

High Fives & Fist Bumps

"I dread handshakes. I've got some problems with my hands, and everywhere I go, people want to impress me with their grip. To make it worse, now women are coming up with that firm shake. So I'll say, 'Gimme five!' If a boy wants a handshake, I'll just give him a hug."

—George Foreman

High fives and fist bumps have become the popular alternatives to traditional handshakes, especially among the younger generations. As a new social norm, they are used as a greeting, an approval, an acknowledgement, a celebration, and a gesture of understanding. High fives and fist bumps are also viewed as a healthier alternative to traditional handshakes because they don't spread germs.

Considerations & Exceptions

- Be mindful of a person's age; be tender with arthritic hands. In that case, a loose and gentler handshake is a gesture of sensitivity and compassion.
- Show interest; even if your right hand is full, offer your left hand.
- Demonstrate respect when you are caught in an introduction while seated; try to stand.
- Be instinctive about when to allow the length of your handshake to linger to express unity, connection, or sympathy.

Hugging

"We can bring positive energy into our daily lives by smiling more, talking to strangers in line, replacing handshakes with hugs, and calling our friends just to tell them we love them."

—Brandon Jenner

All hugs are not created equal. Some people are naturally gifted in showering others with warmth and affection. They can hug with such a sincere intention it transcends a handshake. Their hugs feel genuine, non-threatening, and are emotionally consistent with the relationship they share with the "hugee."

One such person is my friend Brian. He is a deeply compassionate man who was sad to learn that his work colleague, Tom, had lost his 17-year-old daughter to a drug overdose. When Tom returned to work weeks later, Brian approached him and said, "Man, I am so sorry. There are no words to express my condolences."

Brian reached out to hug Tom. At first, he was rigid and on guard, but with Brian's genuine embrace, he felt Tom release into his safety. Tom had had to be so strong for his wife and family, and Brian's hug allowed him to surrender into another man's strength. It was a memorable and powerful step towards healing. Sometimes a hug at the right time, even if spontaneous, can be the kindest thing you can do for another human being.

Assumed Familiarity

Hugging is quite an intimate contact. Considering the studies done on proxemics we looked at earlier; when you get within two feet of another person you are inside their intimate space. There are some people who truly do not want you in their 'bubble' unless you are close friends or they've given you permission. Assuming familiarity incorrectly can destroy rapport, make a bad impression, and risk everything you have done well up to then.

Look for all of the possible missteps in the following scenario. My friend Amy arrived at a consultation with her Hispanic business partner. The African American woman to whom they were delivering their presentation was a long-time friend of her partner's. Her partner was greeted with a hug and Amy was greeted with a handshake. The meeting was a great success.

As it came to a close, the two friends hugged. With enthusiastic affection, Amy went to hug the African American client. The woman took a step, turned her shoulder to block the hug, and looked at Amy with dismissive anger. It was almost a defensive move. Her partner, recognizing this, put her arm around Amy to soften the situation and make light of the inappropriate gesture.

Everything turned out fine, but Amy was baffled by the barrier. She was confused by the woman's reaction since their interaction had been cordial and positive. She wondered if she had been socially insensitive or culturally inappropriate. After much reflection, however, she realized that she had simply been too quick to assume familiarity. Thankfully, she earned and learned the lesson quickly to become more aware. Amy eventually earned the trust of her client and secured her valuable business.

Assumed familiarity can get you into trouble. Be mindful in your dealings so you do not make the same mistake. Offering a hug to someone you don't know well enough yet can be a violation.

Confession

Physical touch is one of my primary love languages. For those of us who share this love language, touching is an endearing gesture of affection, appreciation, and connection. It is not intended to be inappropriate in any way when we hug you upon meeting, pat your back, or squeeze your arm.

For us, it is an enthusiastic demonstration of friendship. However, there are many people who do NOT like to be touched—men or women. In spite of our good intentions, touching can make others feel awkward, offended, and in the worst-case scenario, violated. It is crucial to be vigilant and socially aware enough that you can read people's cues to know when to pull back and contain yourself.

Years ago, I was invited to a cocktail party for an Asian-American networking group. As I introduced myself to a Japanese businessman, I reached out and firmly shook his hand. Much to my embarrassment now, I automatically took my other hand and wrapped our hands in a "hand hug." This is a common gesture of friendship in the South. As his wife approached, however, she appeared appalled and felt disrespected that I was touching her husband. Our cultural differences were marked. Despite this cultural mishap, I was able to redeem myself. We all moved past it and delighted in an interesting conversation. Physical touch is a touchy topic (pun intended), especially when various cultures are involved.

---

66 Seek to make others feel comfortable by demonstrating respect for their individual needs as well as their cultural norms. Your consideration and heightened awareness will guide you well—and help you make a great first impression. 99

8 WAYS TO **MASTER**
The *Art* of BODY LANGUAGE

1. *Energy & Aura.* You release your own distinctive energy signature which naturally produces a physical presence. When you emit positive energy, thoughts, feelings, and vibrations, you attract more positives into your life.

2. *Approachability.* Being warm and inviting demonstrates comfort, care, and emotional safety which encourage engagement. Your openness says, "I'm happy to meet you and am glad you're here."

3. *Mirror, Mirror.* Discreetly use matching and mirroring to sub-consciously demonstrate that you are " more alike than different."

4. *Eye Contact.* Direct eye contact is one of the best compliments you can give to another. You are subliminally telling them that you are listening, they matter, and that what they have to say is important.

5. *Smiling and Expressions of Emotion.* A genuine smile is inviting, contagious, and encouraging. People do read a book by its cover and your expressions provide a glimpse for what they'll find inside.

6. *Poise, Postures & Gestures.* Poise confirms purpose. Postures portray personality. Gestures express emotions. They combine to make a powerful statement about who you are and how you feel about yourself.

7. *Orientation & Proximity.* Be aware of the orientation between yourself and others so that you can be sensitive and responsive to their comfort zones.

8. *Handshakes, Hugs & other Touching.* Learning how to touch appropriately can elevate your presentation, demonstrate respect, and convey confidence.

4

The *Art* of

ACTION

8 WAYS TO INITIATE &
ACTIVATE FORWARD MOMENTUM
FOR POSITIVE IMPACT

The *Art* of ACTION

L ife rewards action. To get from where you are now to where you want to be requires forward movement and momentum. Although you may already know what it takes to bridge the gap, simply knowing what to do is not enough.

Action is the key to creating the changes needed to propel you toward your chosen outcomes and help you achieve your relationship goals. How are you allocating your time, energy, and activities to 'activate your awesome' and contribute to making a positive first impression?

The Art of Action explores specific action steps you can take for personal and professional transformation. Start by taking the initiative to be kind, courageous, and polite. Become a 'good finder' and seek to acknowledge the best you see in others. Move beyond yourself to serve a greater purpose and vision. Learn to mix, mingle, and glow, thus helping others feel more comfortable, at ease, important, and connected.

By being fully present and engaged you will maximize your moments to make every encounter count. Being proactive and intentional will enable you to create a positive experience for yourself and others.

1. *Just be Nice*
2. *Be Brave*
3. *Manners Matter*
4. *Polish the Gold*
5. *Service Beyond Self*
6. *Take the Initiative*
7. *Mix, Mingle & Glow*
8. *Be Fully Present & Engaged*

1. Just be Nice

"Lead the life that will make you kindly and friendly to everyone about you and you will be surprised what a happy life you will lead."
—Charles Schwab

Nice is a little word with a big meaning. How many times did your mother say, "Just be nice?" It's basic manners, yet in our negative world today people often neglect to extend random acts of kindness and simple acts of courtesy. It is no mystery why nice people are well liked and get along harmoniously with others. Being nice makes people feel emotionally safe, allowing for more authentic, trusting, and happy interactions.

Google Proves Nice Counts

On a quest to discover what it takes to build the "perfect team," Google launched the *Project Aristotle* initiative to find the answers. Over a period of several years, they surveyed hundreds of teams, conducted interviews, analyzed studies, and observed how team members interacted with one another.

Google's findings revealed that "psychological safety" is the key ingredient for creating a high-functioning team. It nurtures a healthy environment that encourages freedom of expression, engaging communication, empathy for one another, caring, support, respect and, drum roll please . . . BEING NICE!

Benefits of Being Nice

- You set positive karma into motion.
- What you give is what you get back in return.
- You are more likable.
- People will treat you better.
- You will reduce personal stress.

- You will make friends more easily.
- You can improve someone else's day.
- You will have less drama in your life.
- It takes less energy than being otherwise.
- It makes you a more valuable team player.
- You create a sense of emotional safety for others.
- It can keep you physically and psychologically safe.
- You set a positive example for others to play nicely.
- You will build bridges of cooperation and collaboration.
- You will improve personal and professional interactions.
- Lastly, being nice feels nice!

Paying It Forward

> *"Imagine a world where people look out for each other, where we pay It all forward, where success is measured in selfless acts, where kindness is the philosophy of life."*
>
> —www.RandomActsofKindness.org

In the hit movie, "Pay It Forward," a middle school child dreams of how he can change the world by being the catalyst for kindness. He begins his "social experiment" by performing a selfless act of kindness, and so begins the domino effect. As each consecutive person receives an act of kindness they, in turn, do something nice for another. The kindness becomes contagious and changes hundreds of lives for the better. Think of the global impact we could make if more people would make it their mission to simply pay if forward by BEING NICE.

Being Nice Has Its Limitations

While you will certainly attract more bees with honey, there are times when being nice can backfire. Take it from a naturally kind person, being a "bitch" has its time and place. There will be times when you must engage with mean, rude, and inconsiderate people.

ASK YOURSELF: Have you found that being nice to some people is simply not effective? When might it be wise to throw down the gauntlet and get tough or confrontational?

4 Times to Get Tough . . .

1. **Self-Respect**—You don't have to take everything on the chin and lose the respect of yourself and others in the process. Don't be a doormat or a pushover by allowing people to disrespect or run over you. Stand firm in your beliefs and values.

2. **Self-Preservation**—Understand and set boundaries. Decide what is and what is not acceptable in how people treat you. Claim your power to live life on your terms and not at the whims of others' unreasonable requests and demands.

3. **Protecting others**—If you are a parent of a child or a caretaker of the elderly or disabled, it is your moral duty to defend them to the end.

4. **Self-Defense**—Have you ever felt threatened, unsafe, or abused because of another's behavior? Assert yourself and do whatever is necessary to ensure your safety. Being kind DOES NOT mean you should excuse such behavior.

Build Bridges, Don't Burn Them

> *"It's never too late to be nasty, but once you're nasty,*
> *it's always too late to be nice."*
>
> —Xavier Lim

Some people not only burn their bridges, but they also torch the town! With all their deeds of drama and destruction, they leave behind an aftermath of distrust, disrespect, and disappointment. And for what? This behavior creates immeasurable suffering in all directions. It ruins reputations and business deals, shatters lives—and closes doors which can never be re-opened. These repercussions can be prevented or avoided by simply BEING NICE.

Kindness is a powerful bridge builder which unifies teams, bonds friends, supports loved ones, and spreads good will. Tending to your bridges will fortify your relationships in such way that you will keep your invitations coming and your options open for future opportunities.

UN-Impressives

*"Nice guys finish first. If you don't know that then you
don't know where the finish line is."*

—Garry Shandling

Whoever came up with the idea that "nice guys finish last" must have been either very jaded or downright malicious. Why would a caring, emotionally healthy human being ever think that being "un-nice" is a virtue? Anyone who wants to get ahead in life and have quality outcomes needs to understand that kindness is a strength. You will move forward faster by making friends rather than foes.

Avoid Engaging In . . .

- Bullying
- Blaming
- Criticizing
- Complaining
- Manipulating
- Backstabbing
- Being two-faced
- Breaking promises
- Being rude or pushy
- Discriminating unfairly
- Being mean and intolerant
- Finding humor at the expense of others

17 Ways to Just Be Nice

"No act of kindness, no matter how small, is ever wasted."

—Aesop

1. Be sincere.
2. Be altruistic.
3. Practice patience.
4. Inquire and engage.
5. Keep your promises.
6. Offer help to others.
7. Acknowledge others.
8. Control your behavior.
9. Be situationally aware.
10. Be polite and courteous.
11. Use considerate manners.
12. Greet people with a smile.
13. Practice random acts of kindness.
14. Show respect for yourself and others.
15. Be complimentary and look for positives.
16. Walk in another's shoes to understand their needs.
17. Share of yourself without expecting anything in return.

2. Be Brave

"Be brave. Take risks. Nothing can substitute experience."
—Palo Coelho

Being brave is not for the light-hearted. Bravery takes fortitude—the very act of bravery prevents anyone from knowing you were ever afraid in the first place. Any time you put yourself on the line, you risk (and maybe fear) failing, falling, being embarrassed, or looking stupid—none of which are comfortable. If being brave were easy, more people would be.

Being brave requires taking deliberate action and doing something new that stretches you beyond your comfort zone. It's not bravery unless you are doing something which causes you to feel afraid. Unless there is some degree of fear or apprehension involved, bravery is not even needed.

When it comes to meeting new people, playing well with others, and connecting on deeper levels, there are inherent gaps which can be closed only by being brave. When is bravery needed?

Social Scenarios for Being Brave

"Courage doesn't always roar. Sometimes courage is the little voice at the end of the day that says I'll try again tomorrow."
—Unknown

Stepping out and stepping up can be an intimidating experience, especially in social situations where the outcomes are unpredictable and uncertain. Have you ever been reluctant to . . .

- Say "no?"
- Request help?
- Ask for a raise?

- Stand up to a bully?
- Talk about tough topics?
- Confront a friend or spouse?
- Speak up and share your opinion?
- Begin a conversation with a stranger?
- Deliver a presentation or speak in public?
- Talk about the "white elephant" in the room?
- Befriend people who are much different than you?
- Make sales calls because you don't want to be rejected?
- Approach a new group of people at a networking event?
- Go to an event by yourself where you did not know anyone?

Each of these scenarios can strike fear in the hearts of many because each involves risk and potential discomfort. Life holds endless circumstances with a broad and diverse range of challenge or conflict that require you to be brave.

What is easy for one person may be terrifying for another. Not all people have developed an unshakable confidence to kick butt and conquer. How can meek and quiet wallflowers, both women and men, join the ranks of the risk takers and event shakers? The first step is to ask yourself how you may be feeling stuck and then get moving.

Stuck in the Status Quo?

"If you always do what you always did, you'll always get what you always got!"
—Unknown

If you like the relationship results you have been getting and don't see any need for improvement, your status quo may actually be your sweet spot for comfort and contentment. That is a wonderful place to be.

However, if you are like most of us, staying stuck in your status quo may prevent you from striving, thriving, and growing in your relationship possibilities.

I was once hired by an organization to deliver a workshop on networking. The goal was to provide their engineers with tools and strategies for expanding their circles of influence—to foster innovation, collaboration, and teambuilding. One of the engineers raised her hand in the middle of the program and bluntly said, "I'm happy with the people in my life and don't care to add any more." I respect and appreciate her position and have sometimes felt the same way.

But, as long as we are alive, we will meet, greet, and interact with new people. Even if we are not inviting them into our personal lives, being socially brave will open new doors which may have remained closed otherwise.

Face Your Fear and Do It Any Way

"Your fear is the most boring thing about you. Fear only ever tells you one thing: STOP. Whereas, creativity, courage, and inspiration only ever want you to GO.

Go = motion = change = fascination = possibility = growth = LIFE."

—Elizabeth Gilbert

Fear is the number one reason why people do not take action. The divine irony is that most of the fears we experience are self-generated and born out of our own imaginings, hence the acronym **False Evidence Appearing Real.**

In his book, *Fear is a Thief,* my dear friend Gary Westfal shares, "Let's call fear what it is, shall we? Fear is an enemy—a thief—that robs us of the things we rightfully desire for our lives. It hides behind the cowardly cloak of deception we permit it to wear, effectively allowing it to have more power than it rightfully deserves."

Every one of us, at some time or another, has allowed fear to prevent us from living our best possible life. The first step in conquering our fears is to identify and confront them. Among the most common are fear of . . .

- Failure
- Success
- Being rejected
- Looking stupid
- Financial insecurity
- Falling on your face

- Being vulnerable
- Appearing weak or unhealthy
- Exposing your secrets
- Being alone or unloved
- Upsetting the status quo
- Disappointing others

14 Tips for Cultivating Bravery & Courage

1. **Ground yourself in your character values:**
   Building a solid foundation of integrity and character will fortify your confidence to face down fears and take bold action.

2. **Take a deep breath & relax:**
   When you feel fear, your body tenses up and your thoughts lead you down an anxiety-ridden path. Stop, breathe, relax.

3. **Try something new for the first time:**
   Take a chance. Stretch beyond your familiar limits by taking risks that move you out of your old mindset and into a new perspective. Once accomplished, trying something new bolsters your confidence and boosts your ability to be brave.

4. **Build upon your strengths and talents:**
   What are you good at? What makes you feel confident and personally powerful? Your competencies will ground you and build your strength.

5. **Get involved in a cause you are passionate about:**
   Serving a vision bigger than yourself changes your focus from self-doubt to whatever action is necessary for the vision to succeed. "When in doubt, take it out."

6. **Avoid the bystander effect:**
   Rather than standing on the sidelines watching other people achieve their goals, jump in with both feet and get involved.

7.   **Interview brave people and learn their secrets:**
     Whom do you know that displays courage and confidence?
     Ask them for their best practices, mimic their actions, follow
     their steps, utilize their methods. Ask if they will mentor you.

8.   **Borrow courage:**
     There is inspiration all around you in the form of people who
     are living your dreams, achieving similar goals, and already
     succeeding. Knowing that something can be done is often
     half the battle. Most successful people find great reward in
     helping others reach for goals.

9.   **Change Your Attitude Toward Failure:**
     Many successful people will tell you that if you aren't failing,
     you aren't trying—that failure is an essential precursor to
     achieving worthwhile endeavors. Failing (no matter how
     hard) is one of life's best teachers for winning the next time.

10. **Start small:**
     Taking small, consistent steps for calculated risks will help
     you test your footing. Once you begin enjoying mini-victories,
     you will be able to build upon your small successes to
     escalate momentum and strengthen your courage to take
     bigger ones.

11. **Reduce uncertainty by being prepared:**
     As Zig Ziglar once said, "Success happens when opportunity
     meets preparation." Preparing well for potential outcomes
     will provide you with a safety net if there is a hiccup, glitch, or
     temporary setback.

12. **Practice, practice, practice:**
     Each time you test your bravery you grow your self-assurance
     and increase your comfort to a greater degree. Repetition
     helps build confidence and competence. You did it; now do it
     again!

13. **Do It Scared:**

    Being scared is a precursor to bravery, otherwise it wouldn't be bravery, would it? Mustering the courage to stretch beyond your familiar territory is a rewarding act in itself.

14. **May the Force be with you:**

    Whether you fortify yourself with a positive mental attitude, affirmations, faith in God, prayer and meditation, or an innate sense of personal destiny, you have the power to summon your courage and be brave.

If I Were Brave

By Jana Stanfield & Jimmy Scott

What would I do if I knew that I could not fail?
If I believed, would the wind always fill up my sail?
How far would I go? What could I achieve?
Trusting the hero in me?

If I were brave I'd walk the razor's edge
Where fools and dreamers dare to tread
I'd never lose faith, even when losing my way.
What step would I take today if I were brave?

What if we're all meant to do what we secretly dream?
What would you ask if you knew you could have anything?
Like the mighty oak sleeps in the heart of a seed,
Are there miracles in you and me?

If I refuse to listen to the voice of fear
Would the voice of courage whisper in my ear?

3. MANNERS MATTER

"Manners are not optional, but essential."
—Kingsman Movie

Impeccable manners and courteous behavior are the hallmarks of healthy relations and human interaction. Polite people tend to be more respected, admired, and appreciated than their rude counterparts. Your manners are critical for both making a positive first impression and creating success in life, love, and business.

Without civilized social graces, not only is life more difficult, but a positive first impression can be destroyed as fast as it is made. You already know the difference between being a gracious person versus a rude one. And as is often the case, the people who would benefit the most from reading a book like this are the ones least likely to buy and read it. For you, however, this chapter will serve as a sterling reminder to make your manners shine.

Modern-Day Manners

"The hardest job kids face today is learning good manners without seeing any."
—Fred Astaire

While good old-fashioned manners and etiquette have worked for centuries, new standards and expectations have come into play with the modern world. Behaviors which would have been appalling in the past are now socially acceptable. Likewise, what is a social norm today may have been irrelevant thirty years ago. Regardless of the trends we see in the deterioration of morality, respect, and values, wise people will still strive to take the high road to rise above the ever-increasing rudeness and stand apart from the crowd.

Years ago, I heard a story about a centenarian who was being interviewed on her 100th birthday. She was asked, "Throughout your life, you have witnessed amazing change and innovation. The past one-hundred years have brought the inventions of the car, television, air conditioning, and microwave ovens. What is the most extraordinary change you have seen in your lifetime?" Without missing a beat, she replied, "That a teenager can say "suck" in front of their parents and get away with it!"

While cultural norms may have changed with the times, being considerate of fellow human beings is not an antiquated notion; its time hasn't ended. Quite the opposite is true. In our world today, kindness and politeness are needed more than ever.

19 Manners Which Will Never Go Out of Style

"Manners are a sensitive awareness of the feelings of others. If you have that awareness, you have good manners no matter which fork you use."

—Emily Post

The elegance of etiquette is a timeless expression of class which transcends social status, demographics, educational level, and ethnicity. Good manners say more about you than the person who is on the receiving end. Take the initiative with deliberate steps to be a polite person:

1. Say please when you are making a request or asking for help.
2. Say thank you when a person has said or done something kind or at your request.
3. Ask permission before borrowing something that's not yours.
4. Hold doors open for the next person coming through.
5. Offer a helping hand before being asked.
6. Let the people exiting an elevator step out before you step in.
7. Be kind to people who are in service positions.
8. Keep your negative opinions close to your vest and out of earshot where your words might hurt or offend.

9. Be careful not to curse in front of others.
10. Cover your mouth when you cough or sneeze.
11. Reciprocate a thoughtful word or a good deed in kind.
12. Say "excuse me" when you bump into someone, unintentionally violate someone's space, or need to get someone's attention.
13. Apologize when you've made a mistake or are in the wrong.
14. Live by the "Golden Rule" and treat others the way you would like to be treated.
15. When dining at home or in a restaurant, wait until everyone is served before eating your meal.
16. Acknowledge notable events like birthdays, weddings, and anniversaries.
17. Reply to invitations, regardless of whether you will be able to attend.
18. Acknowledge and show gratitude for gifts and gestures of hospitality.
19. Put things back where they belong. Leave the world a better place than how you found it.

Misplaced Manners

---

66 *All manners are not created equal and can conjure different interpretations based on the environment in which they are being displayed.* 99

What is appropriate in one setting may be entirely inappropriate in another. How you behave at a football game is different than how you behave at your sister's wedding. How you interact with your closest friends will be different than how you engage with your boss.

For more than forty years, Judith Martin has inspired the world with advice on etiquette excellence, proper behavior, and codes of conduct through her critically acclaimed newspaper column, "Miss Manners." In an interview for her book, *Miss Manners Minds Your Business,* Mrs. Martin reminds us that "When you go to work, you want a degree of professionalism which does not involve hearing about all of the sordid details of a person's love life. We are not necessarily all friends, but have a job that needs to be done. A work friend is not always a social friend. One requires distance while the other embraces intimacy."

As our society has become more casual, the line between a person's personal life and professional life has become blurred, especially with the advent of social media. Personal information, your manners (or lack thereof), opinions, and pictures of your private life are available for all the world to see. HR directors, recruiters, and potential employers will often ascertain a person's manners and moral compass from their online presence.

ASK YOURSELF: Are you presenting yourself in the best of all lights, online and off, and demonstrating the dignity of good manners? Make sure of it! If not, it may come back to haunt you.

The Waiter Rule

"Politeness is a sign of dignity, not of subservience."
—Theodore Roosevelt

How a person treats wait staff speaks volumes about their character and values. If they misbehave in this scenario, you can likely predict how they will react when cut off in traffic, when their luggage is lost, or when life doesn't go their way. It is also an indicator to CEOs and hiring managers as to whether a person is a viable candidate for being a considerate team player.

In his leadership book, *Swanson's Unwritten Rules of Management,* Raytheon's CEO Bill Swanson writes, "Watch out for people who have a situational value system, who can turn the charm on and off depending on the status of the person they are interacting with. Be especially wary of those who are rude to people perceived to be in subordinate roles. Your value system and ethics need to be constant at all times regardless of who you are dealing with."

Ernest Hemingway was a champion of the common man. He once said, "There is nothing noble in being superior to your fellow man. True nobility is being superior to your former self."

UN-Impressives

> *"Rudeness is the weak person's imitation of strength."*
> —Eric Hoffer

1. **Not holding doors open for the next person:**
    After a satisfying workout at my gym, I was walking behind a man who was exiting at the same time. He was only about two feet in front of me. As he walked through the door, he let it close behind him, almost hitting me in the face. Was he being intentionally rude? Was he preoccupied and focused on other things?
    No matter whether an offender is being a jerk intentionally, or is simply oblivious to how his behavior is affecting others, rude behavior instantly makes a negative impression. Be aware!

2. **Interrupting another person while they are talking:**
    Interrupting someone in mid-sentence demonstrates that your focus is on yourself, not the person talking. I had a friend who used a humorous retort whenever someone would interrupt him. He would graciously, albeit sarcastically, say, "I'm sorry, I didn't mean to speak while you were interrupting." It always got a laugh, yet he was cleverly letting the intruder know of his infraction without being too confrontational.

3. **Speaking rudely to others:**
   Often, all we need to do to ensure that we do not launch into a rude remark is to pause . . . breathe . . . and smile to ourselves before speaking.
   And when people are rude to you, just remember that they are revealing who they are, not who you are. Don't take it personally. Sometimes being silent is your best response.

4. **Not returning what's been borrowed:**
   Whether you have borrowed money, folding chairs, yard tools, or a popular book, always make sure you return to another person what is rightfully theirs. Lending it to you in the first place was a gift of trust and assistance. Being slow to give back in return may be considered rude.

Chivalry is Not Dead

"A gentleman knows his actions carry more weight than any words spoken."
—Being Caballero

A man worth his salt will treat a lady like a lady and make the effort to be a gentleman. While independent women are fully capable of being self-reliant, the majority whom I know appreciate being treated with respect, consideration, and chivalry. For the women who yearn for the old-fashioned, good-hearted, chivalrous guy, I promise, they do exist.

I am a very lucky lady that my life partner, Daniel, is a true-blue Southern gentleman. Watching him in action not only earns my love and respect, but it also strengthens his countenance and bolsters his reputation as a man.

As a health care provider, he treats numerous patients who are elderly or in pain. Daniel has made it a customary ritual while people are in his care to help them with their coats, provide a stabilizing arm, carry the ladies' purses, and even walk patients out to their cars. While this kindness provides extraordinary customer service, it also demonstrates that small acts of chivalry can make a significant impact on one's reputation, first impression, and overall human-beingness.

16 Acts of Chivalry

*"Some say that the age of chivalry is past, that the spirit of romance is dead.
The age of chivalry is never past, so long as there is a wrong
left un-redressed on Earth."*

—Charles Kingsley

What are some of the things a modern-day knight can do to render service? A chivalrous person will exhibit thoughtful consideration to most everyone he encounters. He will . . .

1. hold the door open for others.
2. place others' needs before his own.
3. move in to help with heavy lifting.
4. show up at the time he promised.
5. brings the car closer when it is raining.
6. return phone calls when he says he will.
7. remove his ball cap or hat when indoors.
8. protect others in threatening situations.
9. walk around the car to open a lady's door.
10. ask for others' thoughts; consider their opinions.
11. stand at the table until all ladies have been seated.
12. remove his sunglasses when speaking face to face.
13. offer his seat on a bus or in a crowded public place.
14. defend others' honor and guard them from humiliation.
15. anticipate another person's needs and offer to be of help.
16. walk along the street side of the sidewalk when with a lady or elder.

4. POLISH THE GOLD

"Anyone can find the dirt in someone. Be the one who finds the gold."
—Proverbs 11:27

As a lifetime optimist, my first tendency has always been to look for the best in others, the best in situations, and focus on what is working rather than what is not. Noticing the good has helped me immensely in life and business and it can do the same for you.

Years ago, I read Andrew Carnegie's metaphor "developing people is like mining gold." He shared that sometimes you must move tons of dirt to find an ounce of gold. Every one of us has dirt because we are all imperfect and fallible. However, within each of us lies a vein of gold. When you find this treasure, regardless of how small, and begin to polish it, a person will shine so brightly the dirt falls away. Polishing the gold in others is easy to do and a valuable habit to develop to transform your relationship results. People will usually rise to the occasion and live up to your positive expectations.

The Greatness of Being a Good-Finder

"Good finders look only for what is good in others and vocally affirm them explicitly and gratefully. We can actively look for the good in everything and everyone, even ourselves; it's just a matter of perception!"

—Amanda Gore

Finding the good in others is mutually rewarding for both you and the fortunate recipient of your kind words. Don't you love being around people who make you feel great about yourself? Don't you want to do business with people who make you feel valued and important? Wouldn't you rather work with people who appreciate and respect you? Of course you would!

Now go out and do that for others! When you become a generous good-*finder* you will infuse **positive energy, optimism, and good will into their lives, as well as your own.**

Polishing the gold in others will not only make them feel better about themselves, but it will also elevate you in their eyes as well as your own. Gifting others with your words of affirmation is an easy yet generous way to spread good will and create a positive experience for everyone.

9 Ways to Polish the Gold & Help Others Shine

1. **Take the time to mine the gold:**
    Actively seek the goodness in others then express your gratitude for it. Excavate the dirt, seek the treasure, and polish their gold to shine boldly and brightly. People will rise to your positive expectations and belief in them.

2. **Say something nice:**
    My wise mother raised us with the philosophy that if you can't say something nice, don't say anything at all. That is a Southern custom if there ever was one! It is easy to find fault, criticize, condemn, and complain—but none of these behaviors will help you enjoy positive relationship results.

3. **Catch people doing things right:**
    Outstanding leaders know that people will be more engaged, perform at higher levels, and be more loyal when they are appreciated and celebrated. Jeff West, international speaker and author of *The Unexpected Tour Guide,* shares that "People will jump over high hurdles, fight fires and break through walls for leaders who find them doing things right. Building that kind of chemistry is essential if a team is going to jell." Capitalize on the opportunity to notice what people are doing right at work and at home and they will deliver their best. As the old saying goes, "A person who feels appreciated will always do more than expected."

4. **Acknowledge their achievements:**
Great achievements require great effort and usually come dressed as hard work. Move beyond merely recognizing the achievement and express admiration for the effort it took to get there.

5. **Be complimentary:**
Find something positive to say to compliment another person. Whether they are being a great parent, dressing nicely, maintaining a gorgeous yard, or winning a recent 5K run, pick something to acknowledge which is noteworthy.

6. **Focus on the positives:**
Focusing on the positives will get you further in business and further in life. Whatever you focus on will expand. If you focus on what you do not like about another person, they will become so intolerable to you that you cannot bear to be around them. However, if you focus on their positives and can find something redeeming, regardless of how small, the positivity needed to experience a more constructive interaction and relationship will manifest before your eyes.

7. **Brag about their accomplishments in front of others:**
For years, I have shared that the definition of a good friend is someone who says nice things about you behind your back. And the definition of a GREAT friend is someone who says GREAT things to others in front of you. One of the kindest things a husband or wife can do for their relationships is to brag about their partner's qualities to other people.

8. **Flip your positivity switch:**
What is your first instinct? If you are quick to find fault, look for the negative, or complain about another person, knock it off! It makes you less fun to be around. When you feel those negative thoughts and judgments coming in, catch yourself and STOP!

9. **Make a list of positives:**
   Whether you would like to nurture a healthy relationship or improve a toxic one, make a list of positives which you admire about the other person. Begin by identifying, acknowledging, and focusing on their good qualities. Your perspective and how you feel about the person will begin to shift. You will find it much easier to polish the gold from a perspective of gratitude and appreciation.

The Art of a Giving a Great Compliment

"I can live for two months on a good compliment."
—Mark Twain

All compliments are not created equal. Some may change the trajectory of a person's life, while others fall on deaf ears. Is it well deserved or earned? People will remember you fondly when you have affirmed them in a positive way. Paying compliments creates good will, happy moments, and makes you more likeable in return. What are the key elements for a fabulous, well-delivered compliment? You . . .

- are sincere and genuine.
- give it freely without expecting anything in return. Your compliment is a selfless gift, not a boomerang.
- are specific and detailed.
- elaborate on why you like something.
- describe how their positive virtue has positively impacted you.
- can use adjectives for more colorful descriptions.
- keep it positive.
- say it like you mean it with intentional impact.
- use discretion and good judgment.
- leave no room for misinterpretation or misunderstanding.
- say the right thing at the right moment and let it flow organically.

Finding sincere ways to compliment others is a powerful way to make a great first and last impression.

UN-Impressives

- When compliments are used as a passive-aggressive way to manipulate others for personal gain.
- Delivering a back-handed compliment which makes others feel bad.
- Dishonesty—you say it but really do not mean it.
- False bravado.
- Manufacturing the moment for your ulterior motives.
- Pandering to win affection, a vote, or approval.
- Exaggerating and being over-zealous.
- Being hypocritical.
- Expressing preferential treatment or making an unfair comparison.
- When it draws attention to a person's weakness, disabilities, or shortcomings.
- When it is inappropriate and off-color.

Graciously Accepting a Compliment

How many times have you offered someone a sincere compliment only to have it thrown back in your face as if your assessment were wrong? How did you feel? Women are notorious for this social misstep and poor maneuver. Why do they do it? Rejecting a compliment makes the compliment-giver feel as though they should have said nothing.

"I love your dress." – "This old thing? I've had it for years."
"Your new haircut is cute." – "I hate it. She made it too short."
"Have you lost weight?" – "Hardly, I've gained ten pounds!"

Refusing someone's kind words can cause the one doing the complimenting to feel bad. Not only might they regret trying to be nice, but you may have cut off your chances of being complimented by them ever again. Being humble is one thing; being rude is another. Practice receiving compliments with grace, dignity, appreciation, and gratitude. The perfect response to a fine compliment is simply, "Thank you!"

Why Polish the Gold?

"When dealing with people, most respond better to praise than to criticism. To be most effective, praise must be: honest, earned, specific, genuine, heartfelt, authentic."

—Nathan S. Collier

- It builds your confidence when you realize that your words have power and can positively influence.
- As you seek to find the good in others, you will enjoy the ripple effect reminder for finding the good in yourself.
- It makes a great ice-breaker to begin a conversation.
- It helps you meet new people and make new friends.
- It strengthens your relationships and builds mutual admiration.
- It brings more happiness and joy into your life.

Praise Lavishly & Often

In his book, *177 Mental Toughness Secrets of the World Class,* Steve Siebold encourages us to use praise as an integral component in our every day interactions with others.

He writes, "The great ones use praise to lighten the load, ease the burden, and warm the heart. They know most people are lonely, afraid, or suffering through some kind of painful situation that is invisible to the rest of the world. Champions are a beacon of light in a cloudy, stormy, predictable world. Armed with praise, they are the ultimate force for good."

5. $\mathcal{S}$ERVICE $\mathcal{B}$EYOND $\mathcal{S}$ELF

"Service is a smile. It is an acknowledging wave, a reaching handshake, a friendly wink, and a warm hug. It's these simple acts that matter most, because the greatest service to a human soul has always been the kindness of recognition."

—Richelle E. Goodrich, Smile Anyway

Service

Service [sur-vis] *noun*

1.   The act of helping, aiding, or doing work for another.

Does this dictionary definition sound simplistic? Well, it is foundational to delivering world-class, game-changing service. Did you notice it didn't mention you? True service takes the focus completely off you and devotes it entirely to the needs of another person.

As you read in *The Art of Being*, having a heart of service and generosity is a powerful state of being and a positive way to make a great first impression through valuing others. "Service Beyond Self" encourages you to take deliberate action steps to rise above self-interest and *ask what you can do for others, not what they can do for you.*

The Service Mindset

When I first began my real estate career at the age of twenty-two, I had a fresh Bachelor's Degree in Marketing in one hand and 'a tiger by the tail' in the other. I was on a mission to be successful in life and in business and make a lot of money in the process. Every goal I set was about *Me. Me. Me!*

I was driven by: How much money could I make? Which property listings paid the biggest commissions? How many calls did I need to make to schedule new appointments? How many listings did I need to have to hit my target?

You can see where I am going with this! Working full-time, nights and weekends, seven days a week, I only made eleven thousand dollars in the first year! I was tired, disillusioned, and knew that I had to either change careers or massively shift my mindset.

I chose the latter. I took ALL focus off me and re-directed my time, energy, and resources to serving my clients. Their hopes, needs, and desires became my primary focus. How could I help solve their problems?

---

66 *Where my previous motivation had been a self-serving ambition, my new service mindset was dedicated to serving a vision greater than myself.* 99

Within a year, I quadrupled my income, and then I doubled it every year thereafter. This service mindset quickly taught me that by helping others achieve their goals, I could more easily achieve my own.

What Is Driving Your Service Engine?

What is the motive behind your services? If it is self-centered, self-serving, and lacking consideration for others, then earning people's trust, rapport, and business will inevitably be more of a struggle. A self-serving agenda throws up red flags which stop relationships dead in their tracks. It can destroy trust, make people wary of your intentions, and push customers to your competition.

However, if your agenda is truly to serve, your ROI (return on investment) will substantially expand. As we know from the "Law of Reciprocity," what you give is what you get. If you are helping people only to see what you can get out of it, your pie stays small and your opportunities stay limited. However, if you sincerely want to help people succeed, you will not only enjoy more success, but expand your possibilities beyond your expectations. Once you see the benefits from all directions, you will not want it any other way!

Service Beyond Self

Service Beyond Self is Essential for Success Because It . . .

- Builds credibility, trust, and customer satisfaction.
- Strengthens your personal reputation and public image.
- Fosters goodwill and makes people feel appreciated.
- Helps you build healthy relationships with others.
- Nurtures collaboration, participation, and cooperation.
- Reaffirms a continuity of service for quality assurance, integrity, and reliability.
- Saves money—it costs less to keep existing customers than it does to create new ones. When you do it right the first time, you don't have to fix it the next time.
- Improves communication and builds rapport.
- Fosters mutual respect and understanding
- By providing other people with what they want, you will get more of what you want!

Service Beyond Self in Action

I once had the pleasure of presenting to the University of North Carolina's School of Government. Upon arriving at the Raleigh-Durham airport, I retrieved my luggage from the carousel and went straight to the Sheraton Hotel kiosk to arrange for their free shuttle service. When I called the hotel, the phone rang endlessly without an answer, much less a recording.

Unfazed, I pulled up their local website on my cell phone to call the front desk. Much to my surprise, the recording said their number was out of service. What? How could this be? They were a prominent hotel and I had a reservation!

Dismayed, I called their corporate number and learned they were going through a major upgrade and launching a new phone system throughout the hotel. So much for a *free ride!* I grabbed a taxi, paid the driver twenty dollars and arrived safely at my destination. As I approached the front desk for check-in, I greeted two ladies with a smile. I asked, "Which one of you is the nicest because I have a very special favor to ask?" They laughed and I moved toward the one who raised her hand first. I shared my experience and she confirmed that their new phone installation had knocked out all their phone service. She went to get her manager and when he returned, he had cash in hand and handed me a twenty-dollar bill for my trouble!

He thanked me for my patience and apologized for the inconvenience. Much to my surprise and delight, when I finally got to my room, there was a gift basket with culinary treats to ensure my warm welcome was complete. Their simple "Service Beyond Self" philosophy has made me a raving fan and loyal Sheraton Hotel customer for life. Think about ways you can adopt this same service mindset.

Moving from Woe to WOW!!!

What happens when you have a disgruntled customer? Is there a way to take a negative situation and turn them from being an unhappy camper into an enthusiastic fan? Absolutely!

I first learned about the L.A.S.T. technique for moving people from Woe to WOW! while working with the Costa Enterprises McDonald's Restaurant group in North Florida. They have made it a part of their core principles to deliver service beyond self throughout all their restaurants.

It is such a timeless and powerful method, I wish I could give its unknown creator credit. I have since observed various organizations throughout the country integrating this outstanding method.

The **L.A.S.T.** acronym will help you remember it for years to come. It will not only teach you how to take a challenging situation and create a positive outcome, but also how to make a wonderful impression which will L.A.S.T!

L—Listen Attentively
- Be fully present and give your customer your full attention.
- Stay calm and remain patient.
- Do not interrupt or become defensive.
- Let the customer express his or her concerns.
- Nod your head and use affirming words to show that you are listening.
- Repeat back and empathize, when necessary. This confirms your understanding of the problem or question.

A—Apologize
- Thank your customer for raising the issue.
- Apologize sincerely–never argue.
- Own the problem, even if it is not your fault.
- Show genuine concern in your gestures, posture, and tone of voice.
- Take your customer at their word without questioning their motives or integrity.

S—Solve the Problem
- Take action quickly and effectively.
- Ensure that your customer is satisfied with the solution.
- Learn from your mistakes.

T—Thank the Customer
- Thank them for bringing his or her concerns to your attention.
- Treat them with respect and empathy.
- Avoid further inconvenience to them.
  "If we consistently exceed the expectations of employees, they will consistently exceed the expectations of our customers."
  —Shep Hyken

PEACE

I love acronyms, don't you? They are quick and easy tools for remembering important lessons that are too good to forget. The PEACE acronym goes straight to the heart of the matter for delivering "Service Beyond Self." When you do this one thing, you will increase your opportunities, earn loyalty and respect, and rock your first and last impressions.

*P*ersistently *E*xceed *A*ll *C*ustomer *E*xpectations

13 Simple Ways to Deliver Service Beyond Self

1. **Make it Easy for People to Do Business with You.**
2. **Be an Awesome, Sincere Listener.**
3. **Listen to Customers' Words** and tone of voice, body language, and how they feel. Ask questions, listen, and meet them on their level. Explain, guide, educate, assist and do what is necessary to help them get the information they need to fully understand their question or issue.
4. **Show Enthusiasm.** Greet customers with genuine interest. Give them your best. Think, act, and talk with positive enthusiasm and you will attract positive results. Your attitude is contagious!
5. **Identify and Anticipate Needs.**
6. **Under Promise & Over Deliver.** Apply the principle of "Service Beyond Self" . . . give more than expected. Meet and exceed their expectations. If you can't serve their needs, connect them with whoever can.
7. **Make them Feel Important.** Our deepest desire is to feel important. People rarely care how much you know until they know how much you care. Use their names, find ways to compliment them—and be sincere.

8. **Golden Voices – Golden Choices.** Your "vocal image" on the phone and in person can make or break your customer's impression. If your voice is confident, clear, and concise, you will be perceived as such. You can't separate your voice from the rest of your body, so breathe deeply, stay hydrated, and speak with confidence.

9. **Take Responsibility for their Satisfaction.** Do whatever is necessary to help them solve their problems. Let them know that if they can't find answers to their questions to come back to you for help.

10. **Treat your TEAM well.** Fellow colleagues are your internal customers and need a regular dose of appreciation. Thank them and find ways to let them know how important they are. Treat your colleagues with respect; chances are they will have a higher regard for customers.

11. **Choose an Attitude of Gratitude.** Gratitude changes your perspective and helps you appreciate the good rather than simply taking it for granted.

12. **Perform, Provide and Follow-Up.** Always perform or provide your service in a spirit of excellence and integrity. If you say you're going to do something—DO IT! There is tremendous value in being a resource for your customer. If you can help them to succeed, they are more likely to help you succeed.

13. **Use Gracious Words.** "Thank you, thank you very much."

6. Take the Initiative

"The critical ingredient is getting off your butt and doing something. It's as simple as that. A lot of people have ideas, but there are few who decide to do something about them now. Not tomorrow. Not next week. But today. The true entrepreneur is a doer, not a dreamer."

—Atari founder Nolan Bushnell

The Start of All Good Things

Your ship will never come in if you don't send any out. Have you ever found yourself dreaming, hoping, and waiting passively for things to change or for your life to get better?

Do you ever sit back and wonder how and why other people are so successful, productive, or accomplished? What is the driver that inspires them to go for the gold, seize opportunities, and make things happen?

Rather than being green with envy, realize that a dramatic difference between the "haves" and "have-nots" is the "do" and "do-nots." If you are seeking positive change and transformation, what can you begin to do?

First, take complete responsibility for your life and current outcomes. Then take proactive steps for the necessary action to move forward in your desired direction. This personal choice is at the heart of your achieving impressive results. Taking initiative is the start of all good things born from action . . .

- Growth
- Creativity
- Enterprise
- Invention
- Success
- Solutions
- Accomplishment
- Development
- Positive Change
- Transformation

Decide today to take a stand, make a plan, and get going. No one ever said it was going to be easy and wouldn't require effort. It will sometimes require that you go against the grain, face great challenge, conquer fear, overcome obstacles, and bounce back when knocked down. Choose to keep moving and don't give up. And if your ship still doesn't come in—swim out to it!

Just Show Up

Guess what? Being in the right place at the right time can't happen without your first showing up. Companies have been started, marriages made, friendships found, careers created, and opportunities seized by those people who *just showed up.* Whether through coincidence, serendipity, strategy, or fate, taking the initiative to show up will reward you in ways which never would have occurred if you hadn't. Just by showing up, you have taken a proactive step to impress people by being there" in person" and demonstrating your willingness to be involved.

Have you ever had a friend in need whose only request was the gift of your presence? When major life changes happen or tragedies hit, you can find out very quickly who your real friends are because they are the ones who SHOW UP.

Years ago, my childhood friend Steve lost his father. Since Steve had left Tallahassee shortly after high school graduation, we had not seen each other for over a decade. Upon learning of his father's funeral, I made plans to attend to "be there."

After the service, I approached the family's receiving line. When Steve saw me, he was stunned that I had made the effort to be there for him. We both cried as we hugged and he said, "I can't tell you what it means to me that you showed up."

---

66 *Showing up sends a message that you are a devoted friend, a team player, a dedicated parent, an inspiring leader, a loyal mate, and more.* 99

The actor, writer, and director Woody Allen once said, **"80% of success is just showing up!"**

You Can Show Up By . . .

- Participating.
- Sharing ideas.
- Being dependable.
- Keeping your word.
- Taking the initiative.
- Volunteering to be of assistance.
- Being there when a friend needs you.
- Raising your hand and asking questions.
- Attending your children's sporting events.
- Taking your place and claiming your space.
- Demonstrating that you have something to offer.

Getting into the Game

"As soon as you say something can't be done, you will be passed by a person who is already doing it."

—Unknown

Do you typically observe the game of life from the sidelines, sit in the penalty box, play your heart out on the field, or show up when the opportunity has already passed by and ask, "What happened?"

Your answer to this question will reveal a lot about your initiative. Granted, various situations call for diverse levels of interest and engagement. However, if you want to rock your relationship results, it is going to require action, effort, initiative, and choosing to get in the game.

Open New Doors of Opportunity

"Go out, take charge of your own prosperity, do some things, take some chances, make some calculated risks because risky is the new safe."

—Randy Gage

When my niece Rachel moved to Boston in her twenties, she needed to secure a new job. With a Bachelor's Degree in Finance on her resume and six years' self-employment work experience under her belt, she quickly accepted a Marketing Executive Assistant position to get her foot in the door of a public corporation. One day there was a Marketing Division meeting off-site, and the President of the North America business unit gave a company status informational speech that included a specific discussion around developing a career path.

In his talk, he shared with his employees that . . . *they were each responsible for taking the initiative to create their own career paths to determine their career story. Opportunities with the company were available; however, each person was ultimately responsible for informing their managers of their desire, and working toward obtaining the skills needed for career growth and progression.*

Upon hearing this, Rachel decided he was right and she took him up on his offer. She took the initiative to make sure she sat at his table for the rest of the meeting to gain an opportunity to introduce herself to him. When she did, she said, "In the spirit of what you just said, I want to come work for you." It just so happened he had an opportunity opening the very next month and he told her to apply for the position; she did and she secured the job working directly for him.

After working with the president for less than one year, Rachel was promoted to the position of "Business Manager," then "Program Manager," and within three years, "Director of Business Initiatives." She has now built an incredible career working with the company's strategy team in which she travels throughout the United States and Europe.

Interestingly, as I am writing this chapter, I am on a plane to Boston to celebrate Rachel's graduation from Harvard University with a Master's Degree in Business Management, an investment her company made in her development. Guess who is coming to the celebratory dinner? The president who not only admired her initiative, recognized her talent, and gave her opportunities to thrive, but also became her mentor and cherished friend.

Be the "Liker"

"If you want to be liked, BE THE LIKER!" This was some of the best advice my enlightened mother ever gave me. Throughout my childhood, teen years, and adulthood, this golden nugget of simple wisdom empowered me to take personal responsibility for developing friendships.

When you want to reach out, make new friends, and increase your likeability factor, step up and "like" others first. They will usually mirror your initiative and like you back.

Will You Be My Friend?

Leaving Florida meant leaving behind all my wonderful fun-loving girlfriends. When I first moved to Madison for love, one of the glaringly painful holes in my heart was that I knew so few people here and didn't have any close girlfriends. I was not sure how to start new friendships, so I became very observant of the women whom I instantly liked and resonated with.

One night, Daniel took me out for a romantic dinner to our now favorite restaurant, the Bonfyre Grill. We took a seat in a round booth, adjacent to the large u-shaped bar. We were discussing how much I missed my girlfriends in Florida and how much I looked forward to making new ones here.

Within only a few feet, there were three ladies sitting at the corner of the bar. They were talking, laughing, slapping high fives, hugging, laughing, sharing, toasting, and having an awesome night. Their energy and joy were delightful and attracted me like a moth to a flame.

Pointing these ladies out to Daniel, I said, "Darlin, that's what I'm talking about! Aren't they awesome? I want what they're having! I have to go meet them."

He pragmatically replied, "No, baby. You don't know those ladies. You can't just go up to them and introduce yourself!" The fastest way to get me to do something is to tell me I can't.

Ignoring his advice, I got up, walked over, gently rested my hands on two of their shoulders and said, "Ladies, I have to tell you how much you have impressed me. I just moved to Madison from Florida and I left behind all my girlfriends. I have been sitting over there admiring your friendships. You remind me so much of my girlfriends back home and I had to come over and speak with you." And without missing a beat, I next asked, "Can I be your friend?" They were so impressed by my sincere request, they kindly opened their circle and invited me in.

Daniel sat back, shaking his head, watching in amazement. We exchanged business cards, followed up, and have stayed in touch. Now, almost two years later, Julie, Peggy, and I have celebrated birthdays together, countless happy-hours, shared holidays, high school graduations, and more. Our sweet sisterhood was born from my taking the initiative to be open and outgoing. The resulting rewards are beautiful friendships which may last a lifetime.

---

66 Begin to take the initiative when you want to meet someone new. Be the one who steps forward first. Simply say hello and begin a conversation. 99

Introduce Yourself

Being confident and outgoing will empower you to approach new people who might be reluctant to take the first step. It is amazing how many people we come in contact with yet pass like ships in the night without any engagement or connection.

I spend a great deal of time on airplanes traveling from one speaking engagement to the next. There have been times when I have sat for hours next to strangers with whom I never made eye contact or uttered a word. But I have also met people with whom I engaged in such delightful conversation that it resulted in new business and referrals.

One morning I was sitting on a bike in a spinning class at my gym. There was a lady whom I did not know sitting on the bike next to me. As we waited for the instructor, I decided to break the silence and start a conversation. I took the initiative to introduce myself and within a few short minutes, I knew her children's names, how long she had lived in Madison, which exercise classes she preferred, and where they went for Christmas. When the class was over, I confirmed that I remembered her name correctly, reminded her of mine and shared that it was a true pleasure meeting her. A simple introduction turned a stranger into a fresh and delightful acquaintance.

Extend Invitations

How many times have you sat at home alone feeling jealous or sad that you were not invited to a party or out to dinner? You may have seen people having fun on Facebook and wondered what it would take to be included next time. And when you don't feel included, it can leave you feeling rejected, dismissed, lonely and excluded. It does not have to be this way. Why do we wait for others to do the inviting? You can change your social life instantly by taking the initiative to reach out and connect with someone.

Be the Inviter

When I began my speaking career, I designed and delivered motivational programs for children teaching them success skills for life. Before going into a middle school one year, I interviewed the principal, Alexis Tibbetts, to ask what words of wisdom her students desperately needed to hear from me. She shared, "Kids can be so cruel. Some of the children never feel included or a part of something special. Please tell them that rather than being lonely and getting their feelings hurt, they can start doing the inviting." Her words were spot-on. Alexis went on to become a well-loved superintendent of schools in Okaloosa County, Florida. Her words of wisdom were game-changing for her students. They can be game-changing for you as well.

Coffee Talk

Jill Franks is a top-producing Realtor in Middleton, Wisconsin who has taken being the "Inviter" to new heights. She began a new tradition which has become her networking trademark.

She actively seeks out interesting people in our community and invites them out for coffee. No selling, no closing, just engaging in stimulating conversation and quality connection. By taking the initiative to have coffee with new people each week, she has made extraordinary new friends, supported others in their goals, grown her business, expanded her influence, and had a blast!

> 66 *Imagine how many new friends you would make, how much new business you could create, and how much fun you could have by simply taking the initiative to be the inviter.* 99

Try it today. Welcome new relationships into your life that would never have occurred otherwise.

Intentional Actions

I disagree with the adage, "The road to hell is paved with good intentions." Good intentions are powerful mindsets which will drive your actions to accomplish the results you want. Setting good intentions sets you up for success by providing you with a vision and a plan to "get 'er done" and make it happen!

"The road to hell" (in the metaphorical sense, of course), occurs when the people who have good intentions fail to act, follow-through, or live up to their promises, all of which creates stress, frustration, and disappointment. People can be earnest and well-meaning, but their words become hollow when actions do not follow their words. By setting good intentions and taking deliberate action to back intentions up, you can transform your results.

Why Do Some People NOT Take Initiative?

- They have a FEAR of . . . rejection, looking stupid, failing, criticism, getting out of their comfort zone, or imposing on other people.
- They are unmotivated or uninspired.
- They get stuck in negativity, confusion, stress, or doubt.
- They don't want to upset the apple cart or the status quo.
- They are lazy, disengaged, or indifferent.
- They have LACK of . . . energy, desire, confidence, self-esteem, skills, creativity, imagination, connections, resources, education.

23 Ways to Take More Initiative in Life and at Work

"There are three types of people in this world: those who make things happen, those who watch things happen, and those who wonder what happened."
—Mary Kay Ash, American businesswoman

1. Set goals.
2. Be curious.
3. Get advice.
4. Ask for help.
5. Get creative.

6. Be prepared.
7. Be persistent.
8. Ask questions.
9. Make a decision.
10. Be a team player.
11. Lead by example.
12. Take the first step.
13. Don't procrastinate.
14. Accept responsibility.
15. Focus on the positives.
16. Be the first to volunteer.
17. Seek new opportunities
18. Simplify! Simplify! Simplify!
19. Make your presence known.
20. Speak up and share your ideas.
21. Deal with problems immediately.
22. Do things without being told or asked.
23. Make a list of what is not working in your life then name one action step you can take today to make it better.

The first step in getting unstuck and moving forward is to examine what is holding you back from taking action. The power is yours to set your intention and take the action needed to create the life you desire. You are in control of your initiative—be proactive.

7. $\mathcal{M}$ IX, $\mathcal{M}$ INGLE & $\mathcal{G}$ LOW

"She coaxes out the wallflowers, notices when drinks need refilling, steers a risky political discussion back to safe ground, flirts with an elderly man, engages a 5-year-old boy in animated conversation. And here's the amazing thing: When you and she are talking one on one, the other 74 people in the room turn into extras. You're the effervescent center of the universe. Her eyes never leave yours. Her words seem meant exclusively for your ears. Moreover, everything coming out of your mouth sounds fresh, riveting."

—Peter Smith

The title of this chapter was inspired by my friend Robyn Bomar. As an event planner extraordinaire, she ran the company Mix Mingle Glow, where she planned, designed, coordinated, executed, and delivered extraordinary events from Florida to New York and California. I was always impressed by her mission to bring people together for memorable moments and amazing experiences.

Robyn now lives in New York City where she continues to work her magic in making people feel special. She is now the founder of The Birthday Project (thebdayproject.com) where she inspires people all over the world with ways to celebrate birthdays and special milestones through intentional random acts of kindness.

Presenting "Mix, Mingle & Glow" in a social context is a lovely way to describe how you can make a great first impression by taking the initiative to help other people shine. Think of the times when you have attended an event where there were a lot of people.

ASK YOURSELF: Do you remember a gracious hostess, an engaging guest, or someone who worked the room like a honey bee in a flower garden?

They would glide from one person to the next, spreading good will and cheer, being the glue that brought everyone together with ease.

Hostess with the Mostest

Think of a time when you have had a party in your home or had friends over for dinner. Didn't you want to make sure they were nurtured, cared for, and well-taken care of? Didn't you want your guests to interact with each other and enjoy the experience so they would remember it fondly?

When we fell in love, Daniel had never formally entertained. When we began dating, however, entertaining friends became one of our greatest joys. Whether we were having a sit-down candlelight dinner for ten or a wine and cheese party for forty, I noticed something very special about him. When in action, he was a joy to watch and a sight to behold. He made it his personal mission to speak to every single person there. He would not let the evening end without consciously making an effort to have a meaningful touch point with each person.

In his book, *Networking is a Contact Sport,* Joe Sweeney advises that when you attend networking events, act as if it is your party and you are the host or hostess. By doing this, you will help others be at ease and demonstrate a heart of service and generosity.

Inversely, when you are in a small group of people or friends and you don't make the effort to speak to everyone, it may be considered as rude. Rather than run the risk of people feeling neglected or dismissed, make the effort to Mix, Mingle, and Glow . . .

Mix

- Be situationally aware and pay attention to the people in the room.
- Introduce guests or help strike up a conversation.
- Be the one who takes the initiative and makes and effort to "work the room."
- Make eye contact and acknowledge others with a smile and friendly gestures.
- Greet people as they arrive, even if it is not your expected role.

- Spot the people who may be first timers or guests and help them feel more welcomed and embraced.

Mingle

- Be the connector—introduce people to each other who may not otherwise connect.
- Be a conversation fire starter; point out what people have in common as you are introducing them.
- Seek out the folks who may appear to be shy, or awkward, or wallflowers. Find ways to build trust and comfort. Engage them with a kind word to pull them out of their shell.
- Arrive early and stay late; connect with people before and after your event.
- Stretch beyond your own comfort level to speak with, sit with, and start conversations with people whom you do not know.
- Offer to refill someone's drink or clear their plate.
- Encourage introductions: "There is someone whom I would love for you to meet . . ."

Glow

What can you do and how can you be in order to bring out the best in others and truly help them shine?

- Be complimentary; say something nice.
- Be a great listener and make them feel like you are hanging on every word.
- Create enthusiasm and anticipation for the person they are getting ready to meet.
- Act like you have personally invited them to the party and help ensure they have a wonderful time.
- Give people an experience, not just a conversation.

You're Not Alone

When I was speaking to thousands of teenagers a year, I interviewed my niece Sarah Jane, who was a high school student at the time. I asked, "What do you think would be helpful for kids to know that would make a difference in their lives."

She said, "I was terrified, but I put on a happy face so that no one else would know. What I didn't realize is that everyone else was as scared as I was."

Knowing others may feel the same way as you can make social situations feel less awkward. When approaching new people, find ways to put those at ease who might be reluctant to approach us otherwise. Where Can You Begin to Mix, Mingle & Glow?

8. Be Fully Present & Engaged

"Your daily life is your temple and your religion. Whenever you enter into it take with you your all."

—Kahlil Gibran

Be Here Now

Do you feel fully present and engaged in the way you live your life? Do you immerse yourself in the moment or do you strive and struggle as you negotiate the distractions of our modern world? It's easy to have blind spots regarding how you are showing up for life when you are consistently bombarded with distractions, commitments, and personal preoccupations, isn't it?

---

66 *Your life is happening in the NOW, yet the present moment is often squandered by your thinking about what has happened in the past or may happen in the future.* 99

When you are "off somewhere else" people notice. Have you found yourself in conversations in which you're so concerned about what you are going to say next, that you don't even hear what the other person is saying? Guilty as charged, right?

A lack of engagement sends the message that you may not care, are not interested, are too busy, or that the other person does not matter to you. Even though this is rarely your intention, it can happen when you're not being mindful and deliberate to connect in the moment.

In their New York Times Bestseller, *The Power of Full Engagement*, Jim Loehr and Tony Schwartz state that, "To be fully engaged, we must be physically energized, emotionally connected, mentally focused, and spiritually aligned with a purpose beyond our immediate self-interest."

Being 100 percent in the moment and focusing on the person you're with is one of the finest compliments you can offer. One of the most respectful and considerate things you can do for another is to truly be with them in the here and now.

Employee Engagement

"Employee Engagement" has become a very hot topic in recent years. The escalating statistics for disengagement are alarming. In 2015, the Gallup Polls' "The State of the American Workforce" survey found that only 32.5 percent of the U.S. Workforce is engaged and committed where they work, and 54 percent say they would consider leaving their companies if they could receive a 20 percent raise elsewhere. Disengagement not only lowers performance, morale, and productivity, but it's costing employers billions of dollars a year. It's a growing problem, which has many companies baffled.

Why is this disengagement epidemic becoming the new norm? A few reasons I have witnessed in speaking with companies across the country include . . .

- Information overload
- Distractions
- Stress/overwhelmed
- Apathy/detachment
- Short attention span
- Fear, worry, anxiety
- Rapidly changing technology
- Entitlement
- Poor leadership
- Social media
- Interruptions
- Multitasking
- Budget cuts
- Exhaustion
- Boredom
- Conflict
- Social insecurity
- Lack of longevity

- Preoccupation

These challenges not only create separation and work dysfunction, but we are seeing it happen in relationships and personal interactions.

Full and present engagement is a valuable commodity! Wikipedia describes an "engaged employee" as "one who is fully absorbed by and enthusiastic about their work." And as a result, "they take positive action to further the organization's reputation and interests."

When you are fully present and engaged in your workplace, you will demonstrate that you care about the success of your organization, are a team player, have a can-do attitude, and will go the extra mile to fulfill and exceed expectations.

These qualities make a great impression on your boss, your teams, and your customers. You will be more respected, noticed, and appreciated in the process.

As your own "CEO of Self," projecting this positive level of engagement furthers your own personal reputation and interests for healthy communication, networking, and positive first impressions. An added bonus is that YOU will receive great benefits from putting forth this type of effort. Whether it be self-esteem, new training, cooperation, experience, or a raise or bonus, the rewards are extensive and many.

11 Ways to Be More Engaged

1. Care about others.
2. Be 100 percent in the moment.
3. Keep focus on the person you are serving.
4. Try to get involved, engaged, and interactive.
5. Show interest in what matters to other people by listening, acknowledging, and responding.
6. Arrive in the moment anticipating creating a valuable interaction for yourself and others.
7. Move towards the things that inspire you and provide a sense

of joy and connection.

8. Reconnect with the essence of yourself and be grounded in that essential relationship.

9. Maintain eye contact and deliver the non-verbal cues that you are fully with the other person.

10. Limit distractions—close the door, silence your phone, hold calls, put tasks aside, etc.

11. Show up to the moment being your best and giving your best.

8 WAYS TO **MASTER**
The *Art* of ACTION

1. *Just be Nice.* Nice—this little word has a big meaning. Use it generously. Being nice helps people feel emotionally safe, allowing for more authentic, trusting, and happy interactions.

2. *Be Brave.* Being brave requires taking deliberate action and doing something new that stretches you beyond your comfort zone. Face your fear and do it anyway!

3. *Manners Matter.* Courteous behavior is the hallmark of healthy relations and human interaction. Manners ensure you will be more respected, admired, and appreciated. Thank you!

4. *Polish the Gold.* Be an optimist; look for the best in others, the best in situations, and focus on what is working rather than what is not. It's golden!

5. *Service Beyond Self.* Value others; have a heart of service and generosity. Rise above self-interest. Ask what you can do for others, not what they can do for you.

6. *Take the Initiative.* Be proactive. If you want to rock your relationship results, it is going to take action, effort, initiative, and choosing to get in the game—so, step up, step out, and show up!

7. *Mix, Mingle, Glow.* Stretch beyond your own comfort zone to speak with, sit with, and start conversations with people whom you do not know. Take the initiative to help other people capture the spotlight and shine.

8. *Be Fully Present & Engaged.* Being 100 percent in the present moment and focusing on the person you're with is one of the finest compliments you can offer. One of the most respectful and considerate things you can do for another is to truly be with them in the here and now.

5

The *Art* of

COMMUNICATION

8 WAYS TO CONFIRM CLARITY & UNDERSTANDING FOR POSITIVE IMPACT

The *Art* of COMMUNICATION

Communication is the *soul* of all relationships. More than any other skill, it is the heartbeat of success in sales, marketing, marriage, business, friendship, communities, and beyond.

Wouldn't it be wonderful to be a natural communicator and know exactly what, when, why, and how to speak so that your message is conveyed and received as you intend?

Communicating negatively (gossiping, bragging, bullying, and criticizing) can be disastrous to your reputation, cause you to lose the respect of others, and leave a terrible impression. Why leave this essential expertise up to chance when it can make or break the success of your relations?

The Art of Communication shares insights to help you communicate with a higher awareness and focused intention and meet people on their level to increase clarity and understanding. When you begin conversations with confidence and listen attentively, you will become more flexible and adaptable in most any situation. Since we are all unique and individual, being cognizant of different personality styles will help you better recognize where others are coming from to minimize barriers, build trust, and catapult your newfound relationship into a meaningful connection. The savvy socializer knows this all.

1. *Mindful Awareness*
2. *Conversation Starters*
3. *Active Listening*
4. *Voice Value*
5. *Using Names*
6. *Wise with Your Words*
7. *Communication Styles*
8. *Savvy Socializing & Synchronicity*

1. Mindful Awareness

"Mindfulness is the awareness that arises through paying attention, on purpose, in the present moment and non-judgmentally."

—Jon Kabat-Zinn

Mindfulness means paying attention to what is happening at this very moment and being keenly aware of your surroundings and the people in it. Whether your awareness is focused on your own emotions and perceptions or directed toward the preferences, needs, and feelings of others, being mindful (aware and attentive) will enable you to respond more appropriately.

---

66 *This deliberate focus and sensitivity allows you to "put yourself in another person's shoes and walk around a while" to better understand where they are coming from and what they are all about.* 99

Developing this ability instills a sixth sense for navigating human relationships with dignity, grace, and discretion, thus making an intentional and thoughtful first impression.

Mindfulness is a quiet strength and deeply rooted value which many other cultures understand and often practice better than we do. It can be puzzling to people from other countries as to why Americans are so task-driven and action-oriented.

As Americans, we typically move full steam ahead without much regard to mindfulness or thoughtful reflection, often to one's own detriment. Yet it is that same propensity for bold action which makes fulfilling the "American Dream" possible—where an immigrant can come to our country with nothing and achieve extraordinary things.

Although it may serve you well, any strength or skill which is overused can become a limitation when it forces you to constantly be moving and looking for the next best thing. Distractions, interruptions, and incessantly chasing after the golden ring become the norm. Your encounters will be more successful when you slow down, pay attention, and become more mindfully aware of the world around you. Heightening your awareness in your social, situational, contextual, orientational, and cultural scenarios will improve your agility as you adapt to new social settings.

Social Awareness

With your mind alert and your eyes wide open, you will be better able to assess your space and your place for optimizing exchanges and your communication impressions. Becoming more socially aware involves greater understanding of the dynamics of social interactions to assure you achieve harmonious outcomes.

---

66 When you are socially aware, you will realize whether you are forcing yourself into a conversation or have actually been invited to participate. 99

Sometimes you must earn the right to be included. Otherwise, you may appear awkward or pushy.

At a Chamber of Commerce networking breakfast, two of my friends and I were standing in a circle talking. A stranger approached, interrupted our little reunion, and gave each of us her card. She then began talking about herself and her business without a hint of social awareness, or care about her interruption. She even had the tactless gall to ask us for referrals. When she left our small circle, we looked at each other and laughed, "What was that?"

Do you attend networking events to give out as many cards as possible or is it your intention to deliver something of value? When you are busy charging ahead with your own agenda, you're not meeting the needs of anyone but yourself—and it's obvious!

When people can't *give* anything and are only there for themselves, why should others use their time and energy to get involved? There's no benefit.

Sometimes it is better to refrain from engaging in conversation, because making no impression is better than making a bad impression.

When a person is focused completely on self it is nearly impossible to be mindful of others at the same time. That is a contradiction for healthy communication, networking, and relationship building.

Situational Awareness

"Situational variables can exert powerful influences over human behavior, more so than we recognize or acknowledge."
—Philip Zimbardo

Situational awareness enables you to observe your periphery with clear vision and emotional foresight, which may inevitably keep you socially, physically, or professionally out of harm's way. Connect the dots. When you enter a room, a social situation, or a business meeting, be mindful of cues; read between the lines to better understand people and events. What do these things tell you?

Ask Yourself. . .

- Who is sitting where?
- Who is speaking first?
- Who is dominating the conversation?
- What is the tone of the meeting?
- How are people interacting?

My friend Amy Tolbert, Ph.D. (eccointernational.com), runs the global business communications company ECCO International. As an expert in multi-cultural diversity, Amy trains companies worldwide on how to be effective in business with other countries. She has a keen understanding for the importance of mindful awareness in all circumstances at all levels.

Amy had an important meeting with a new client to whom she had already submitted her training proposal and expert solutions. She noticed that the client (who was running the meeting) was open, talkative, and clearly in charge. Amy jumped right in and began sharing her ideas. The woman got her back up and became rigid. Being situationally aware, Amy stopped speaking immediately. One of the participants explained that their boss—the woman—was not aware of Amy's credentials yet and asked if they could take a few steps back for her to share her background. Without situational awareness, the meeting would have gone down fast and been an epic failure.

The one-hour presentation which Amy had prepared was thrown completely out the window because the woman had many questions which needed to be resolved before they could move forward. The woman was testing her and once Amy passed the test, she was able to continue. She quickly changed her entire approach and delivery to accommodate the needs of her client. Adaptability is the mark of a true professional.

How do you know when to advance the conversation or when there's something still unresolved? When you are situationally aware, you watch the body language and notice the cues that are given to you. Listening and observing are being mindful in the best sense of the word.

Appropriate Awareness

"Because of the diverse conditions of humans, it happens that some acts are virtuous to some people, as appropriate and suitable to them, while the same acts are immoral for others, as inappropriate to them."

—Thomas Aquinas

Being "appropriate" means being suitable, fitting, relevant, or proper in a situation. What may be appropriate in one circumstance can be terribly inappropriate in another. How does one discern? Sometimes it is simply a matter of maturity and experience.

When I was fifteen years old, my uncle's brother died. As we were getting dressed for the funeral, I decided to wear my favorite new red dress. My mother was appalled and said, "Surely you are not wearing a red dress to a funeral. It is disrespectful." Rebelling against being told what to do, I wore that silly dress. My mother was not happy. Not only was I being immature for not respecting my mother's wishes, but it made a bad impression on others as I sat in a sea of black. When my funeral comes around, I hope everyone will wear bright, vibrant colors, as is appropriate given my personality and wishes—no black allowed!

While attending a conference in Atlanta, my friends and I enjoyed lunch at a restaurant in the CNN tower. Only two tables away, Ted Turner was engaged in a business meeting. I told my friends, "I have to go meet him!" My friends said, "Susan you can't do that. It would be rude to interrupt and highly inappropriate." As a twenty-three-year-old, my enthusiasm overruled my discretion. Fortunately, my friends overruled me! As you develop appropriate awareness, you will begin to give focused attention to being respectful and conscientious toward other people.

Contextual Awareness

Contextual awareness represents a continuum of behaviors, which illustrates how and why groups of people unite or divide among cultures.

Amy was on the MARTA train in Atlanta after attending a meeting at the Federal Reserve Bank. She was dressed professionally and carrying her rolling briefcase. The sweet elderly gentleman sitting next to her started talking and inquired about what brought her to Atlanta.

After sharing that she was visiting to train the executive team at the Federal Reserve Bank, he tapped her on the knee and said, "That's so sweet, little lady." He actually touched her knee! Not to mention the indifference he showed to her professional success.

Because of the context, she was not at all offended or angry and simply thought he was kind of endearing. She recognized that he probably rode the MARTA every day to speak with people to prevent being lonely. If a younger man, a male foreigner, or a male street person had said and done the same thing, it would have been outrageously inappropriate and highly offensive. The interpretation of events and experiences changes when the context of the interaction changes.

Orientational Awareness

When you have **orientational awareness,** your perceptions and impressions are based on location and proximity. Orientation may imply hierarchy, position, and prestige, or be the result of habits, traditions, and perceptions.

In America, when a man walks in front of a woman it may imply that they are not equals and he is exerting dominance over her, or being arrogant and rude. In a different culture, however, it may be presumed that he is someone worthy of profound respect and is protecting her by going first.

On a recent business trip, I reunited with a friend I had not seen in twenty years. After having a lovely lunch meeting, we came out of the restaurant to walk towards the parking lot. He automatically moved me to the inside of the sidewalk as he walked along the curbside. His orientational awareness illustrated a chivalrous gesture of protection and respect which impressed me greatly.

Cultural Awareness

"We live with a cultural lens, through which we see the world."
—Amy S. Tolbert, PhD, CSP, Principal ECCO International

This cultural lens is so much a part of us that we are not even aware of how obvious it is to others. Like the nose on your face, you may forget that it is there, but everyone else sees it. I can't look at you and not see your nose.

Being grounded in your lifelong culture and your own perspective, you are comfortable with the way you see things and may believe it is the best and only way. Sociologically speaking, as Americans we often lack social, cultural, and mindful awareness. We hear the stories of how our arrogance has been known to offend, confuse, and alienate people from other cultures. Arrogance is the thief of mindfulness and it happens from both directions.

Amy's keen cultural awareness helps her keep her own reactions in check when she experiences behaviors which may be considered rude and offensive to others. At a recent international conference, the men from India and China rushed in and out of the elevators without paying any notice to the people they were pushing past. She found herself getting irritated that they were being so rude. One day, as she struggled with multiple bags, a couple of African-American men were extremely courteous: they held the door open and offered to help.

The other men were not being rude, they were simply from cultures where things move very fast. In their countries, where people compete in tight spaces, they shove past anyone and everyone to keep the line moving. They don't slow down. When they cut in line at an airport they're not intending to be rude. They are simply displaying a culturally acceptable behavior different from our own. Likewise, a friend told me that she spent two days saying "Excuse me," when bumping into people in Seoul, Korea, until she discovered their pushing and jostling was intentional and normal. Maybe not like us, but not rude either!

Clarifying Why Confusion Occurs

To gain greater understanding, clarity, and awareness, you must become aware of your own values and beliefs. Think of a triangle or an iceberg. **Below the waterline, your beliefs and your values build the foundation for your behavior.** Your foundation defines for you what is good, bad, impossible, or possible in your world. This ultimately drives your behavior, choices, opinions, and actions.

We will judge others based on their behaviors with little to no understanding or regard for their beliefs or values—standards we may not know, nor typically see. When we do this, things can be taken completely out of context because we are assessing their behavior against our expectations, which are produced from our own personal value system.

Navigating relationships within our own culture can be challenging enough. When diverse cultures are involved, however, a huge potential for misunderstanding, disrespect, miscommunication, and intolerance is present.

It is crucial to understand that there are myriad interpretations of behavior. When you subscribe only to yours, you may begin to think that everyone else is wrong and thus limit your flexibility and possibility. Developing cultural awareness will make your diverse relationships easier and more productive.

4 Steps for Understanding Each Other

1. Identify your beliefs and core values; ask how they determine your behaviors and habits.
2. Realize with whom you are interacting and try to identify how their values are explaining their behavior.
3. Assume positive intent.
4. Seek ways to adapt your behavior to help bridge the cultural gap.

Prepare yourself well by learning how to be more mindful in each interaction. The effort you put forth to gain insight will empower you to make a better impression on others, while enriching your opportunities to build enlightened, trusted relationships.

2. CONVERSATION STARTERS

"The measure of a conversation is how much mutual recognition there is in it; how much shared there is in it. If you're talking about what's in your own head, or without thought to what people looking and listening will feel, you might as well be in a room talking to yourself."

—Dylan Moran

Conversation starters. Icebreakers. Openers. However you choose to label them, that moment when the first words come out of your mouth can make or break the outcome of your entire conversation. Been there, done that, right? Your first words will not only shape your first impression, they can create amazing connections, lead you to your dream job, or help you discover a new best friend—or accomplish exactly the opposite.

Your first words will outlive your conversations and impact how you are remembered, liked, or regarded. Wouldn't you enjoy opening conversations with ease and mutual recognition? The challenging part is that it can be . . . awkward!

Meeting someone for the first time has significance, but for some people, the awkwardness can be so great that they avoid a conversation altogether. The person who may be shy, introverted, or afraid of sounding stupid may just choose to remain silent rather than take the risk of engaging in embarrassing dialogue.

The space between meeting a stranger and making a new friend can be a short distance or a gaping chasm. By understanding how to open a conversation well, you will be better able to bridge the gaps and build rapport more successfully.

How do you minimize the awkwardness in that moment? What are some of the conversations starters you've used to open, encourage, and support enjoyable and beneficial conversations? You can certainly take the easy road and use the predictable and boring defaults like:

- How are you doing?
- How about this weather?
- What do you do for a living?
- Hi. My name is _____. What's yours?
- Blah, blah, blah, blah . . .

Break out of the defaults you have been using for years. Shake it up. Make it fun. Make it memorable. Dive in with more engagement and interaction. Taking the initiative to be more creative will help you build a bridge to close the gap.

10 Bridge Builders

1. Simply say hello with a smile.
2. Ask them what they love about their work.
3. Ask natural questions out of genuine curiosity.
4. Get a person talking about what's important to them.
5. Compliment something positive which you've noticed.
6. Engage them with questions which are easy to answer.
7. Introduce them to someone whom you think they'll enjoy meeting.
8. Ask them if they have any trips or vacations planned.
9. Look for something you may have in common so that the conversation begins with shared interests.
10. Think of questions that begin with h*ow, what, when, why* and *where.*

Winning Ways to Open a Conversation

"You can discover more about a person in an hour of play than in a year of conversation."
—Plato

Add a fresh twist of creativity to make a stellar impression which people won't soon forget. Granted, your venue will determine how far you can stretch and how creative you can be. Making small tweaks to your conversation starters can make a memorable impact!

14 Awesome Conversation Starters

1. What do you do for fun? Hobbies, recreation . . .
2. What are your super powers? Gifts, talents, strengths.
3. Good morning! It's great to see you!
4. What is your story? Tell me about yourself.
5. What brought you to _____?
6. Do you have anything special happening in your life (or your business)?
7. What's the best thing that's happened this week?
8. Are you living your life purpose or still searching for it?
9. What gives you passion and makes you happy to be alive?
10. Do you have any pets?
11. How do you know the host?
12. When you were a child, what did you want to be when you grew up?
13. If you could go anywhere in the world, where would it be?
14. What's next on your bucket list?

Speaking on Stage

Speakers and presenters have only a few short seconds before their audience members begin forming opinions. True professionals know that beginning with impact determines audience engagement, the energy in the room, positive feedback, the quality of the experience, and whether or not their performance will be a success. A few of the popular methods which you can use to break the ice from the stage are:

- Using music.
- Using quotes.

- Telling a joke.
- Citing statistics.
- Showing a video.
- Asking questions.
- Stating a problem.
- Sharing acronyms.
- Sharing a personal story.
- Laying down a challenge.
- Using analogies and comparisons.
- Taking surveys; raise your hand if . . .

Once you refine, define, and discover great conversation starters, you will enjoy renewed confidence for communicating well with new people.

3. Active Listening

"Courage is what it takes to stand up and speak; courage is also what it takes to sit down and listen."
—Winston Churchill

Listening is one thing; however, ACTIVE listening is quite another. The first is a passive act which does not require great involvement, whereas, the latter is a consciously aware and deliberately focused effort to actively participate in the conversation.

Think of the communication that takes place in your own life on a continuous basis—at home, at work, with friends, and beyond. When you actively listen to people, you enhance communication. Listening actively confirms for people that you are positively receiving and thoroughly understanding the message they are conveying. By your practice of active listening, everyone involved benefits because you . . .

- are more engaged and engaging;
- demonstrate that you are interested in others and what they have to say;
- make others feel important, respected, understood, and appreciated;
- improve your memory and retention;
- affirm to others that you are an authentic, caring, and compassionate person;
- make a great first and last impression.

If the skill of participatory listening came effortlessly and easy for everyone, there would not be so many misunderstandings, communication breakdowns, irritations, and frustrations. Active listening is key to all healthy and effective communication, however, it doesn't necessarily come easily.

The Listening Dilemma

"The word 'listen' contains the same letters as the word 'silent.'"
—Alfred Brendel

While active listening is crucial for optimal communication, we are faced with a dilemma which can perplex even the most sincere and engaged of individuals.

Through the years, I have heard that the average person speaks at about 150-160 words per minute, but can listen at a rate of about 1,000 words per minute. What is going on during all that extra mind time?

- Our minds are racing ahead and preparing for the next thing we are going to say.
- We are preoccupied with other thoughts, priorities, and distractions.
- Our subconscious filters are thumbing through our database of memories, judgments, experiences, perspectives, and opinions to frame how we are going to interpret what we think someone is saying.

To make matters even more complicated, research has shown that we remember only 25-50 percent of what we hear. This inclination not only compromises our connection with another person, but we can fail to retain vital information. All this evidence demonstrates that it is imperative that we intentionally pay closer attention and strive to become an in-depth listener.

UN-Impressives of the Poor Listener

- Thinking about what you should have done, could have done, or need to do.
- Allowing your emotional reactions to take over.
- Interrupting the person talking.

- Replying before you hear all the facts.
- Jumping to conclusions and making assumptions.
- Being preoccupied with what you're going to say next.
- Getting defensive or being over-eager.
- One-upmanship—feeling the urge to compete and add something bigger, better, or more significant than what the speaker has to share.
- Imposing an unsolicited opinion.
- Ignoring and changing the subject altogether.

Being Present

Years ago, I attended a conference where the keynote speaker encouraged everyone to BE HERE NOW! It grabbed people's attention and reminded us that living, loving, listening, and laughing all occur in the present moment.

Active listening requires being fully present and engaged in the moment. When you are mindfully focused, the person with whom you are communicating feels that you are making them a priority—that you value their time and their perspective. It is in these moments that we can go to deeper levels of discovery, exploration, and connection. It is one of the most valuable gifts and finest compliments you can give to another.

Listening in Layers

> *"The soul has been given its own ears to hear things the mind does not understand."*
>
> —Rumi

When you become an actively engaged listener, you will develop the mindful awareness that active listening involves multiple layers and distinct levels. You can have the perfect message, but it may fall on deaf ears when the listener is not prepared or open to listening.

These listening "planes" were first introduced by the American composer Aaron Copland (1900-1990) as they pertain to music . . .

1. **The Sensual Plane:** You're aware of the music, but not engaged enough to have an opinion or judge it.
2. **The Expressive Plane:** You become more engaged by paying attention, finding meaning beyond the music, and noticing how it makes you feel.
3. **The Musical Plane:** You listen to the music with complete presence, noticing the musical elements of melody, harmony, pitch, tempo, rhythm, and form.

ASK YOURSELF: Does your listening during a conversation occur the same way? Notice the various levels above to ensure that you achieve clarity, understanding, and communication success—the next time and every time.

- Observe a person's physical presence to see how their body language aligns with their message.
- Recognize what is being said on the surface.
- Engage your intuition to hear the meaning, purpose, and motivation behind their message.
- Be aware of your own internal responses and how you are feeling.
- Put yourself in their shoes to better understand their perspective.

Become keenly aware of these three layers to discover whether you're listening with interest and intent for excellent communication and understanding—or are you unintentionally sabotaging potentially phenomenal conversations. Knowledge of the listening planes will raise your awareness. And as you apply these, enjoy the surprising difference.

An Empathetic Ear

Empathetic listening is a finely tuned ability to go beyond words to discover the thoughts and feelings which live beneath a person's surface presentation. Becoming an empathetic listener helps you to better understand how another person feels and why they communicate as they do.

Your heightened awareness of their perceptions, experiences, emotions, and personality styles can reveal why they feel the way they do so that you can choose your responses wisely and compassionately.

My friend John is an urgent care physician who has several patients who come to see him for various ailments on a regular basis. In addition to being brilliant and taking wonderful care of his patients, he has a unique ability to empathetically listen to his patient's needs.

One of his patients is a repeat visitor, even when she's not exhibiting symptoms. He takes the time to listen to how she's feeling and responds with kindness, empathy, and caring. He has come to realize that her visits are filling her deep need to feel validated, cared for, and understood in ways which she does not receive at home. His empathetic listening delivers incredible customer service for patient care and makes him a better health care provider. Wouldn't it be incredible if this was the manner for not only doctors, but all professionals?

Listening is Love

When my son Nick was five years old, he was sitting at the kitchen bar while I prepared dinner. In typical busy mother fashion, I was multitasking—cooking, cleaning, running the laundry, answering the phone, and attempting to listen to what he had to say.

Nick became very impatient because I was half-listening and not fully hearing his message. That sweet little man came over to me, put his little hands on each side of my face and turned my entire head to face him. Once we were looking at each other eye-to-eye and he had my complete attention, he proceeded to share his thoughts and continue the conversation.

It was an important lesson and loving reminder that great listening requires full attention. The process of attentive listening makes the other person feel important, valued, and heard. For Nick, listening was, and still is, love. I've never forgotten that precious moment—and the lesson!

Think about the people in your life with whom you have the most engaging dialogue—the ones who will listen to you and consider your opinions regardless of the topic. They'll stop whatever they are doing to give you their full attention. They become completely present and hear you.

Listening is one of the finest ways to demonstrate our love for another human being. How many marriages could be saved, friendships healed, careers made, and opportunities enjoyed if people would simply stop what they are doing and listen deeply to what another person has to say. If practiced by everyone, this principle could be a world-changer!

The Physical Language of Listening

Active listening is a physical process which transcends simply hearing. Your body language speaks on your behalf as to whether you are fully present and engaged . . .

- Make eye contact.
- Nod your head; confirm.
- Use your eyebrows and expressions of emotions to show that you're paying attention.
- Lean forward.
- Listen patiently to demonstrate respect and sensitivity.
- Open your physical presence to encourage them to continue.

Active listening is not only a matter of making yourself available to hear someone talk, but it is showing the sender, physically, that you are receiving and understanding their message on all levels.

Sensational Customer Service

"Your most unhappy customers are your greatest source of learning."
—Bill Gates

Active listening is the ultimate "Golden Rule" for sensational customer service. Just as the important people in your life will feel more valued and appreciated when you actively listen, so will your customers. **Active listening is one of the best services a company can provide.**

Have you ever had a legitimate complaint as a customer which made you angry, upset, or frustrated? How was it "handled?" If you were dealing with an inept, uncaring, or untrained employee, they may have made matters even worse by being rude, defensive, or apathetic. Simple acknowledgment and validation of your complaint is sometimes all that is needed. Without it, you're left frustrated or upset.

If you have ever experienced this type of unprofessional treatment, I doubt you would even consider giving them business in the future. Interrupting, ignoring, patronizing, or antagonizing a customer is like pouring gas on a fire and creates a more explosive situation than the original complaint. Still, it continues to happen every day, costing companies millions in lost revenue.

Now let's look at the flip side. When a diligent and caring person receives your complaint, they have the power to turn a challenge into a triumph. Through active listening, they demonstrate that your satisfaction is their top priority. They not only seek to solve your problem, but they are dedicated to re-earning your trust, your respect, and keeping your business.

ASK YOURSELF: How can you utilize active listening to provide sensational customer service? How will this help resolve complaints from unhappy customers?

- **Give them your full attention** and listen without interruption or defensiveness.
- **Thank them** for bringing the issue to your attention.
- **Take their concerns seriously** and share their sense of urgency to resolve the problem quickly.
- **Ask questions and focus** on what they are really saying.
- **Listen** to their words, tone of voice, body language, and most importantly, how they feel.
- **Beware of making assumptions** or rushing to conclusions before you hear their concern fully.
- **Explain, guide, educate, assist,** and do what's necessary to help them reach the resolution.
- **Treat them with respect and empathy.**

When you do an amazing job of resolving an unhappy customer's problem, you may end up impressing them more than if the problem had never occurred. You may have just earned their loyalty . . . forever!

Growing Your Business

For sixteen years, I had a spectacular real estate career in Tallahassee, Florida. I loved receiving telephone inquiries and making cold calls. I knew that if I could meet people on the phone, I could usually turn them into buyers.

My success with customers on the telephone wasn't by using pushy sales methods, but by engaging people in meaningful conversations which could lead to friendships on the phone before I ever met them. I would ask questions, listen to their stories, respond to their needs, develop rapport, and earn their business. When we would finally meet in person, it felt less like an introduction and more like a reunion. It was not only good business, we had fun in the process!

This method enabled me to expand my territory and create a strong network of loyal customers for referrals and repeat business. Make **active listening** a deliberate part of your business plan and success strategy. You will not only grow your business, but also make wonderful friends along the way.

14 Ways to Become an Incredible Listener

1. Be present and provide your undivided attention.
2. Seek first to understand, then to be understood.
3. Listen attentively and respond appropriately.
4. Minimize or eliminate distractions.
5. Focus your attention and energy with singleness of purpose on what the other person is saying.
6. Quiet your mind and suspend your thoughts to make room in your head to hear what is said—in the moment!
7. Ask questions and demonstrate empathy.
8. Use your body language and nonverbal cues constructively and pay attention to theirs.
9. Follow the rhythm of their speech; hear their tone.
10. Repeat and summarize what you have heard them say to confirm understanding.
11. Be open-minded and non-defensive.
12. Respond rather than react.
13. Be respectful, calm, and positive.
14. Try to resolve conflicts, not win them.

4. $\mathcal{V}$OICE $\mathcal{V}$ALUE

"From the first word you hear a person speak, you start to form an impression of the person's personality."

—Phil McAleer, University of Glasgow, Scotland

Every time you speak, you are using your voice to connect with others, whether it is in person, on the phone, or in a recorded message. Is your voice value delivering the image you wish to convey? Is your voice coming across as smart, friendly, and positive or ignorant, rude, and negative? The way you deliver the words you say becomes your "vocal image."

This "vocal image" can make or break your first impressions, impact your communication, and determine how people respond to you. According to the communications firm Quantified Impressions, their 2012 study found that "the sound of your voice matters twice as much as the words you say."

What can you do to ensure that your **voice value** translates into **impression value?** Every professional voice coach worth their salt will bring you back to the importance of tone, pace, and pitch. While these concepts were introduced earlier in *The Art of Body Language* section, we can now elaborate and take a deeper dive into how you can use your voice to improve your communications.

Vocal Tone for Emotional Expression

Your tone of voice is less about *what* you say and more about *how* you say it. It enhances or diminishes the language you use, how you construct your sentences, and the way your words sound. Tone of voice represents the emotional expressions of your thoughts, feelings, and attitude. It is generally believed that nearly 40 percent of your first impression will be set from the tone of your voice. Your vocal thermometer can be more impactful than the actual words you use.

Your tone demonstrates . . .

- Energy
- Volume
- Sincerity
- Confidence
- Happiness

- Sadness
- Preoccupation
- Anger
- Efficiency
- Empathy

Your tone of voice can be conveyed in both the words you speak and in the words you write. Your tone can represent the character of your business and the strength of your resolve, and express the depths of your conviction.

Does your tone match your intention? Is your tone of voice confusing or clarifying? Are you coming across to others as you had hoped? Once you begin to notice your tone, you can adjust as needed to make it work in your favor.

Heed Your Speed

Are you a *fast* or a *slow* talker? Be mindful towards the person with whom you are speaking to ensure that your message is being comprehended, understood, and absorbed. If they are listening at a slower rate than you are speaking, disconnect can occur.

As a professional speaker, I speak rather quickly with enthusiastic energy and emotion. This doesn't always sit well with people who like to speak at a slower pace and need more time to process. What I have learned through years in this profession is that to be more effective I must adapt my pace to the comfort level of my audience. When I am speaking to academics, engineers, and doctors, I speak with a slower pace than the one which I use with sales people, customer services teams, or teenagers.

Aligning your voice value with the tone, pace, and pitch of your listeners will help you connect on all levels.

Pitch

Have you ever paid notice to the full sound range of your voice? If you have ever been in a chorus or a singing group, you already know that they will separate the group based on each singer's pitch and assign their roles accordingly. While my speaking voice has a soprano pitch, my singing voice is a lower alto.

Your pitch represents how high you can fly and how low you can go. Different pitches get different responses and interpretations from your listener. And this does indeed impact impressions.

A high-pitched voice may sound less authoritative, more youthful, and less experienced, whereas, a lower pitched voice may be perceived as being more authoritative, confident, and credible. It is unfortunate that listeners will make assumptions based on these differences before even knowing the depth and value of your message. Play with your ranges and find a comfortably low pitch. Practice it to see if it makes a difference in conveying more authority and brilliance.

Articulation

When your speaking style is clear, confident, and concise, your listeners will perceive you as such. Developing your eloquence and enunciation will reduce the likelihood of misinterpretation and misunderstanding, making your delivery more powerful. By speaking in a competent and confident way, your message will sound more relevant and appropriate, reflecting you in a favorable light.

Variety is the Spice of Life

Voices come in all shapes, tones, and sizes. Some are compelling and effective, while others are grating and agitating. The list below begins to illustrate how different personalities can be assigned to different vocal qualities . . .

- Warm
- Loving
- Breathy
- Gravelly
- Dull

- Nasal
- Rough
- Hoarse
- Gruff
- Melodious

- Whiny
- Sultry
- Twangy
- Energetic
- Shrill

Your Signature Sound

"A lively, expressive voice is one of the most powerful instruments in the world, especially when it's resonant and sparkles with changes of pitch, speed, and volume."

—www.simswyeth.com

In music, voice value is categorized for singers, composers, and listeners. Whether a performer's voice type is soprano, alto, tenor, baritone, or bass, they all have unique characteristics that make them unique and impressive. You, too, have a signature sound that is uniquely yours and makes you stand apart from the crowd.

Neen James (NeenJames.com) is an eloquent and successful international speaker who stands at four-feet-eleven with a rich Australian dialect and a high-pitched voice. For years, fellow speakers with good intentions told her she needed to take voice lessons to lower her pitch to give her more depth for a compelling stage presence. With complete confidence and loyalty to her uniqueness, she ignored the naysayers and her amazing signature voice which has become a powerful brand.

My loving man, Dan Futch, was Southern born and bred. Although he has lived in the northern Midwest for almost thirty years, he has never lost his deep, syrupy, Southern drawl. It has become his brand which makes him memorable, charming, and truly unique.

Most people are familiar with the rich, resonant tones of James Earl Jones and Morgan Freeman. Their signature voices bring strength, authority, and lyrical enjoyment. Are there aspects of your voice that you can capitalize on to make a great impression and be simply unforgettable?

5. *Using Names*

"Remember that a person's name is to that person the sweetest and most important sound in any language."

—Dale Carnegie

Think of the times that others remembered your name and used it kindly. How did it make you feel? When you use someone's name it makes him or her feel recognized, appreciated, and special. Using names with respect and consideration tells a person that you care, are present and engaged, and that you are genuinely interested in making a connection. You make them feel remembered!

A Sign of Respect

As our world grows more casual, we observe a tendency for everyone to use first names rather than surnames. "It is a pleasure meeting you, Mrs. Young," has a completely different connotation than "Nice to meet you, Susan."

What determines whether the usage is acceptable or inappropriate? If you want to make a great first impression with positive impact, it is essential that you know there is a difference.

Using titles such as Mr., Mrs., Miss, Dr., etc. demonstrates respect. In previous generations, it was a social necessity and simply good manners. One would consider you rude and uncultured if you were so presumptuous as to go straight to a "first name basis." First names can imply an intimacy that does not exist and it may offend a new person until they know you better. Be wary of making assumptions.

I was raised in an era when part of respecting your elders was to call them by Mr. or Mrs. When my children were growing up, an occasional child would call me Susan. It was jarring, felt disrespectful, and I did not like it. We reached a mutual agreement and their friends began calling me Ms. Susan. Perhaps this is more prevalent in the

South, however, your awareness and consideration can help prevent social missteps.

It is wise to use titles for people in positions of power, higher education, seniority, or maturity, unless otherwise instructed. This may sound old-fashioned, but practicing respectful traditions will earn you points and inevitably make you seem more cultured and sophisticated. This is especially true with older generations. To call certain people, such as your boss, teachers, professors, doctors, your parent's friends, etc. by their first names might be considered disrespectful. It is best to err on the side of caution until you know what is appropriate.

Asking Permission

Asking permission to call someone by their first name is a gesture of gentility and consideration. And once permission is granted, the gate is open for mutual respect and mutual purpose. "Dr. Qubein, may I call you Nido?" Simply demonstrating this courtesy before making an assumption is impressive. Once permission is granted, you have earned points on both sides.

Uh-Oh . . .

One year I was the guest speaker at an annual conference. The person who coordinated the agenda mistakenly typed my name as "Sue" rather than "Susan." I felt odd and a little disrespected because they didn't take the time to ask the spelling of my name. It felt awkward when I saw it on all the tables throughout the ballroom, to say the least. I asked, "Please make sure that you introduce me as Susan because I've never been called Sue." The initial impression was sticky for an instant, but they quickly made it right. The correction was shared and everything turned out fine. Even an innocent and unintentional name error can impact your first impressions. Making a joke about it once I was on stage was a light-hearted way to confirm my *real* name.

Make It Fun

Have you ever been publicly acknowledged or called upon in a room filled with people? Depending on your personality type, it can be either exhilarating or mortifying. It certainly does grab your attention, as well as everyone else's!

When I am working with groups of thirty or fewer people, there is a powerful name exercise that I do to break the ice, start with humor, and begin my program with positive energy. One by one, each person will introduce themselves using an adjective that describes their personality that starts with the first letter of their name. "Spontaneous Susan," "Dependable Dave," and "Happy Helen" are a few quick examples. The benefit for the participants is twofold: it makes each person feel good and it makes people laugh. Additionally, it enables me to learn their names so that I can integrate them into the entire presentation for full engagement and participation.

Wearing Nametags

On Yourself: The purpose of wearing nametags in the first place is for people to see your name. Otherwise, why bother? We have all seen nametag placements that range from proper to downright raunchy. People can get pretty creative about where they place them and it is not always appropriate. For this book, we will focus on the best practices.

To make a positive first impression, where is the best place to wear a nametag? Since we shake hands with our right hand, placing your nametag on the right side of your body will make it quickly visible for the best eye contact. Within a few inches of your collar bone and right shoulder will provide greater visibility even when you are sitting down.

On Others: I enjoy reading nametags and calling people by their names before we have officially met or been introduced. It provides an instant icebreaker. Walking up to someone and saying, "Hi Brenda!

I'm Susan!" creates a quick connection that might not have happened were her name not displayed.

When I eat in a restaurant, I will either ask for the name of the wait staff or read their name tag. As I use his or her name throughout the meal, I receive better and more personalized service. Start doing this with cashiers, bellmen, salespeople, and other service people who commonly wear name tags and you will find yourself on the receiving end of great customer service.

Business Cards

Do you attend events where business cards are exchanged in a networking environment? My friend Brian Haugen is a networking ninja. His gregarious personality and love for people have enabled him to easily win friends and influence people. He has a lot of tips, but one of his best is regarding how to best handle business cards.

When I asked him for his thoughts on being an effective networker, he shared that there is an art to how to receive someone's business card with respect and interest. He continued by saying, "When someone hands you their card, take a moment to hold it, read it, repeat their name and then make a comment or ask a question. And make notes on their card to help you remember the exchange."

This small action communicates you are genuinely interested and want to remember them. Too often when people hand us their cards, we quickly slip them into our pockets or purses without giving notice to what it says. Subliminally, it tells the other person that we don't care or are not interested. Take a moment to demonstrate your interest; this will help your newfound relationship be off to a good start. Small actions can make a significant impact!

"Why is it so important to use people's names? A person's name is the greatest connection to their own identity and individuality. Some might say it is the most important word in the world to that person."
—Joyce E.A. Russell, Vice Dean and Director, Executive Coaching and Leadership Development University of Maryland

10 Terrific Tips to Remember Names

Have you ever met a new person and within seconds forgotten his or her name? It can be embarrassing, can't it? Many people will laugh, brush it off, and say, "I simply can't remember names!" But you should take remembering seriously. Below you will find a few simple memory techniques that will help ensure you don't get caught in this common and socially awkward moment.

1. **Wash, Rinse, Repeat**—Repeat the name upon introduction, throughout the conversation, and as you bid farewell. Try it both in your mind as well as out loud. Avoid nicknames unless otherwise invited.

2. **Visual Imagery**—Connect the name with a mental picture that will remind you of that person. If his name is Barry, think of berries. If her name is Cheri, imagine her drinking cherry punch.

3. **Rhyming, Rhythm, Adjectives, and Alliteration**—Use rhyming (trim Kim), rhythm (Sally sells seashells), adjectives (kind Kevin), and alliteration (Mike likes milk). These ideas may sound silly, but they stimulate your mind to improve your memory.

4. **Association**—Creating a connection to something that has been important to you will give a name sticking power. Did you go to the same college? Did you work for his company at one time? Does she have the same car as your best friend? Begin looking for associations and it will make the names more memorable.

5. **Create a New Contact**—Saving someone's name shortly after meeting will help you retain it longer. Whether it is on a piece of paper, your cell phone contacts, "friending" him on Facebook, or inviting him to join your LinkedIn network, adding the name to your contacts will make it easy to remember him for a long time into the future.

6. **Pay Attention**—Minimize distractions and focus on what they are saying. Making a concerted effort to concentrate will help you improve your memory.

7. **Make a Connection**—Connect their name or a feature on their face with something you already know. This connection will help anchor their name in your mind for future recall.

8. **Use Mnemonic Devices**—What does their name sound like? What words can you connect the sound of their name or voice to trigger your memory?

9. **Write it Down!**—Whether you write their name down on the back of a card, a receipt, a handout, or in a notebook, this simple act will help you remember.

10. **Introduce a "Just-Met" to Someone Else**—Introduce your newfound acquaintance or friend to someone else. As you share her name with another person, the name will become locked into your memory.

"Where Everybody Knows Your Name" was the theme song for the popular 1980s television show "Cheers." Gary Portnoy and Judy Hart Angelo's song, captured the sense of family, acceptance, and welcome we feel when other people use our names:

"Sometimes you want to go where everybody knows your name, and they're always glad you came. You wanna be where you can see, our troubles are all the same. You wanna be where everybody knows your name."

6. Wise with Your Words

"Be Impeccable with Your Word. Speak with integrity. Say only what you mean. Avoid using the word to speak against yourself or to gossip about others. Use the power of your word in the direction of truth and love."

—Don Miguel Ruiz

The Words You Think

Your thoughts lay the foundation for your life's experience. Are you utilizing your thoughts for your highest good or are they harmful to you and others? Are your thoughts building you up or tearing you down? Notice the quality of your words and ask yourself these questions.

Your self-talk is a silent force working behind the scenes that determines how you present yourself to the world. Without saying a word, your thoughts are being projected and are written all over you. Your thoughts become your attitudes, which become your actions, which become your behavior, which become your habits, which become your lifestyle, and inevitably determine your outcomes. Utilize this circular truth by using positive thoughts to create positive outcomes. It is a choice you get to make every day. Choose wisely.

The directive we have so often heard, "Change your thoughts, change your life," is indeed based on the power of words. The key to your happiness, well-being, and interactions with others begins, continues, and concludes with the nature and quality of the words you hold in your mind as thoughts. Make them work for your highest good.

The Words You Speak

"The words you speak become the house you live in."

—Unknown

Your words have the power to shape your thoughts, your opinions, your attitudes, your self-esteem, your goals, your self-image, how others perceive you, your reputation, your behavior, and more. Your words are incredibly powerful, whether they are being used for good or for bad.

The "Law of Attraction," based on the principle of cause and effect, is not only a process of reaping what you sow through your actions. Its magnetic impact derives from the words you use, attracting and reinforcing whatever you are thinking about and putting out into the world through your speech. If you want to attract greater success, prosperity, health, and to enjoy more fulfilling relationships, craft your speech to affirm and manifest them.

The Words You Write

Few things scream 'unprofessional' faster than a poorly written letter or resume filled with errors, misspellings, misuse, and negligence. Your written words show up in a variety of forms:

- Emails, texts, and memos
- Blogging and publishing
- Your website and social media
- Letters of correspondence
- Advertising, marketing, and promotion

Even with my focused intention to be eloquent and reflect perfect grammar, syntax, and punctuation in my writing, I still flub up occasionally. Thank heavens for spell check, auto-correct, and the brilliance of my amazing editor Elizabeth Dixon. None of us is perfect, but our editing needs to be as thorough as possible if we hope to make a great impression.

Having a second set of eyes to review what you do is an effective practice. Sometimes you will be so close to your own work that your blinders will cause you to miss tiny details which can create huge errors, and reflect poorly on your intelligence and expertise.

Review and reread your work before you hit send, post, or publish. Thankfully, many of the social media channels allow you to edit what you have created after they have been posted. However, there will be times when what you send out will be un-retractable. In some cases, they are there forever. So choose your words wisely!

Your Grammar

"Your grammar is a reflection of your image. Good or bad, you have made an impression. And like all impressions, you are in total control."

—Jeffrey Gitomer

Growing up with well-educated parents and an older sister with her Master's Degree in English Language and Literature, I was left with little wiggle room as a child to use poor grammar. When I would inadvertently slip, I would be corrected in a matter of moments— excuse me, seconds! While it may have been irritating for a 10-year-old, I am eternally grateful as an adult that the grammar police kept me in line.

As a professional speaker and author, excellent grammar is crucial in my profession. Without the proper use of words and language, I would lose credibility and respect.

Your grammar is crucial to your image, brand, and reputation. It reflects upon your level of intelligence, education, experience, upbringing, and native geography. Poor grammar can totally bomb a job interview, make someone delete your email request, cause people to judge you behind your back, or dismiss you as being a poor communicator. It is all preventable!

Rather than using these pages for a boring English lesson, I will simply encourage you to become keenly aware and pay close attention to your articulation and grammar.

UN-Impressives

- Lying.
- Bragging.
- Gossiping.
- Cursing and using foul language.
- Making self-deprecating comments.
- Regularly expressing worry and anxiety.
- Criticizing and condemning people and situations.
- Demonstrating a lack of emotional intelligence or compassion.

7. COMMUNICATION STYLES

"To effectively communicate we must realize that we are all different in the way we perceive the world and use this understanding as a guide to our communication with others."

—Tony Robbins

Personality Styles

The wonderful world of human relationships is a rich mixture of backgrounds, perceptions, habits, preferences, behaviors, and motivators. These differences can create barriers to communication and connection, creating a lack of understanding or clarity. Just as we each have our own genetic DNA that makes us unique, we also have personality traits that do the same.

A fast way to get a clear understanding of yourself and others is through personality profile assessment. Many companies and hiring managers administer these tests to ensure that personalities are well matched to positions. They also help build dream teams to optimize the combinations of strengths and complementary qualities among their people.

Understanding a wide range of personalities will help improve your communication, connection, and engagement not only at work, but in your relationships at home, in life, and in love.

To master *The Art of First Impressions for Positive Impact,* it is imperative to understand some basic personality differences so that you can navigate and nurture relationships from a position of awareness, empathy, and acceptance. This understanding will greatly enhance your communication skills, regardless of the differences, so that you can make positive impressions on people who are different from you.

Not until the writing of this book had I gathered such a powerful list of personality assessment resources. I enthusiastically invite you to visit ten of my favorite assessment tools to explore, discover, learn, and grow in your emotional and relationship intelligence . . .

1. DISC   www.EverythingDisc.com
2. Colors   www.ColorCode.com
3. Fascinate   www.HowToFascinate.com
4. Myers-Briggs   www.mbtionline.com
5. Xyting Insight   www.Xyte.com
6. Predictive Index   www.PredictiveIndex.com
7. 5 Love Languages   www.5LoveLanguages.com
8. Strengths Finders   www.GallupStrengthsCenter.com
9. Emotional Intelligence   www.EmotionalIntelligence.net
10. Kiersey Temperament Sorter   www.keirsey.com

Is there overlap and similarity among the assessments? Absolutely! Although each assessment packages information differently, you will recognize the common threads for basic personality differences which apply throughout humanity—and gain great material for your relationship toolbox!

The "spot-on" accuracy of the results may astound you. Once you understand yourself and realize that other people have their own sets of unique traits and preferences, you can find ways to communicate more effectively with them.

Some will reveal how you interact with the world around you, where you direct your energy, how you make decisions, how you approach work, and how you tend to communicate. Others will reveal how you give and receive love and what it takes to feel appreciated.

I am sharing this wonderful information with the caveat that I am not promising, endorsing, guaranteeing, judging, or predicting any outcomes for you. I'm simply providing you with tools which I have enjoyed and hope you will too!

Different Strokes for Different Folks

"Feelings of worth can flourish only in an atmosphere where individual differences are appreciated, mistakes are tolerated, communication is open, and rules are flexible—the kind of atmosphere that is found in a nurturing family."

—Virginia Satir

First things first—differences abound! Race, creed, color, gender, national origin, handicap, age, familial status, socio-economics, education, politics, religion, geography, and job status. Does that list look like a poster ad for the ACLU? Add in our vastly different life experiences and things really start to get interesting.

As if these diverse characteristics weren't enough, bring them all into a social context where we must work, live, love, and engage with people different from ourselves—is it any wonder that communications can be challenging? The fact that someone is *different* from you does not make them wrong—it just makes them *different*. Why would we ever want everyone to be alike anyway? That would make the world boring!

The following ideas can give you better relationship expertise so that you can navigate differences with compassion and confidence.

Introvert, Extrovert, or Ambivert?

"There is no such thing as a pure introvert or extrovert. Such a person would be in the lunatic asylum."

—Carl Jung

Labels have always represented limitation, conformity, and narrow-mindedness to me since the human personality is multi-faceted and continuously evolving. Perhaps that is why I am so intrigued by the concept and labels of "introvert" and "extrovert." Neither description accurately defines the state of my social interactions. What about yours?

The concept is made even more fascinating when you consider it as a psychological spectrum. Imagine a sliding scale of personalities that range from being an "introvert" to an "extrovert" and placing "ambivert" smack dab in the middle.

Introvert	**Ambivert**	**Extrovert**

|-----------|-----------|-----------|-----------|-----------|-----------|-----------|-----------|

This linear scale illustrates a continuum of experiences, because these descriptions do not apply to every person at all times. We all have tendencies, preferences, and comfort zones that change according to the people we are surrounded by, the environment we find ourselves in, and our levels of confidence in the moment. Using the scale above, where do you typically fall in the spectrum?

Although my sister, Liz, is socially engaging and very confident with people, she tends to more of an introvert. She generates energy from the inside, from center to circumference, and would rather have one-on-one conversations to connect quietly and deeply.

I, on the other hand, am energized by walking into a room filled with three hundred strangers; I like to meet as many people as possible and walk out with new friends. After all that excitement, however, I am content to go home and curl up with a good book in complete silence.

Is one of us right and the other one wrong? No. We are just different. It is not unusual for people to believe that their way is the best way—that they are right and everyone else is out-of-sync or mistaken. The divine irony is that since we are better at being ourselves, how can we expect others to be less like themselves to fulfill our expectations? We cannot change who we are wired to be and neither can others.

By becoming aware of the differences and developing an understanding of each person's uniqueness, you will improve your interactions to make more positive first impressions.

So, how does all of this impact your first impressions for communicating. The summaries below help to illustrate how the Myers-

Briggs Type Indicator (MBTI) Assessment describes the differences.

Introverts

MBTI defines the distinction by stating that introverts get their energy from spending time alone, are thought oriented, seek depth of knowledge and influence, and prefer more substantial interaction. Introverts need time to process information and would rather give you a contemplated response than a quick reaction. In addition, they . . .

- Process information internally. It is normal for them to continuously contemplate, generate, circulate, evaluate, question, and conclude.
- Are rejuvenated and energized by rest, relaxation, and down-time.
- Need time to process and adapt to a new situation or setting, otherwise it is draining.
- Tend to be practical, simple, and neutral in their clothing, furnishings, offices, and surroundings.
- Choose their friends carefully and focus on quality, not quantity. They enjoy the company of people who have similar interests and intellect.
- May resist change if they are not given enough notice to plan, prepare, and execute. Sudden change creates stress and overwhelm.

Extroverts

In contrast, MBTI explains that extroverts are action oriented, seek breadth of knowledge and influence, prefer frequent interaction, and get energy from spending time with people. In addition, they . . .

- Process information externally by verbalizing, collaborating, brainstorming, discussing, sharing their ideas, and communicating until they achieve desired results.

- Are rejuvenated and re-charged by being around people, interacting with friends and family, and having dynamic conversations.
- Enjoy the excitement and adventure of a new situation or setting.
- Tend to be more colorful, unpredictable, daring, stylish, and cluttered in their clothing, home furnishings, offices, and surroundings.
- Love meeting new people and making new friends. They enjoy variety and engaging on all levels.
- Are very spontaneous, resilient, and adapt well to change.

Ambiverts

An ambivert navigates the introvert/extrovert spectrum with ease since they do not fit directly into either category. Since neither label applies to them, they are social chameleons who adapt to their environment to maximize their interaction and optimize their results. In addition, they . . .

- Can process information both internally and externally. They need time to contemplate on their own, but consider the opinions and wisdom from people whom they trust when making a decision.
- Love to engage and interact enthusiastically with others, however, they also enjoy calm and profound communication.
- Seek to balance between their personal time and social time, they value each greatly.
- Are able to move from one situation to the next with confidence, flexibility, and anticipation.

Not everyone is going to like us or understand us. And that is okay. It may have nothing to do with us personally; it's often more about who they are and how they relate to the world.

In his book, *The Four Agreements*, Miguel's Ruiz encourages us to "not take things personally; people behave for their reasons not ours." Our personality differences and life experiences shape how we perceive, engage, react, and respond.

Conversational Chameleon

We know that chameleons are lizards that are famous for their ability to change their colors and fit in as their environments require. This ability enables them to change themselves for safety, survival, and healthy well-being. Their colors adjust to reflect their mood, their surroundings, and serve as camouflage when necessary. Fossils prove they have been on this planet for over eighty million years, so they must be doing something right. Their innate ability for adaptability deserves appreciation, respect, and further consideration. It obviously works!

When you strive to become a conversational chameleon, you can more swiftly adapt to your environment and surroundings for your own safety, survival, and healthy well-being. Learning the personality styles of others will further heighten your awareness of differences to enhance your social agility. When you gain clarity on what is important to others and why they act as they do, you will be better able to engage confidently with their energies and personalities to thrive in most any situation.

Susan RoAne (SusanRoAne.com) is the bestselling author of *How to Work a Room: The Ultimate Guide to Savvy Socializing in Person and Online*. She is known worldwide as the Mingling Maven and is a respected expert, author, and keynote speaker on networking, connecting, and conversations. In her book, she shares the roadblocks and remedies to help people become savvy socializers and succeed at networking.

She recently shared with me that putting labels on personality styles can sometimes create bias and limitations. She said, "We've spent so much time crystallizing our differences that it can be to our detriment. It is more important to simply engage with people on a respectful and authentic level.

Being a **conversational chameleon** allows you to do that. One day I may be speaking to the CEO of a global company and the next to my four-year-old nephew. Just as you would not talk to your eighty-year-old grandmother the same way you would talk to a twenty-three-year-old co-worker, adapt your own behavior to the person with whom you are speaking."

Understanding Personality Styles Helps You:

- Communicate more easily with others by understanding their perspectives.
- Adapt your behavior to resonate with others.
- Develop deeper levels of compassion, patience, and communication.
- Deliver personalized customer service.
- Build trust and rapport faster.
- Nurture existing relationships.
- Make more sales.
- Feel more confident networking.
- Realize that people behave the way they do for their reasons, not yours.
- Appreciate the diversity of teammates, family members, friends, and work groups.
- Unify your teams and get the best out of your people by focusing on their strengths, aligning their styles with their assigned positions, and knowing how to motivate and reward them.

Effective communication requires an elevated level of self-awareness, and desire to understand and appreciate one another. As you move forward in life, seek to build upon your understanding of our communication and personality differences so that you are well-prepared to arrive and thrive in your first (and lasting) impressions.

8. SAVVY SOCIALIZING & SYNCHRONICITY

"The measure of a conversation is how much mutual recognition there is in it; how much shared there is in it. If you're talking about what's in your own head, or without thought to what people looking and listening will feel, you might as well be in a room talking to yourself."

—Dylan Moran

Savvy Socializing

When I asked Susan to share a few of her golden nuggets about being a savvy socializer, she replied, "It is really a lot easier than most people think. The savvy socializer has a firm grasp of social etiquette and social manners. For example, you must learn when it is time to exit a conversation graciously. You have to know when it is time to thank people. If you got a new job from a personal referral, you need to acknowledge them before they find out from a third party three months later. Savvy socializers keep people in the loop and understand social nuances."

The Gift of Gab

She continued by saying, "Many people dismiss small talk as being a waste of time. If you think small talk is not worthy of your time you are making a big mistake. It is actually one of the best ways for you to get to know someone. Don't be afraid to share a little bit about yourself so that you give another person enough information to ask questions. Small talk is the biggest talk we do."

My man Daniel sees twenty patients a day, many of whom he has never met before their appointment. With only fifteen to twenty minutes to spare, he has no choice but to use the gift of gab to connect quickly. He said, "Small talk is easier than big talk, especially with someone you do not know. It is an easy stepping stone to help you break the silence for more comfortable conversation. This initial form of communication opens the door for big talk." Find ways to start small talk with new people and they will be impressed by your friendly disposition and sincere interest.

Savvy Synchronicity

The Swiss psychiatrist Carl Jung (1875-1961) first introduced the concept of "synchronicity" to describe the meaningful coincidences which occur in our lives and connect us all in our humanity.

The synchronicity found in nature extends to the rhythm and patterns in our relationships; it explains how random events can come together to achieve harmony, flow, and order. Similarly, social synchronicity plays a large role in the art of constructive communication by helping us understand how social patterns can positively impact our relationships.

Groundbreaking research at Cal Tech has now revealed that humans not only tend to synchronize their movements, such as clapping in unison or walking at the same pace, but they also synchronize their social interactions as well. It is in this synchronicity that we can find social solutions for engaging, connecting, and communicating with ease.

The gracious timing of social synchronicity helps the sender's message align and resonate with the receiver's ability to recognize, receive, comprehend, and appreciate the intended message. When the sender and receiver are "in sync," the clarity and synergy created are powerful and affirming.

However, being "out of sync" happens all the time . . .

- Have you ever begun a discussion when the timing was not right and your message was subsequently rejected?
- Have you ever said the right thing at the wrong time and ended up looking stupid or inappropriate?

- Or perhaps rather than having a positive or a negative effect, your message fell on deaf ears and had no effect at all?
- Has your poor timing ever resulted in social awkwardness, humiliating rejection, or alienation?
- Has anyone ever attempted a serious discussion with you in the middle of your day when you were overwhelmed by phone calls, emails, and appointments?

Knowing *when* to say something is as important as knowing *what* or *what not* to say. You may have the perfect message, but it can be negated by imperfect timing. Being "out of sync" can be exasperating. Seek to synchronize to increase your chances for success and positive outcomes. Just because your timing is good for you does not mean it is a good time for another person.

Finding the right time is like discovering a social portal which opens a gate for others to receive your message and "get you." You only get one chance to make a first impression and if the gate begins to close, you may never get another opportunity to walk through it. Watch for the openings and synchronize your movements with your intended recipient.

All in Good Time

The ancient Buddhist saying shares, "When the student is ready, the master will appear." When the timing is right, lessons are learned and miracles can happen. However, when the timing is "out of sync," even the best of intentions can be met with resistance.

I love to read. However, there have been times when certain books did not resonate with me because the timing was off kilter. Their lessons fell flat because their messages were not pertinent, relevant, or interesting to me at the time. Then, when I would re-read the same book years later, it could rock my world and change my life for the better. The message was more in alignment with where I was at that moment in time. With most anything, just because your timing may not be good now, does not mean it won't be better later.

The Power of the Pause

"Pausing is a vital skill for audience engagement. In fact, punctuation is to readers as pausing is to your listeners. Whether you are in front of a crowd, sitting around a conference room table, or having a one-on-one phone call, visualize that what you are saying is the story you are telling.
It needs punctuation."

–Keith Bailey, Decker Communications

Eloquent speakers, communication experts, seasoned actors, and musicians all understand the transforming power of the pause. They know all too well that strategic silence and a well-placed whisper can speak louder than words in delivering a memorable presentation. It captures people's attention . . . creating eager anticipation for your next words.

5 Reasons to Develop the Power of the Pause. It . . .

1. encourages your communication partner to express their thoughts without interruption.
2. provides a moment of silence to calm incessant talking.
3. allows time for your brain to catch up with our mouth.
4. provides your listener with space to process your message.
5. highlights important points for your message to have more impact.

Getting into Sync

People feel the most comfortable with and gravitate more quickly to the people with whom they are the most alike. You will receive your best results by seeking first to understand and then to adjust your energy, movements, posture, words, gestures, and behaviors to synchronize with theirs. This alignment will build a sense of rapport and commonality which will help your conversations progress smoothly and more successfully.

Free Flowing Dialogue

"Dialogue is the flow of meaning between or among us. But meaning can only flow between or among us when we listen and respond to each other."
—David Bohm

Have you ever been engaged in a conversation which was so dynamic that you were both firing on all cylinders, in perfect harmony and at warp speed? Years ago, one of my girlfriends and I were going on a road trip and our destination was four hours away. We started an amazing conversation as our trip began. We arrived four hours later, but it felt like we had been driving for only half an hour. Have you ever been so immersed in the free flow of conversation that it transcended time, space, and effort? That is the beauty of being in flow.

The Rhythm of Relationships

It's not a mystery that there are certain people with whom we "click" and others with whom we don't. In the movie, Forrest Gump, Forrest proclaimed that he and Jenny got along like "peas and carrots." I once heard Tony Robbins say that if you are with the right person, a relationship does not take a lot of work. When relationships are in rhythm, everything is made easier.

Coincidence & Serendipity

Social synchronicity will help you stay open-minded regarding coincidence and serendipity. It is worth considering whether people are showing up in your life for a purpose or by accident.

Ask Yourself:

- Have you pondered a question and someone ironically shows up with the answers?
- Have you ever been thinking of a friend and within moments they mysteriously call or come by?

- How many times have you seen a meaningful relationship start because the right people were in the right place at the right time for the right opportunity?

These "God Winks" may be an answer to prayer, a warning to change course, or a reward for doing things right. Become mindful and aware of how these cosmic puzzle pieces come together to enrich your life and your relationships. It is both affirming and entertaining to consider. Be open and grateful.

Bull in a China Shop

The metaphor "bull in a china shop" appropriately describes how a clumsy (or socially awkward) person can sometimes find themselves in a quite delicate position. Have you ever been in a social situation where it was prudent to bite your tongue, smile and nod, choose your words carefully, or remain silent all together? One in which, if you didn't—it could cause damage?

You can be a bull. And you can be in the china shop. But, just don't break anything! Even the biggest, baddest, most boorish bull can skate carefully through a china shop with dignity and grace if he exercises mindfulness and consideration.

Delicious Dialogue

"A conversation is a dialogue, not a monologue. That's why there are so few good conversations: due to scarcity, two intelligent talkers seldom meet."
—Truman Capote

We've all known the proverbial conversation hog who dominates a discussion and pays little notice to another person's input. They're so busy talking about themselves, we can barely slide a word in edgewise. Don't be that guy! An engaging conversation is a two-way street. Learn to delight in dialogue to ensure mutual respect and consideration.

8 WAYS TO **MASTER**
The Art of **COMMUNICATION**

1. *Mindful Awareness.* Be fully involved in the moment—right now! Developing this ability instills a sixth sense for navigating connections. Be intentional and thoughtful; listen and care.

2. *Conversation Starters.* Your first words will not only shape your first impression, but they can create amazing connections, lead you to your dream job, or help you discover a new best friend.

3. *Active Listening.* Practice this skill. You enhance communication; this confirms that the message another conveys is well received and thoroughly understood. You get it!

4. *Voice Value.* Your voice makes a first impression. Is your voice coming across as smart, friendly, and positive or ignorant, rude, and negative? The way you deliver the words is your "vocal image."

5. *Using Names.* Calling a person by name makes him/her feel recognized, appreciated, and special. It shows respect and that you are genuinely interested in making a connection. You make them feel remembered!

6. *Wise with Your Words.* Speak words that support your highest good. Are your thoughts building you up or tearing you down? Your best first impressions ride on the quality of your words.

7. *Communication Styles.* Understanding the wide range of personalities will help improve your communication, connection, and engagement not only at work, but in your relationships at home, in life, and in love.

8. *Savvy Socializing & Synchronicity.* The savvy socializer has a very good grasp of social etiquette and social manners. They understand the rhythm of relationships in social interactions. It is in this synchronicity that we can find social solutions for engaging, connecting, and communicating with ease.

6

The _Art_ _of_
CONNECTION

8 WAYS TO ENRICH
RAPPORT & KINSHIP
FOR POSITIVE IMPACT

The Art of CONNECTION

Communicating on the surface can be easy. But when you want to dig deeper and connect with more profound impact, you'll need to achieve greater understanding, especially when others have personalities, experiences, needs, and preferences different from your own.

We all have individual ideas and agendas for managing our days and our lives. However, it is when we foster a sense of wonder and nurture a sincere curiosity that we can move beyond the predictable and mundane. Expressing and demonstrating genuine interest for people can connect you on levels you may never have imagined.

In *The Art of Connection,* you will learn simple, yet powerful ways to build trust and rapport for connecting with ease. By being personable and friendly, you will receive more positive and welcoming reactions.

Encourage others to talk about themselves by asking questions and listening with genuine interest. Demonstrating such mutual respect will make you all the more fascinating for kinship and camaraderie.

As you use fun and humor to reduce tension and connect with laughter, light-heartedness will prevail. Exercising discretion and good judgment in your communication will leave your listener feeling like they have met a person of substance and style.

1. *Building Trust & Rapport*
2. *Personable & Friendly*
3. *Be Interested & Interesting*
4. *Be a Discovery Expert*
5. *Commonality & Camaraderie*
6. *Make Others Feel Important*
7. *Use Fun & Humor*
8. *Discretion & Good Judgment*

1. BUILDING TRUST & RAPPORT

"Trust is the glue of life. It's the most essential ingredient in effective communication. It's the foundational principle that holds all relationships."
—Stephen Covey

Trust and rapport are essential for moving a positive first impression forward to create a meaningful and lasting connection. They are the heartbeat of business, the backbone for high performing teams, and the secret sauce for healthy relationships. When we trust someone or something, we place our faith and confidence in their word, reliability, and deeds. Without trust and rapport, a relationship can be cut short before it ever gets started. Strengthen your first impressions by making the intentional effort to first earn people's trust, and rapport will naturally follow.

Earning Trust & Cooperation

The number one thing which stands between you and meeting a new person is *tension*. What is the number one thing which stands between a sales person and their prospect? You guessed it . . . tension. One of our first priorities as we initiate a first impression must be to focus on how to effectively minimize or eliminate tension.

Regardless of your relationship or venue, when tension is high, trust and cooperation are low. When tension is reduced, trust and cooperation increase. It is an inverse relationship. So, how can you move to reduce tension in your first impressions to increase trust and cooperation? Put yourself in their shoes and seek to relate to them with equal footing on a level playing field. Demonstrate how you can bring value to their lives.

Can I Trust You?

*"We can all be successful and make money, but when we die, that ends.
But when you are significant is when you help other people be successful.
That lasts many a lifetime."*

—Lou Holtz

Years ago, I heard Lou Holtz speak at a national conference. His rock-solid reputation preceded him—he is the only coach in the history of college football to take six different teams to a bowl game. He is not only well-respected for his ability to elevate football programs, but to elevate individuals as well.

During his humorous and entertaining keynote, he taught a few small lessons which carried big meanings. He shared that every person you meet is privately asking themselves three questions:

1. Do you care about me?
2. Do I like you?
3. Can I trust you?

When you make an authentic, sincere, and dignified effort to create a positive first impression, you increase your chances of receiving a "Yes!" to those questions. Unfortunately, if someone you meet answers "No!" you've got an uphill battle to earn their business or develop a friendship.

ABCD Trust Model

A discussion on building trust and rapport would not be complete without mentioning *The New York Times* bestselling author and leadership expert Ken Blanchard's *ABCD Trust Model*.

In his book, *Trust Works! Four Keys to Building Lasting Relationships,* Dr. Blanchard shares four essential elements for transforming your relationships. Once understood and applied, they serve to replace tension with the respect, collaboration, engagement, and psychological safety we all seek.

1. **Able**—Does the person demonstrate competence for delivering quality results, solving problems, helping others, and doing their best?
2. **Believable**—Are they honest, sincere, respectful, humble, and trustworthy? Do they admit when they have made a mistake and do their utmost to make it right when they are wrong?
3. **Connected**—Do they care about others and show it through listening, praising, showing interest, being empathetic, and being a team player?
4. **Dependable**—Are they accountable, consistent, reliable, responsive, and organized?

Whether you want to make a positive first impression or secure a lasting one, these four qualities help move us beyond our initial encounters to dive deep and create meaningful connections.

When Trust Is Broken

"Whoever is careless with the truth in small matters cannot be trusted with important matters."
—Albert Einstein

When trust is broken, foundational cracks occur which weaken the entire relationship. As with concrete, no amount of filling and patching you apply with the hope of fortifying the fracture will ever repair the weakness caused by the rift.

As soon as someone believes you cannot be trusted, you are stopped dead in your tracks. Whether this perceived loss of trustworthiness is true or false, the perception alone can be damaging.

Sometimes we break people's trust accidentally. An infraction such as not returning a phone call, missing a deadline, being late for an appointment, divulging a confidence, or speaking out of turn can damage our perceived character and reputation.

---

66 *Take steps to be humble, sincere, and authentic, and apologize if necessary. If a relationship is valuable to you, it is worth your concern and effort to make it right.* 99

I've Got to Trust You to Like You

People want to do business with people whom they like and trust. If anything in a business presentation raises concerns or doubt about your trustworthiness, everything shuts down. And then there's little hope of moving forward in a positive way—you're done.

Years ago, my mentor, Mary Seals and I shared a mutual acquaintance who was successful in sales, but had a questionable reputation. I told her, "I really like him, but I can't trust him as far as I can throw him." Mary bluntly replied, "Susan, if I can't trust someone, I don't like or respect them."

Her comment caused me to reconsider always giving people the benefit of a doubt and to instead be wary when someone demonstrates a lack of integrity.

Going with Your Gut

Your natural instincts are a great barometer for a person's trustworthiness. Listen to your gut when something feels amiss. When your natural "Spidey-Sense" kicks in, it may be alerting you to red flags you would not see on the surface otherwise.

People consider trust differently. Some approach a new relationship with a degree of skepticism and want the other person to earn their trust before it is freely given. Their reluctance is often influenced by a previous experience when they were hurt, betrayed, or let down by others.

I, however, typically trust people until they prove me wrong. As an energy-sensitive person with a highly intuitive nature, I pick up on clues as to whom I can trust or should be wary of. I will take my chances and continue living with my heart wide-open. Having faith in humanity and expecting the best from others improves my happiness and well-being.

What are those behaviors that make us take pause to think twice about a person's trustworthiness? Guarded body language, lack of eye contact, nervous fidgeting, interrupting, speaking ill of others, lying, arrogance, and gossip to name a few.

Rock Your Rapport

"Rapport is the ability to enter someone else's world, to make him feel that you understand him, that you have a strong common bond."

—Tony Robbins

Trust and rapport are listed in that order because without first building trust, healthy rapport is not possible. Rapport allows you to create a friendly compatibility and easy companionship which feels comfortable and enjoyable. As you rock rapport, you will open doors, earn loyalty, establish long-term relationships, and promote mutually respectful interaction. How can you break the ice and move toward creating a positive connection?

11 Tips for Building Rapport

1. Adapt to the other person's energy level.
2. Assume rapport.

3. Be open and friendly.
4. Exude warmth and approachability.
5. Find common ground or mutual agreement.
6. Keep your commitments and always follow through.
7. Make eye contact.
8. Soften your voice, your smile, and your eye contact to convey openness and interest.
9. Match and mirror a person's gestures and body language.
10. Pay attention.
11. Validate the other person by asking questions and showing sincere interest in their answers.

Good for Business

Trust and rapport are the connective tissue for gaining and maintaining healthy relationships. They provide people with the comfort and reassurance that they are doing business with an organization who cares.

Top sales professionals will confirm that nurturing their "sphere of influence" is essential to their success. When trust and rapport are well cultivated, it can yield tremendous bottom-line results.

For leaders, it can make all the difference in the viability of their teams. When there is mistrust or low connectivity, teams can falter and fight—making productivity and profitability suffer. When a leader nurtures an environment of trust, respect, and honesty—business soars, creativity and problem-solving are inspired, and collaboration enables people get more done in less time.

The bottom line is that, as human beings, we all crave belonging and connection. This only happens when trust is established and continuously cultivated.

2. Personable & Friendly

"Lead the life that will make you kindly and friendly to everyone about you, and you will be surprised what a happy life you will lead."
—Charles Schwab

Animation. Enthusiasm. Sincerity. Excitement. Acceptance. Have I just described your family dog? You're happy to see him because he is so happy to see you. It is no wonder dogs are called "Man's Best Friend" with attributes like that. Their natural propensity for joy makes them among the most personable and friendly creatures on the planet. Human beings could learn a thing or two from their eager and earnest approach to life.

People who exude these qualities are treasures indeed—not only to the friends they make and strangers they meet, but to the companies who employ them. These special people are genuinely warm, sincerely kind, and put people at ease with their inviting nature and light-hearted conversation. They are easy to talk to, easy to like, and bring a positive vibe to even the most stressful situations

Wise leaders know that this is the highly-prized personality for employees who are meeting, greeting, and engaging on the front lines with customers. They are the real ambassadors of good will who make positive first impressions for the organization. Their affinity for being personable and friendly can boost the attractor factor for winning business, loyalty, and rave reviews.

It's the Southern Way

The South is known for its "Southern Hospitality," and I feel fortunate to have grown up in such a friendly and caring culture. Our remarkable mother has always exemplified these qualities and has been a consistent role model for making other people feel valued and important.

She will approach new people in most any situation to gift them with a smile and a moment of her time. Regardless of their role, position, or stature, she confidently engages others with animation, enthusiasm, and interest. Her gentility makes people feel emotionally safe and cared for. This degree of friendliness melts resistance, lowers barriers, and opens hearts by valuing humanity. Almost always, her personal connections develop with feelings of mutual respect, appreciation, and friendship.

What About the Social Introvert?

Perhaps you don't want to talk! Maybe you prefer to speak only when responding to another person. If you tend to be more reserved and less gregarious, the expression on your face will speak volumes. A pleasant expression and a genuine smile communicate friendliness and approachability that will lead you to a positive experience. Your body language engages—without words.

10 Ways to Be More Personable and Friendly

We all know that person—the one who wakes up on the right side of the bed; the one who surely consumed a bowl of sunshine for breakfast; the one who asks how you're doing and means it. How does she emanate that much light? How can we also appear more friendly and personable? How can we be that light for others?

1. Listen more than you speak.
2. When you do speak, ask questions of the other person before volunteering your own story.
3. Show a genuine interest in what the other person has to share.
4. Keep the focus on the other person. People love to talk about themselves—their kids, their significant other, their pets, their job, etc.

5. Keep a positive attitude, a smile, and eye contact.
6. Be the glue that holds the conversation together. And learn to be the glue that keeps other groups of people together.
7. Laugh at other people's jokes.
8. Take the initiative to say hello and introduce yourself.
9. Get in tune with other people's emotions.
10. Embrace small talk as a positive way to begin new conversations.

It can be a mean world; sadly, there is no shortage of rude people. Throughout my travels, I pleasantly discovered that if you are friendly to others, they will usually mirror the same in return. Regardless of which cities or countries I visit, the majority of people I encounter tend to be friendly, personable, and caring.

---

66 *Most people want, need, and respond positively to gestures of kindness and goodness. This universal friendliness connects humanity.* 99

Not Just a Personality Trait

While some may consider being friendly an appealing personality trait, I challenge you to see it as a valuable skill. In a world where we are continuously bombarded with negativity and anxiety is at an all-time high, a warm and friendly person is a welcome relief. Training yourself to be the friendly "calm in the storm" makes you a true asset to your business, your family, and your community.

Think about the impact you have on the people around you every day. How do you interact with them? Is your presence uplifting or are do you bring a dark cloud?

Don't Let Circumstances Throw You Off Track

Is it possible to be friendly and engaging every day? Of course not. Everyone has their moments. I once read a quote from an anonymous author who said, "It's okay to have a bad day— just don't unpack and live there." I love that. As an example, imagine waking up and stubbing your toe as you get out of bed. You can respond in one of two ways. You can allow it to start your day off on the wrong foot and go through the rest of your day in a bad mood—souring everything and everyone in your path.

OR . . . you can say, "Oh great—sh*t happens, the day's got to get better from here!" Then set your intention to look for the good things that head your way for the rest of the day. You have the power to pick.

Fine-tune your rebounding and resiliency skills. Teach yourself different ways to stay mentally in the moment by projecting a friendly and positive vibe in everything you do. Remember, your vibe attracts your tribe. So be conscientious of your impact—it's powerful!

Make the Right Choice

We can choose how we present ourselves to the world—and we should. From a sales perspective, who would you rather work with? Someone who is friendly and amiable or someone who is stiff and unyielding?

From a leadership lean, are you the BOSS that creates fear and rules with an "iron fist" or are you a LEADER who listens and connects with your team members to create a culture where collaboration and creativity can thrive?

Are you the one who strives to brighten other people's days or are you the one waiting for others to do that for you? These are choices that can and do make a huge difference in the value you bring to the table, personally and professionally.

3. INTERESTED & INTERESTING

"When you speak to me about yourself, you are a bore. When you speak to me about others, you are a gossip. When you speak to me about me, you are a brilliant conversationalist."

—Unknown

Is it better to be interested or interesting? Good question. People will be more interested in you when you first demonstrate that you are interested in them.

If you want to impress someone with how much you know, the best thing you can do is talk to them about . . . *them*. People typically love to share their stories and are delighted when others show genuine interest in hearing about: their families, what they do for fun, their opinions, where they are going on vacation, their happiest memories, their hobbies, or even where they grew up.

---

66 *By taking a personal interest in other people's lives, you are demonstrating selflessness, grace, and respect.* 99

Rather than trying hard to be interesting and focusing on yourself, turn your attention to filling that need in others.

ASK YOURSELF: Your closest friends want to know all about the details of your life and want to hear what is happening in your life. How can you be that type of person for others?

How Can You Show You Are Interested?

When you are genuinely interested, your authenticity reveals itself in your body language, attitude, facial gestures, eye contact, and overall responsiveness. You clearly communicate your interest when you:

- Pay close attention.
- Ask how you can help.
- Ask probing questions.
- Practice great listening.
- Invite people to participate.
- Express curiosity without judgment.
- Find a way to help others achieve their goals.
- Keep your mind open to innovative ideas.
- Make introductions and connect like-minded people.
- Get to know people first before talking about yourself.
- Consider how and why they feel/think/believe as they do.

Curiosity

What makes you curious about someone when meeting them for the first time? Do they have a fascination factor? Is there something special about them that stands out? What makes you want to learn more?

Be fiercely curious about **who they are, what they do, what they like,** and **what they need.** If you pay attention to them, they will pay attention to you.

Ask questions and learn to listen without words being spoken. Hear with your heart, eyes, head, and intuition. Your natural curiosity can be your own best friend for revealing how to engage with genuine interest.

Lenee's aunt is a master conversationalist who can enter a party of strangers and leave with a handful of new best friends. When she walks into a room, she is on a mission to learn everyone else's story. Her focus is so completely dedicated to hearing about others that her own story is irrelevant to the conversation. It feeds her feelings of joy to get to know others and hear their stories. Try it!

Memory Makes Magic Happen

Have you ever been away from someone for a while and when you are reunited after a long absence, they ask about something or someone whom you talked about previously? My friend Teresa Palm is an amazing massage therapist. Months can go by between our appointments, however, without missing a beat, she can start up our conversations exactly where we left off ages ago. Her memory has always impressed me and demonstrated that she is interested enough to remember things which were meaningful to me. She always conveys a sincere interest which makes me feel great.

❝ If you truly want to impress someone, remember points they shared in previous conversations and mention it when you reconnect. ❞

How do other people feel when they're around you? When you ask people about themselves, are you just being polite or do you truly want to know? It is obvious. When you focus your intention and questions on them, it makes them feel special and valued. However, if you don't sincerely want to know, it can backfire as appearing insincere.

"You can make more friends in two months by becoming interested in other people than you can in two years by trying to get other people interested in you."
—Dale Carnegie

Take Note

A wise business practice is to become a prolific note-taker if you aren't already. When you've had a great conversation or interaction with someone—whether it is on a conference call, Skype, in a meeting, or even in passing—jot down a note or two about your time together. Then you can reference it the next time you see each other or speak again. Since most of us don't have as extraordinary a memory as my friend Teresa Palm, taking notes is a smart and easy way to show that you are interested and care.

Check Your Ego at the Door

A big part of creating valuable, long-term connections requires setting your ego aside. For some, it's a struggle to not be the center of attention, of the conversation, or of the universe! People feel more valued, respected, and connected when they feel seen and heard. And that's hard to do if it's always all about you. Once you get into the practice of connecting and communicating with people in a way that draws them to you, conversations will be more engaging, and the end result is much more rewarding.

Show Them You CARE

In the business world, mastering conversational skills and paying attention to the details can take you to the top and help keep you there!

Teddy Roosevelt has been credited with saying, "People don't care how much you know until they know how much you care." Think about that from a sales perspective.

We've all known that one salesperson whose primary motivation in a transaction is to earn a commission—regardless of their customer's needs. From their body language to their self-driven talking points to the "close three times and then some" techniques–they come across as egocentric and uncaring.

On the other hand, when presented with a service-minded professional who strives to deliver the best possible experience, aren't you duly impressed? They are genuinely interested in learning about your wants, needs, and desires to help ensure you achieve your goals. They are the kind of person you'll turn to again and again—not only for your own business but to refer to others as well.

4. Be a Discovery Expert

"The quality of our lives is directly related to the quality of our thinking. The quality of our thinking, in turn, is determined by the quality of our questions, for questions are the engine, the driving force behind thinking."
—The Miniature Guide to the Art of Asking Essential Questions

Inquiring Minds Want to Know

Be inquisitive. You already know what you know. A straightforward way to learn something new is simply by asking questions. The more you ask, the more you can learn . . . about life and work, about other people, and about yourself.

Whether you master the art of asking questions to become a skilled communicator, start conversations, or to connect in a more meaningful way, questions can help you build rapport and strengthen relationships. Curiosity adds depth to what you know and to your life experience.

Open Ended versus Closed Ended Questions

When you sincerely want to connect on deeper levels and encourage other people to talk about themselves, use open-ended questions to stimulate your conversation and get the ball rolling.

Well-crafted **open-ended questions** typically begin with *What, Why, When, Who, How,* and *Where*, all of which can prompt the most delightful of conversations. Open-ended questions open doors for new discoveries and opportunities. They encourage others to speak their truths, share their experiences, and express their ideas.

A **closed-ended question,** however, is one which could be answered with a one-word answer or a simple "yes" or "no." It can bring a dynamic dialogue to an awkward halt or stalemate. You can easily flip the encounter around by making a little more effort.

Encouraging quality communication will make it easier for you to establish rapport, gather information, and increase understanding. You can use this "fishing" technique for personal relationships, social events, sales calls, and professional correspondence.

Spot On Answers

"Listen to your patients. They are telling you their diagnosis."
—Sir William Osler

In medicine, prescription before diagnosis is malpractice. Asking the right questions will help you discover a person's needs and concerns so that you can respond intelligently and appropriately.

Yet salespeople, consultants, or managers often try to push their solutions on you before they even know what your needs are. This is a fast way to alienate people and push you toward their competitor, isn't it?

In sales, this tactic comes across as pushy, arrogant, and uncaring. It doesn't have to be this way. Admittedly, it may take great restraint to resist the temptation to dominate a conversation, but when you do, you are rewarded with an appreciation for your interest and attentiveness. Simply by changing your approach and becoming a discovery expert, you will receive relevant answers for how to better connect and serve others.

Socratic Teaching

Socrates would teach his pupils by asking them intelligent and probing questions. By using their critical thinking skills and problem-solving abilities, they could discover the answers for themselves and retain their lessons longer. By using this same approach for Socratic Selling or Socratic Communication, there is no telling how much you might teach and solve for another person, all the while creating a memorable encounter.

Push versus Pull Marketing

Who wants to be pushed around? I certainly don't. Statements push and questions pull. Don't you prefer the latter? Questions pique interest and can keep the dialogue flowing when your other alternatives aren't as attractive or magnetic.

Use questions to find out where people are, where they want to be, and how you can help them cross the great divide. When I was in real estate, there were times when brand new clients would get into my car for a day of touring and house hunting. In many cases, I had never met them before and my first goal was to break the ice and build rapport as fast as possible so that our time together would be enjoyable, interactive, and successful for all of us.

So, how can you move beyond awkward silence with virtual strangers to becoming new friends? By asking great questions! Once a few inquiring questions were placed, I would let them do all the talking.

In sales, there is a questioning funnel for building rapport in which you start with broad questions and discreetly and respectfully move to the more specific. If you don't honor this progression, you risk coming across as pushy. As you build rapport, you earn standing to get more personal.

People love to talk about themselves and when you provide them with an opening and a platform for them to do so, you will be amazed by how your conversations can blossom.

Make It Fun

"Adults are always asking kids what they want to be when they grow up because they are looking for ideas."
—Paula Poundstone

What do you do? It's amazing how people will qualify, quantify, judge, assess, and form complete opinions about you based on that one age-old question. It is a boring, uncreative default setting for attempting to engage a new person.

Spice it up and try something new. Instead, ask "What do you do for fun?" Your creativity will make you more memorable and help you stand apart from the crowd.

"Tell Me About Yourself . . ."

"Tell me about yourself" is one of the best icebreakers and conversation openers you can have. Learn to ask questions using this phrase as the guide. Let the other person do the talking and they will think you are the most delightful conversationalist they have ever met. When you make the effort to do this for others, they feel relevant and valued.

UN-Impressives: Questions with Dubious Intentions

I once knew a woman who had a reputation as a snob and a gossip. I would avoid her at parties because I did not want to participate in her judgmental inquisition. It rarely felt like her questions were based on genuine interest and caring, but rather an attempt to gather information that she could use behind my back. I had her number and could see past her overly eager friendliness. Her attempts to be the expert on everyone else's business have continued to make a poor impression on me these many years later. If your gut reaction is "Why do you want to know?" trust your instincts.

Leading the Witness

Know the difference! Using questions to manipulate, coerce, or lead people in directions which are not in their best interests connotes dishonesty, fraud, disrespect, and a lack of integrity.

11 Benefits of Asking Questions

1. Builds rapport.
2. Nurtures creativity.
3. Grows your knowledge and awareness.
4. Exercises critical thinking and problem-solving skills.
5. Makes the other person feel valued.
6. Helps you make thoughtful decisions.
7. The better our questions, the better our answers.
8. Keeps you agile and open to new ideas.
9. Improves your memory and retention.
10. Helps you stay informed and relevant.
11. Enables you to discover a new world of possibilities you would not have known otherwise.

In her book, *Communicate with Confidence!,* communication expert Dianna Booher (booherresearch.com) teaches that there are right ways to ask questions without being intrusive. She shares, "Most people like to have others show interest in them. When you seek out another's opinion or ask about someone's experiences or interests, you are complimenting them. That warmth builds rapport."

> *"The important thing is not to stop questioning.*
> *Curiosity has its own reason for existing."*
> —Albert Einstein

5. COMMONALITY & CAMARADERIE

"We must stop concentrating on our differences and focus on what we have in common. Then we can realize our full potential and achieve the greatest good in the world."

—Bonnie L. Oscarson

Finding commonality with another person can help you create an instant bond by transcending social differences and going straight to creating rapport. Finding common ground allows you to connect the dots in the big picture to discover what feels most comfortable, how to connect, and where you might fit in when meeting new people.

When people are like you, conversations flow naturally and feel more relaxed, don't they? You know what to say, how to talk, what to expect, and how to understand them on an intuitive level.

Wouldn't it be wonderful to enjoy this level of simplicity in all relationships, regardless of differences? You can. Begin taking the initiative to find common ground with others and you will soon lay solid foundations on which to build great first impressions.

Social Certainty

The romantic notion of "opposites attract" works well in fairy tales, however, science proves that "like attracts like" for healthy communication and successful relationships. Social psychologists have long relied upon the "Similarity Attraction Theory" to explain why we are more positively inclined toward people who are the most like ourselves.

Similarity reduces uncertainty and gives us a comforting degree of psychological safety. It is no wonder, then, that "birds of a feather flock together." Our tribe understands our vibe.

It is easier to do business and work with people who are most like ourselves. Establishing social certainty helps you build trust, develop rapport, and strengthen your connection. However, the right questions might lead you to find a niche of commonality in someone who is very different from you. It can be professionally and personally rewarding.

Discovering Things You Have in Common

"We all have something in common. It's just a matter of taking the time to find out what it is."

—Susan Gale

In his book, *The Attractor Factor,* Joe Vitale shares five simple ways for building wealth (or anything else) from the inside out. Along with the "Law of Attraction" there is also an "Attractor Factor" for easily building camaraderie and commonality for making a positive first impression. Seek to find:

1. Shared History
2. Shared Stories
3. Shared Interests
4. Shared Attitudes
5. Shared Experiences
6. Shared Beliefs and Values

Identifying, developing, and connecting on these points of reference will provide you with a rich resource of information from which to engage in stimulating conversations and connect on meaningful levels.

Once you start looking, you will discover unlimited links and openers for nurturing camaraderie. Do you drive the same car? Did you attend the same college? Do you both write with your left hand? Love vacationing in Paris? Prefer sushi over pasta? Both have twins? Attend the same church? Each run marathons? Enjoy the same television shows? Have the same breed of dog? While downright basic, these shared commonalities can often bring a sense of familiarity and affection even for people whom you have never met.

Strategic Commonality

Social media has capitalized on helping people find others who share their similar interests shared experiences and common passions. With social media, we are easily able to target potential customers who would be ideal for our business pursuits and professional development.

Instant Access

When my twins were born, I moved abruptly from being a professional career woman to a full-time, stay-at-home mom. The role shift opened a new door of commonality which surprised and delighted me. I was instantly welcomed into a special "Motherhood Club," where before I never would have related. It felt as if I was suddenly bonded with mothers worldwide. It's important to remember—nothing stays the same, nor do we. Sharing a commonality with others can connect you with others in ways you may never have imagined.

Professional Networking

The first week I lived in Madison, WI, I sought a local chapter meeting for ASTD (American Society for Training and Development). Having belonged to the same organization in Florida, I knew it would be a comfortable way to meet new people and make new friends. Knowing we would have a lot in common, I entered the room of strangers feeling confident and hopeful.

As everyone took turns introducing themselves, it was easy to see our common denominators. I briefly mentioned that I was new to the area, was a professional speaker, and a member of the National Speakers Association. Within minutes of mentioning NSA, a fellow participant approached me, shared that she was a member too, and our lively conversation began. The positive first impression we made on each was so powerful and captivating that we continued our conversations for months to come. Now, two years later, Tina and I are the best of friends and I have every confidence we will be for life. You never know when an amazing person will walk into your life when you seek common bonds and camaraderie.

How About This Weather We Are Having?

When all else fails, Mother Nature has provided you with a great social default for finding commonality with others. Since weather is a universally shared experience, it enables you to jump into a conversation with anybody and everybody. While discussing the weather may sound boring, trite, and predictable, it is a safe and the certain ice-breaker that can help you build commonality regardless of who you are addressing. As I write this, we have icy rain! It's never a boring topic.

Venturing Out

In our high-tech world today, there are unlimited ways with which you can search for people, places, and events to connect you with like-minded people. Food enthusiasts? There are local cooking classes. Gardening fans? There are flower shows and garden expos. Kids in school? Join the PTA and get involved. There are clubs and groups for almost any interest these days and venturing out to make those connections is a powerful way to expand your insights, your network, and even your business.

I recently heard of a real estate professional who LOVES to cook. So, her niche market? Foodies. She attends local restaurant events and cooking classes and turns strangers into friends and clients. Her closing gift to new homeowners? A recipe box. Then she sends new recipe postcards every month to tuck inside. Isn't that a smart way to stay connected in a meaningful way?

6. Make Others Feel Important

*"People will forget what you said. They will forget what you did.
But they will never forget how you made them feel."*

—Maya Angelou

What Makes You Feel Important?

What gives you your sense of importance and makes you feel special? Who and what bring out the best in you? What does it take to make you feel like a million bucks and ready to take on the world? When people make you feel important, doesn't it elevate them in your eyes? Learn to do the same for others.

We all have an innate desire to feel important, be special, and feel appreciated. Considering the universal drive to have those needs met, it is one of your best ways to move past making a positive first impression and turn it into a lasting one.

This insightful quote I once heard stays with me: "Tell me what gives you your sense of importance and I will tell you what you are. That is the most important thing about you. That is what determines your character."

Some people get their sense of importance through their charitable works and community service. Some get it through the diplomas on their walls and the letters behind their names, while others may get their sense of importance from the cars they drive, the balance in their bank accounts, or the size of their homes. Different strokes for different folks.

Regardless of what their motivators may be, notice what a person's hot button is and you will have the key to nurturing your new relationship in a positive way.

The Gift that Keeps on Giving

I once had a lovely real estate client named Jane who was an elderly lady living alone. Her sons lived far away in the Pacific Northwest and she rarely saw them. I became her Realtor when she decided she needed to down-size from her larger home and buy a smaller one. Throughout this transition, we would talk, laugh, share, and bond. After we successfully completed her transactions and got her comfortably situated in her new home, I stayed in touch to nurture our friendship.

Over a year later, I got a call from her son in Seattle who was calling to inform me that his mother had passed away. And at the reading of her will it was revealed she had requested that when it the time came to sell the property in her estate, they were to call Susan Young. By making her feel special and important, I earned not only her friendship, but her loyalty and continued business.

Tune into WIFM

Most everyone has the classic question stamped on their forehead that asks, "What's in It for Me?" It is not a matter of being self-centered, arrogant, or narcissistic; it is simply a natural and instinctive response to gauge how we are going to best interact and deal with another person.

When the people we meet demonstrate that their presence brings value, consideration, or contribution, we are much more likely to be open, trust their motives, and engage on meaningful levels. However, if their behavior demonstrates that they are only out for themselves, we are more likely to resist, reject, or in some cases, run away.

Do you approach people with a heart of service or with a hidden agenda? Make no mistake, they will feel your intentions, even when not spoken.

Sensational Salesmanship

International speaker and business consultant Jill Konrath authored the book, *How to Sell to Big Companies.* Jill shares that when sales people make prospecting calls to large companies, they may have only one-and-one-half minutes on a voice mail to make a great first impression. If they don't captivate their customer in that brief moment, their phone call will probably not be returned.

---

66 *Many sales people make the mistake of talking about how great they are and what they bring to the table. If they would simply take a breath, shift their mindset, and instead present ways to help solve their client's problems, they would capture more new business.* 99

Every time a new client hires me for a keynote, workshop, or coaching session, the first questions I ask them are, "What are the 3 top challenges your organization is dealing with? What are your goals? What problems would you like for me to help solve?"

Using their own answers, I am able to design a program that is customized specifically around their needs. It takes my focus completely off of *Susan* and centers my attention towards making *them* feel important.

Make Me Feel Special

Mary Kay Ash, the founder of the Mary Kay Cosmetic empire, taught her teams that most people have a sign hanging around their necks that says, "Make me feel special." Answer that need in others through nurturing words, deeds, and actions, and you will be amazed by the ease with which people respond to you. What can you do to make other people feel special?

13 Ways to Make Other People Feel Important

1. Ask people questions about themselves, their interests, their families, their passions and their lives.
2. Catch people doing things right, pat them on the back, and acknowledge them for a job well done.
3. Celebrate their successes.
4. Be lavish in your compliments and sincere in your praise.
5. Be appreciative and say thank you.
6. Listen with genuine interest.
7. Respect their opinions.
8. Encourage people with words of affirmation and validation.
9. Brag about people behind (and in front of) their backs.
10. Make the time and space to be fully present and engaged.
11. Spend quality time together.
12. Share your authentic self and be real.
13. Offer comfort and compassion.

Go Old School

In our digital world today, handwritten notes are an "old school" way to make people feel important. Email is easy and Facebook birthday messages are now the norm, however, taking that extra step makes your efforts extra special.

Whether it is a thank you note, birthday greeting, or a card of congratulations, taking the time to extend this personal consideration makes a person feel like you care. Be the surprise in someone's day and make them feel important.

7. *Use Fun & Humor*

"Laughing together is as close as you can get to a hug without touching."
—Gina Barreca

People love to be happy, enjoy a hearty laugh, and simply have fun. When you're happy, everything feels right in the world and life is good. Knowing that this is a universal yearning, what can you do to feed the need and bring out the best in others?

Having a sense of humor can be one of your greatest assets and equips you with an undeniable "attractor factor." The benefits extend far past a quick wit and spontaneous laughter. It can help you lower stress levels in yourself and others, diffuse difficult situations, interact more easily, and provide health benefits for improved well-being.

Humor lightens our spirits, comforts us through the challenge, brings people together, and helps us to remember the positive sides of life. When your presence and personality bring this welcomed delight and joy to others, you are a pleasure to know and you leave them wanting more.

But What If I'm Not Funny . . .

"Everybody laughs the same in every language because laughter is a universal connection."
—Jakob Smirnoff

When I was a young and aspiring speaker, I sought mentorship from a man who had been a Dale Carnegie trainer for decades. Eagerly wanting to know how to improve my stage presence and build my career, I contacted Dr. Joe Carnley in Destin, Florida and invited him out to lunch.

After we placed our order at the Harbor Docks Restaurant, he dove right in and gave me some of the best advice of my life. He said, "Susan, you have to make them laugh! When they leave your presentations, you want them to feel better and leave happier than when they came in. Help them enjoy your time together."

He continued to describe the magical power that humor has over the human spirit. When we craft humor into our speeches, we can take our audiences on a journey they will never forget.

Immediately after our delightful lunch ended, I drove straight to a Books-a-Million store and headed for the humor section. Since I was not a particularly funny person, I needed all the help I could get. For over an hour I stood there reading titles, flipping through funny books, and enjoying outrageous belly laughs, giggles, and snorts. People were staring, and probably thinking, "I want what she is having!"

The humor section was one of the smallest in the entire bookstore, but it may well have been the most important. When I turned around I noticed the opposite aisle was the "Self-Improvement" section. It ran half the length of the store and displayed hundreds of books. At that cathartic moment, I had a huge "Ah-Ha" moment.

------

66 *If people would read more of these humor books, they wouldn't need all those self-improvement books!* 99

"Follow your heart, but take your brain with you!"

After buying an armload of funny books filled with clean jokes, one-liners, and speech openers, I discovered how truly "spot-on" Joe had been. Inserting humorous zingers throughout my programs has worked like a charm and improved my presentation skills.

ASK YOURSELF: How's your humor? What can you do to have more humorous lines to use in the right place at the right time? I highly recommend it! Laughter is the best medicine indeed. Not only will you enjoy the experience yourself, but the people around you will enjoy the entertainment.

So, what if you are not naturally funny? Don't get discouraged. Do your research, gather ideas, and find your fun. Seek ways to laugh. Not only will doing this provide you with new material for making a great first impression, but laughter will bring you personal delight and satisfaction. Putting a smile on someone's face is one of the best gifts you can deliver.

Find the Funny Side of Life

"A person who knows how to laugh at himself will never cease to be amused."
—Shirley MacClain

- **Clown Around.** Nancy Weil of The Laugh Academy gives people she meets red clown noses and shows them how to use them. Promoting laughter as a cure for stress and negativity, she makes a positive and memorable impact and gives others permission to play.
- **Watch, Listen, & Learn.** Broaden your sense of humor by watching funny movies and shows, reading funny books, visiting live comedy shows, or enjoying YouTube clips.
- **Find Your Funny Bone.** Life provides plenty of material for things for you to laugh at. Seek irony, coincidence, and the abundance of simple humor in life's little absurdities.
- **Expand Your Repertoire.** Professional humorists and comedians, like Jeanie Robertson, maintain joke files filled with assorted topics, anecdotes, and titles. When something outrageously funny happens, she makes a note of it, puts it away, and saves it for the day she can integrate it into her hilarious presentations.
- **Laugh Easily.** Life wasn't meant to be so serious. Enjoy life, be fun, spend time with people who make you happy, widen

that smile, and laugh out loud. Learn to laugh at yourself.

"Humor offers immense physiological and psychological benefits. It reduces stress hormones, dulls physical pain and promotes social bonding."
—Dr. Steven M. Sultanoff

When Humor Falls Flat

Humor is not a "one-size fits all" guarantee. What is hilarious to one person may be offensive to another. By being emotionally intelligent and self-aware, you can discern how, when, why, or where to be funny . . . or not. You might be walking on thin ice and risk making a damaging first impression if you use humor that is:

- At the expense of others.
- Thoughtless sarcasm.
- Belittling or condescending.
- Hitting below the belt.
- Creepy or profane.
- Raunchy humor with sexual innuendo.
- Politically incorrect.
- Mean-spirited.

Know your audience! With the high level of cultural sensitivity these days, it is often better to err on the side of caution. If you don't want your humor to come back and bite you, don't hurt one person to entertain another. We can have humor without making fun of other people.

I have noticed generational humor exists as well. Since our frames of reference and cultural influences vary, there is a lot of room for misinterpretation and the potential to not "get it."

Don't try to make a joke just to make a joke. Sometimes, as human beings, we so want to fit in and connect that we try TOO hard to be something we are not. It's okay if you're not the life of the party. It's fine if you're not a stand-up comedian. Just be you. Real life provides real humor when we're paying attention to it. Share what makes you laugh.

Think of fun ways you can connect with your business or social circles. When you're with your tribe—or like-minded people—they'll laugh and learn right alongside you.

Stories Often Outshine Jokes

My friend Scott Friedman (ScottFriedman.net) is a motivational humorist who specializes in employee engagement, celebration, and customer service. He teaches organizations that when their organizations are happy, they enjoy increased productivity, higher performance, better engagement, and elevated levels of health and well-being among their people.

In his book, "Happily Ever Laughter," Scott shares, "Personal stories are excellent (and entertaining) catalysts both for communicating big ideas and for presenting your most original humor. Better yet, stories let you provide more substance in less time. Jokes, on the other hand, have less reach substance-wise. Why? Because a joke is meant to entertain. A story, on the other hand, has inherent meaning. Stories allow the audience to get to know you, your imperfections, your flaws, and your foolishness. You can be vulnerable right there with audience watching. You can entertain, enlighten and teach all in the same effort."

Choose the Happy Side of Life

Seek ways to bring humor, laughter, and joy to work. It will not only make work more fun, but it can positively impact your bottom line.

Humor can heal the heart, instill hope, bring people together, and remind them that life isn't meant to be so doggone serious. Why not use it for good? There is no denying that humor's uplifting, energizing, and positive impact can transform lives for the better.

"Humor is mankind's greatest blessing."
–Mark Twain

8. Discretion & Good Judgment

The flagrant lack of decorum, reckless behavior, and poor judgment exhibited in our world today continues to astound. Even those who never dreamed they'd be caught in their most embarrassing moments risk public exposure from the ever-present smart phones and non-stop social media. Dare I mention reality TV?

Indiscretion and poor judgment not only can destroy a positive first impression, they also can have lasting negative consequences from which there is no return. Even years into the future, moments of indiscretion in the past can come back to bite you when you least expect it.

The best safeguards you have are to live with dignity, love, and self-respect, and to make choices you can be proud of in the first place. Even as an adult, I still think to myself—*what would my mother say?*

The dictionary defines discretion as the quality of showing discernment, the ability to make responsible decisions, and behaving or speaking in such a way as to avoid causing offense to others or revealing private information. Doing what is right is not always easy and can require uncommon courage. Be brave my friends, living right is its own reward.

Discretion is the Larger Part of Valor

Discretion represents both your personal self-respect and the respect you have for other people. A discreet person has the wisdom to differentiate between good and bad, right and wrong, and favorable and unfavorable. A discreet person . . .

- is strong, yet humble;
- expresses genuine concern and interest;

- exercises caution to avoid unnecessary risks;
- knows intuitively when a situation or conversation is heading in the wrong direction;
- does not need to tear others down to build himself up;
- refrains from using foul language or speaking brashly;
- regulates her reactions and responds appropriately;
- takes the higher road rather than wrestling in the mud;
- remains gracious and poised in the heat of the moment;
- refrains from unnecessary confrontations;
- does not break confidence or share other people's secrets with which they have been entrusted;
- communicates with deliberation and confidence.

To Disclose or Not Disclose

I just saw a poster: "Dirty laundry goes here (laundry basket) not here (Facebook logo)."

Online and in person, withholding personal information is a discreet way of regulating what people learn, think, and know about you. There are times when keeping it real and keeping it honest will reveal your authenticity and trustworthiness, but there are other times, however, when things are better left unsaid or locked away. Hence the term TMI, meaning "Too Much Information!" Discretion is part of "keeping it real" in professional (and self) respect.

You are the only one who can determine what feels right to you. Before baring your soul to the world and telling it all, consider a few scenarios which deserve your discretion.

- Does your date really need to hear what a jerk your ex was and why your marriage ended?
- Will disclosing details of your childhood betray the people who love you the most?
- Will disclosing your health history create unfair bias?

- Will revealing the dysfunctions of your last team help you get that new job or improve the new team?
- Will telling someone how you screwed up alienate their affection or friendship?
- Will exerting your opinion alienate others and make them avoid you?
- Will talking smack about your competitor build consumer confidence?

Usually this kind of self-serving "honesty" will sabotage your success. **If you can't say something nice, don't say anything at all.** Realize that sometimes your own words can, and probably will, come back to be used against you.

Oversharing

Why do some people feel the need to share their deepest, darkest secrets with complete strangers or on social media? How could saying too much, too soon possibly help their case or earn the respect of others? Perhaps their insatiable need to share every sordid detail of their existence satisfies a yearning to get attention, gain sympathy, or make friends.

The irony is that their enthusiasm for personal revelation can backfire badly and have the opposite effect. People become their own worst enemies and don't need anyone else's help in making themselves the brunt of gossip, judgment, and ridicule. A person who overshares demonstrates a lack of dignity, maturity, and discrimination, and it may also be a strong indicator of self-absorbed narcissism and exhibitionism.

Even if you're not broadcasting your personal life to the universe through social media, choose your confidants wisely and with discretion. Your ability to keep your personal details close to your vest will encourage others to feel that you are trustworthy enough to be trusted with *their* personal details.

Zip Your Lip & Bite Your Tongue

The discreet communicator knows when it's time to speak and when it's time to listen. He conscientiously refrains from opening a topic of discussion if it is bad timing or inappropriate. He will stop, look, learn, and listen for cues to ensure he doesn't get caught with his foot in his mouth.

There will be times when you would be wise to err on the side of caution. And rather than making a magnificent misstep, zip your lip and bite your tongue for personal and professional self-preservation.

Let Sleeping Dogs Lie

"You don't tug on superman's cape. You don't spit into the wind. You don't pull the mask off that old Lone Ranger. And you don't mess around with Jim."

—Jim Croce, Lyrics from "You Don't Mess Around with Jim"

When I hear someone expressing an adamant opinion which is diametrically opposed to my own, I have a strong temptation to try to convince them otherwise. But what value is there in attempting to prove another person wrong? How would that solve anything?

The variety of political positions shared on Facebook in the 2016 Presidential Election was both entertaining and, sadly, destructive. I observed friends of a lifetime divide into different camps and sacrifice their friendships through argument and debate. As an avid reader and political junkie, I had to hold myself back from expressing my opinions or presenting factual evidence which would obliterate others' claims. Why would I jump into the fray? All it would do is hurt the friendship. Rarely does arguing political positions change an opinion or belief.

Learn to choose your battles carefully. When you exercise discretion, you will realize that most fights are best avoided. **Let those sleeping dogs sleep!**

The Truth Can Hurt

Honesty is one of your most valuable virtues, however, when used without discretion, it can reap unfavorable repercussions. Have you met people who are so set on exerting their position that they are oblivious to the feelings of others? That their being right is more important than being kind? We all must consider which stance is the most beneficial. Might I suggest . . . *kindness?*

Why do some people feel the need to throw a person's errors or weaknesses in their face or criticize their shortcomings? What benefit can they possibly receive from proving someone wrong to prove they are right? This level of insensitivity and self-centeredness leaves collateral damage in its wake and destroys positive impressions.

The truth may be true, but a discreet person understands that speaking the truth isn't always helpful. It can also be hurtful and harmful.

UN-Impressive Acts of Indiscretion

- Forwarding other people's emails without getting permission.
- Throwing other people under the bus to save yourself.
- Talking loudly, being boorish and insensitive to the others around you.
- Flagrant cheating.
- Burning bridges.
- Talking smack.
- Dissing your competitor to your customer.
- Oversharing and revealing too much personal information about yourself and others.
- Breaking trust by sharing someone else's secrets.
- Being passive-aggressive to manipulate a situation or person.
- Saying one thing and doing another.
- Being two-faced.
- Lying by omission.
- Dispensing bulls#@%!

8 Ways to Shine a Positive Light on Others

1. **Let the other person appear smart.** The person who desperately tries to be the smartest person in the room inevitably comes off as the least.

2. **Don't bring attention to anything which may embarrass another person.** Whether your conversation partner has poor grammar, a pimple on his chin, or lacks social grace, a discreet person does not say or do anything which would make another feel ashamed, embarrassed, or humiliated. Allow the other person to maintain his own grace and dignity.

3. **Ask their opinions, seek their advice, ask them inquiring questions.** By allowing them to reveal their opinions and knowledge, you will demonstrate respect and make them feel important.

4. **Practice patience.** Sometimes it takes a person a moment to gather her thoughts, process information, or respond appropriately. Your patience is respectful and appreciated.

5. **Maintain your calm.** Rather than react with anger or defensiveness, regulate your response and shift the energy into a more positive direction.

6. **Put your ego aside.** Allow another to triumph and enjoy the spotlight.

7. **Be aware and concerned for the feelings of others.**

8. **Purposely seek ways to put others at ease and make them feel comfortable.**

"Watch your thoughts, they become words; watch your words, they become actions; watch your actions, they become your habits; watch your habits, they become character; watch your character, for it becomes your destiny."
—Unknown

When we look at our words and deeds in this context, it strengthens our resolve to be incredibly selective. Everything we say and do becomes a part of who we are and how we connect with others.

8 WAYS TO **MASTER**
The Art of **CONNECTION**

1. *Building Trust & Rapport.* Trust and rapport are the heartbeat of business, the backbone for high performing teams, and the secret sauce for healthy relationships.

2. *Personable & Friendly.* People who are genuinely warm and sincerely kind are easy to talk to, easy to like, and bring a positive vibe to new encounters and social situations.

3. *Interested & Interesting.* People will be more interested in you when you are interested in them. If you want to impress, talk to them about . . . them.

4. *Be a Discovery Expert.* Be inquisitive. A wonderful way to get to know someone is simply by asking questions. The more you ask, the more you can learn . . . about people, work, life.

5. *Commonality & Camaraderie.* By identifying, developing, and connecting powerful points of reference to others, you will have a rich resource of information from which to engage in stimulating conversations and connect on amazing levels.

6. *Make Others Feel Important.* We all have an innate desire to feel important, be special, and feel appreciated. In your words and behavior help others feel important.

7. *Use Fun & Humor.* Humor lightens spirits, comforts through challenge, brings people together, engages, and entertains. Bring delight and joy to others and you will leave them wanting more.

8. *Discretion & Good Judgment.* Don't share your most embarrassing moments with public exposure. Doing what is right is not always easy and can require uncommon courage. Be brave my friends, living right is its own reward.

7

The *Art* of

a

POSITIVE
LASTING
IMPRESSION

8 WAYS TO GAIN &
RETAIN A GREAT REPUTATION
FOR POSITIVE IMPACT

The *Art* of a POSITIVE LASTING IMPRESSION

The fact is, you don't get a second chance to make an outstanding first impression. Up to this point, the lessons in this book have been focused on what it takes to make your first moments fabulous and unforgettable. But once that is achieved, what does it take to keep the good vibe going, especially since it can linger for years to come?

A great first impression can be quickly erased by your doing one stupid, negligent, or thoughtless thing. What steps can you take to prevent this from happening? How can you confidently maintain a positive impression long after the initial interaction has occurred?

My friend and customer service expert Shep Hyken (Hyken.com) says, "People say the first impression is important. I would say that equally important is the last impression. The last impression is a *lasting impression!*" Indeed.

Create happy endings by leaving conversations without feeling rude or awkward. What tips can you apply as you say goodbye? Always try to leave others feeling better than you found them by adding value, keeping promises, and leaving the door open to reconnect in the future.

Even when you don't have direct contact with a person, you can set an extraordinary example by how you treat your team and the people around you. Turn every first impression into a positive lasting one.

1. *Happy Endings*
2. *Share it Forward*
3. *Humility & Gratitude*
4. *Class, Tact & Diplomacy*
5. *Play Well with Others*
6. *Follow-Up & Follow-through*
7. *Reputation & Respect*
8. *Making Moments Memorable*

1. Happy Endings

*"If you want a happy ending, that depends of course,
on where you stop your story."*
—Orson Welles

A great first impression is not only made in the first few seconds; it continues to be made throughout your entire interaction. How you end a conversation is as important as how you began it. Making a great first impression is marvelous, but it can quickly get undone when your parting becomes cumbersome, awkward, abrupt, or overdone.

So, how's it done right? When you meet someone for the first time how can you end on a high note? There is a proactive way to end your conversations and bring them to a positive conclusion to make the experience memorable and positive.

Bringing Conversations to a Close

Whether it is by way of a genuine goodbye or a commitment to take another step, ending a conversation graciously sets a positive opinion in the eyes of your listener. Sometimes conversations will come to a comfortable conclusion, but there are also times when you need to exit politely.

Here are a few easy sentences that you can add to your repertoire to end a conversation on both accounts:

- "It was a pleasure speaking with you today."
- "Thank you for taking the time to meet with me."
- "I look forward to hearing about your project."
- "Is there anything special that I can do for you?"
- "I look forward to us meeting again."
- "Take care until next time."

When leaving a networking event, my friend Brian takes the time and make the effort to close the event with each person he has met like a bee who is pollinating flowers—he never slows down as he waves, hugs, smiles, and extends his "adios amigos"—he makes everyone feel special and nurtured.

On the opposite end, have you ever been engaged in conversation with a person but you are growing weary, bored, and want to escape? You don't want to be outright rude, so you stay and listen, and listen, and listen . . . counting the seconds for the conversation to end. I have great news! There are ways to gracefully exit without hurting feelings.

10 Things to Do When You Feel Stuck

1. Pass the baton. Introduce them to someone else and then graciously excuse yourself.
2. Ask them to introduce you to someone else so that attention is focused elsewhere.
3. Be considerate of their time and frame your exit from their point of view, saying something like, "I imagine you would like to meet a few other people. I enjoyed our time together."
4. Call on your friends. Excuse yourself to speak to a friend who has been waiting.
5. Notice the power of the pause. Where there is a lull in conversation or it is beginning to be filled with "ums, anyways, and well . . . ," politely end the conversation.
6. Let your body language do the talking! When you turn your feet and shoulders into a direction for retreat, they will hopefully pick up the subliminal message that you are soon leaving. Eye contact, as if you are looking for someone who is expecting you, will also discreetly convey that you need to leave.
7. Make an excuse; "I need to get going." or "The bathroom beckons." or "I'm going to get a refill."
8. Excuse yourself to make a phone call.
9. Suggest a future meeting or to reconnect at a later date.

10. Create anticipation for your next meeting. Give them something to look forward to. 'Next time we will . . . .'"

Happy Trails to You, Until We Meet Again . . .

I love the Hawaiian word "Aloha" because it means hello *and* goodbye. There are no final goodbyes. Instead, there is an open-ended understanding that you may reconnect again in the future. Adopting this attitude makes farewells less final.

Daniel has treated thousands of patients during his career. He has a tender bedside manner that is warm, inviting, and respectful. He reassures his patients they are going to be okay. As they are leaving his office, he tells them that if they need anything to please call. He thanks them for coming to see him and entrusting him with their care. This fond farewell creates a an open invitation for them to return again—exemplifying excellence in customer service.

How May I Help You on Your Journey?

One of my brilliant mentors, Joe Sweeney, ends every conversation by saying, "Please let me know how I can help you on your journey." He continues to impress me every time because he genuinely means it. His generous willingness has been such a positive influence in my life that I have begun saying it to others. When it comes from an authentic space of true caring and service, it is hard to beat.

Exiting an Organization

Most, at some point in their lives, decide it is time to move on from one position to the next. In fact, according to a study done by the Bureau of Labor Statistics, employees change jobs on average, every 4.6 years. How you start—and finish—every business relationship is crucial because those transitions are part of your employment career history forever.

You never know when a past alliance will serve you in the future, so it is wise to move forward with dignity and discretion. The folks whom you are leaving may be the same people who will provide you with a raving review later. Wherever you go to – and wherever you leave from – always strive to go with grace.

4 Ways to Leave a Job with Integrity & Professionalism:

1. **Tell the boss first.** It's the right thing to do. While, especially in difficult circumstances, it might be tempting to test the waters with co-workers, you ideally don't want leadership to learn from someone else that you're resigning.

2. **Be honest and steer clear of gossip.** Be honest about making your move. Rumors, gossip, and innuendo can all be career killers. Once they start, they become the adult version of a game of "telephone"—where a story morphs into distorted truths and flat-out falsehoods. They serve no purpose and cause more harm than help. Always take the high road.

3. **Be fair and flexible.** Two weeks' notice is considered a fair exit strategy time-frame. Depending on your position and viability in the company, and your commitments to your new position, if you are needed a little longer and have that capacity, it is a gesture of professionalism and courtesy. In some cases, when leadership views leaving as a betrayal (which certainly can be the case), they may ask you to leave immediately. If that's the circumstance, be the bigger person and leave knowing you've given proper notice, and have your affairs in order.

4. **Express gratitude.** In EVERY situation, there are things to be thankful for. In a difficult work environment, it may feel very inviting to take the "burn the bridges" approach to your departure. Reconsider. You want your reputation to exemplify a person who showed grace under pressure—and wisdom when faced with difficult choices. Thank leadership and colleagues for their part in your journey and move forward with the peace of mind that you handled yourself with strength and diplomacy.

2. Share it Forward

"Carry out a random act of kindness, with no expectation of reward, safe in the knowledge that one day someone might do the same for you."

—Princess Diana

Pay It Forward

In the movie, *Pay It Forward*, 11-year-old Trevor McKinney, played by Haley Joel Osment, receives a homework assignment in his seventh-grade social studies class. He is to put an idea into action that could change the world for the better. He proposes that every time a person receives an act of kindness, he or she go out and 'pay it forward' to three more people. The act of kindness must be something the recipient would not have been able to do for themselves. His idea for the "networking of kind acts" takes off like wildfire and sweeps the country with good will and virtuous deeds. In the end, he changed the world for the better. And you can, too.

This movement of paying goodness forward is not reserved for Hollywood and fictional characters.

_____

66 *It is a powerful philosophy that you can live daily: doing for others without asking or expecting anything in return. This selfless gesture is the mark of fine character that demonstrates compassion for humanity.* 99

_____

I have known many people who share this quality of the servant's heart and have earned the reverent respect and admiration of others. This approach to living not only creates a great first impression, but nurtures a long lasting positive one.

Share and Shine

Have you ever been in line to buy coffee and once you get to the register to pay, you find out that a kind soul in front of you has already paid your tab? If so, you understand the glow it puts in your heart and the smile it puts on your face. What you don't see is the glow of the person who did it for you. They did not do it for praise or with the expectation of reward. They did it to add kindness to the world and with the hope that you would continue to share it forward with others. It's an uncomplicated way to sweeten what might be someone's otherwise bland day. It happened to me in a Starbucks' drive-through, catching me off guard. I passed it on to the car behind me, and I could see their startled faces.

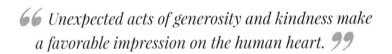

❝ *Unexpected acts of generosity and kindness make a favorable impression on the human heart.* ❞

Beyond making someone else's day, random acts of kindness, praise and compliments—*are free!* They cost nothing to give, but mean the world to get. If you're looking for ways to be more personable and friendly, this is it. Though your gifts may be humble and not seem like much of a sacrifice, others are paying attention to the things you say and do. It really stands out with a stranger!

Years ago, I attended a Sunday service at the Shoreline Church in Destin, Florida. It was held in a movie theater with a casual atmosphere, and tithings were collected in popcorn buckets. After hearing a wonderful program about paying and sharing kindness forward, the ushers passed the popcorn buckets around again. Rather than expecting more donations, the buckets were filled with envelopes of money. They gave the money back!

The envelopes contained various bills ranging from one dollar to twenty dollars. Pastor Eric asked everyone to select an envelope as the bucket passed by, and when they left the church, to use it to do something nice for another person. I was stunned by this activity and deeply impressed. My envelope contained five dollars. On my way home, I crossed a bridge with a two dollar and fifty cents toll. I asked the booth attendant to apply my five dollars to the next two cars behind me. The rest of the day I felt lighter, happier, and more positive.

---

66 *Think of the joy it will bring to your life to do something like this on a regular basis. Even if the recipient never learns your identity, you will have done your part in helping to make the world a kinder, gentler place.* 99

How Can You Begin?

"The point is not to pay back kindness, but to pass it on."
– Julia Alvarez

People will often not ask for help because they are reluctant to impose on you or they are afraid of looking needy. Don't wait for them to ask before you extend kindness. You can begin to "share it forward" by asking yourself these questions:

Ask Yourself:
- To whom can I lend a helping hand?
- What can I do to help another succeed?
- Who would benefit from my experience?
- Who can I introduce to one another so that they can help each other?
- Who do I know that is struggling and could use assistance?

Ask Another:
- What can I do to help you achieve your goals?
- What do you need help with during this time?
- What resources would help ease your challenge?
- Can we get together to see how we can help each other?
- What is the one thing you need to move your business forward?

These impactful ways of sharing it forward will leave a positive lasting impression, demonstrate your heart of service, and help you keep the door open for future connection and collaboration. With just a smidge of extra effort, you are encouraging a continuous relationship and the flow of good feelings. It is only a matter of when you can get started . . .

11 Things You Can Share Forward

1. Your time.
2. Your help.
3. Your wisdom.
4. Your creativity.
5. Your brilliance.
6. Your expertise.
7. Your connections.
8. Your consideration.
9. Your physical possessions.
10. Your solutions and insight.
11. Your money and resources.

Who do you know who needs a boost? What have you learned the hard way that can save someone else the headache? When and how can you share skills you've mastered? You will reap meaningful rewards by helping other people along their path. How can you move from service to significance and make a positive impact?

Seek Out Inspiration

"Any random act of kindness can cause a positive ripple effect restoring our faith in the love and compassion of the human spirit."

—www.PayItForwardDay.com

While doing research to write this section, I was both surprised and delighted to learn that there is an actual Pay It Forward Day on April 28th. Their international website shares ideas, insights, and stories about selfless giving and random acts of kindness.

In fact, as of this writing, 82 countries participate in this annual celebration! Isn't that wonderful? When your spirit needs a lift, or you're eager for ideas on how you can also share it forward, consider reading the incredible stories at PayItForwardDay.com. They detail not only how others have shared it forward to make a difference, but the tremendous impact it has made in the lives of the fortunate recipients. It is heartwarming and hope-filled.

Spearhead a Cause

My dear friend Julie Escobar writes for an organization that creates marketing materials and tools for real estate professionals. Two years ago, after watching the company's sales growth rate increase rapidly, she approached the organization's leadership team with an idea to choose a charity that everyone could passionately support and make it a part of their company's culture. They agreed!

They chose to be a business partner for St. Jude Children's Hospital. They created an easy option for customers to donate to the cause in their checkout processes and even offered to match their customer's donations dollar-for-dollar. To date, they've raised more than $35,000 to help the kids and families suffering from childhood cancer.

While it is satisfying to feel the rewards of helping a cause or volunteering as an individual, there are powerful benefits for rallying your team to join forces. An organizational cause . . .

- Nurtures team unity and morale
- Increases employee engagement
- Encourages participation and collaboration
- Provides a sense of company pride
- Sets a good service example within your company and your community.

---

*66 What can you and your organization
do to Share it Forward? 99*

Consider this thought from Canadian Psychologist Paul Bloom, "We are constituted so that simple acts of kindness, such as giving to charity or expressing gratitude, have a positive effect on our long-term moods. The key to the happy life, it seems, is the good life: a life with sustained relationships, challenging work, and connections to community."

3. Humility & Gratitude

"True humility is not thinking less of yourself, it is thinking of yourself less."
—C.S. Lewis

Humility is one of the seven virtues which engenders trust and admiration. A humble person sets aside his own agenda and operates from a place of truthfulness, authenticity, gratitude, and a spirit of service. A humble spirit does not need to steal the show, make himself the center of attention, or take credit. A humble spirit does not participate in one-upmanship, but rather, enjoys sharing the limelight and encouraging other people to shine brightly.

Humility is especially impressive in a person who has a lot to be proud of but does not flaunt it and remains humble. Someone who has accomplished extraordinary things but does not behave pridefully inspires even greater respect and appreciation.

We instinctively know the difference between someone who is humble and someone who is not. Arrogance, conceit, and egomania are personality traits we could all use a little less of, don't you agree? One of the best phrases I have heard regarding these people is, "Egomania—it is a very strange disease. It makes everyone sick except the person who has it!"

We can be consumed with thinking about ourselves. Adapting an unassuming nature can shift a self-absorbed focus into a humble one.

I read this beautiful thought recently:

"Work for a cause, not for applause. Live life to express, not to impress. Don't strive to make your presence noticed, just make your absence felt."
—Source Unknown

Tall Poppy Syndrome

While writing this book, I was discussing the concept of humility with my friend Kirsty Blattner. She shared that in her home country of Australia there is a phrase called the "Tall Poppy Syndrome." With a profound respect for the quality of humility, Australians frown upon people who are being braggarts, overachievers, arrogant, and flamboyant.

Wikipedia defines "Tall Poppy Syndrome" as "a social phenomenon, in which people of genuine merit are resented, attacked, cut down, or criticized because their talents or achievements elevate them above or distinguish them from their peers."

Maintaining humility in the midst of accomplishment can be challenging, can't it? While we strive to do and be our best to achieve our goals and improve our lives, our successes and personal excellence can intimidate, or worse yet, alienate others who are jealous or insecure. Interestingly, sometimes this comes from a person or persons from whom you would least expect it.

Focus on Another Person

When you make your efforts about another person, it is much easier to be humble. As a professional speaker for almost twenty years, my greatest reward comes from changing the direction of a person's life for the better.

---

66 *Each time I have the opportunity and pleasure to speak in front of people, I pray or meditate before I start so that I may say exactly what my audience needs to hear.* 99

When I speak, it is not about Susan. If people in my audience hear just one golden nugget that makes a difference to them, then my efforts are successful. Focusing on the needs of the audience keeps me humble and eliminates any presentation "butterflies." Try it sometime!

Gratitude

"Gratitude unlocks the fullness of life. It turns what we have into enough, and more. It turns denial into acceptance, chaos to order, confusion to clarity. It can turn a meal into a feast, a house into a home, a stranger into a friend."

—Melody Beattie

Having a humble and grateful heart moves you from raw ambition to a greater vision. What are you grateful for? It has been said that a prayer of gratitude is the most powerful prayer you can have. It ignites the law of attraction by multiplying and enriching that for which you are grateful.

When you give sincere compliments to other people, not only does it make them feel great, it also encourages them to feel good toward you. When you thank others for their gifts, their help, or their giving, they're more likely to give again when you need them next time. When you're grateful for friendships, you will attract more friends and deepen the relationships you already have. Gratitude stimulates magnetism for more good things to come into your life. And it simply feels good.

Have you ever written in a gratitude journal? It is an exercise that helps you put your life into perspective, focus on solutions, stay humble, and appreciate your blessings. Before going to bed at night, write down ten things you are grateful for which happened that day. It clears out the cobwebs and improves your sleep. It takes your mind off your worries, fears, and those *woulda-coulda-shouldas.* Expressing why you're grateful is a great stress release. Adopt an attitude of gratitude and you will attract more abundance, love, and tranquility.

---

66 *Demonstrating gratitude will positively impress others by showing them that you do not feel a self-absorbed right of entitlement, but that you genuinely care about and will share with others.* 99

Entitlement

"Even after all this time, the Sun never says to the Earth, 'You owe me.'
Look what happens with a love like that. It lights the whole sky."

—Hafiz

There is no place in a healthy working environment or relationship for a sense of entitlement and privilege. In fact, an attitude of being owed will more likely cause resentment and avoidance of others. Even though the world really does not owe us anything, most of us enjoy a bounty of blessings. Taking a quick inventory, most of us can tally up many things we can be grateful for—family, friends, health, love, knowledge, prosperity, travel, music, the beauty in nature, delicious food, pets—endless reasons to be happy and grateful! Take the time and make the effort to express and show your appreciation to those who care about you. Thank those who have taken their time to teach you something new and acknowledge them for the value they have brought to your life.

UN-Impressives

People who do not practice humility and gratitude may not even realize how poorly they are presenting themselves to others. And if they do realize, they frankly don't give a damn! People who lack humility and gratitude may:

- Be arrogant braggarts and masters of one-upmanship.
- Have a knack for offending and alienating others.
- Believe they know better than anyone else and that their opinion is the one that matters most.
- Not think twice about being late and lack consideration for other people's time.
- Be "in it" for themselves, and care most about what they will get out of something in return.
- Truly believe they are better than others and may even go so far as to tell them so.
- Abruptly end conversations when things are not going their way.
- Be dismissive while listening, regardless of others' opinions.
- Not let other people finish speaking before they interrupt or answer.

We have all experienced the personalities that turn us off and turn us away. If they only knew how they were being perceived! After a professional event, my fellow National Speakers Association friend Kristen Brown (kristenbrownpresents.com) shared, "I got a good reminder this week. I was at a meeting with a few people who didn't know each other well. One of the women continued to reinforce how successful she was by talking about her high fees, assistant, etc. Another woman, whom I know is very highly paid, was mostly silent about her success but shared tips and knowledge with the group.

After the meeting, I heard a couple of the other attendees in the bathroom say how obnoxious and annoying the woman was who kept talking about herself and how awesome the other woman was who shared valuable tips. There is such a fine line between powerful presence and showboating. It reminded me to be hyper-aware of what and how to share!"

Keys to the Kingdom

Basketball coaching legend Rick Pitino shared, "Humility is the true key to success. Successful people lose their way at times. They often embrace and overindulge from the fruits of success. Humility halts this arrogance and self-indulging trap. Humble people share the credit and wealth, remaining focused and hungry to continue the journey of success." This is powerful, isn't it? And relevant and true for creating a positive and lasting impression on others.

The practice of humility—and the mindfulness which it creates—encourages each of us to be a student of life. Where we recognize our gifts, of course, but also seek to find a learning experience in every day, with every opportunity, and in every new engagement with a fellow human being.

That, in itself, is a golden key to the kingdom of success. It is also an amazing reminder that humility and gratitude are about much more than making a first impression—they are about your positive impact on the world.

4. CLASS, TACT & DIPLOMACY

"Remember that poise and power are inseparably associated. The calm and balanced mind is the strong and great mind; the hurried and agitated mind is the weak one."

—Wallace D. Walters

- **Class:** showing excellence in style, taste, and manner; decency, respectability.
- **Tact:** the ability to do or say things in a discreet way that does not upset or anger another person.
- **Diplomacy:** the art of dealing with people in a sensitive, empathetic, and effective way.

How Dignified is Done

The qualities of class, tact, and diplomacy are grouped together because they interweave into a rich tapestry of refined presence and distinction. You would rarely find one without the others.

You've known people who lack class, lack tact, and lack diplomacy, haven't you? How did their careless, boorish, insensitive behavior affect your impression of them? I would venture to guess that it left a lingering negative impression that was hard to shake.

The proverbial "bull in the china shop" earned his title well by being clumsy, unaware, thoughtless, and indifferent to the environment around him. With all the steps you are taking to create a great first impression, don't let these downfalls be your undoing. Acting with class, tact, and diplomacy will leave such a positive lasting impression that people will remember it for years to come.

ASK YOURSELF: Do you hold high standards for your behavior and discretion? Do you bite your tongue when commenting would be inappropriate? Do you regulate your responses with thoughtfulness and consideration? Do you think before speaking? Do you consider how your manner is impacting others?

Classy vs. Trashy

Classy . . . or not? Years ago, I attended a beautiful wedding of a friend who managed a fine jewelry store. He had been a lifelong bachelor because he had never quite found the classy lady he yearned for to share his life. We all gleefully celebrated that he had finally found "the one." As she walked down the aisle, we oohed and aahed over her grace and elegance, happy for him to have met his match. Yay!

Everything was going amazingly well . . . until the reception. His beautiful, classy, elegant bride began to drink and carouse. It was her party and it was all about her, right? And as if becoming inebriated were not enough, she danced and ran around barefoot (in her white gown), kicking up her dirty heels with a cigarette in one hand and a beer in the other. Add a few colorful curse words and sexual innuendos and the tawdry picture was complete.

In the right setting that kind of conduct might be fun. But we knew our friend. We knew his taste, behavior, and standards. Those of us who knew him well and had travelled far to attend his wedding looked at each other, shook our heads, and said "Uh oh. They won't make it." Sure enough, within a year they were divorced. And now, over twenty-five years later, her lack of class has left an eternal bad impression.

"Show class, have pride, and display character. If you do,
winning takes care of itself."

—Paul Bryant

14 Ways to Be a Class Act

When I began writing a list of classy virtues, I was amused by the fact that every single one I came up with was already a chapter in *The Art of First Impressions for Positive Impact* book! For a fun and quick recap of a few, classy people are . . .

1. Loyal.
2. Honest.
3. Discreet.
4. Gracious.
5. Engaged.
6. Authentic.
7. Respectful.
8. Thoughtful.
9. Always learning.
10. Confident and brave.
11. Emotionally intelligent.
12. Interested and interesting.
13. Taking care of themselves.
14. Keenly aware of themselves, others, and their environment.

Tact & Diplomacy

"Diplomacy is more than saying or doing the right things at the right time, it is avoiding saying or doing the wrong things at any time."

—Bo Bennett

To distinguish the difference, **tact is knowing when and how to speak or not to speak** and **diplomacy knows what to say and how to say it.** As Will Durant so eloquently expressed, "To say nothing, especially when speaking, is half the art of diplomacy."

Great leaders utilize diplomacy to lead, strengthen, encourage, motivate, and support their people. They wisely acknowledge that the differences among their people require them to adapt their communication accordingly.

Diplomatic people are able to distinguish which information can be shared and what information is best withheld. They know how to navigate challenging situations by intelligently forging ahead with thoughtful deliberation. Diplomatic people remain calm, cool, and composed in the heat of conversation and can express their thoughts with intuitive grace.

---

66 Diplomacy is the patina that washes over our interactions to give them a polished shine and make them sparkle. 99

A Cool Head & an Even Keel

Adopting and practicing class, tact, and diplomacy can be game-changers regarding the way people perceive you. When you master these valuable qualities, you will become one of the most trusted and appreciated people in the room.

Why? Because honoring these traits teaches you to keep a cool head in any situation. They allow you to be the steady hand at the rudder—keeping life, relationships, and business on an even keel regardless of what storms are raging. In a world often mired in chaos, people will always need a calm and steady force to lead. Be that force.

5. $\mathcal{P}$LAY $\mathcal{W}$ELL WITH $\mathcal{O}$THERS

"You can discover more about a person in an hour of play than you can in a year of conversation."

—Plato

How to Play Well with Others

As long as you are living on this planet, you will encounter, engage, and interact with other people. Your ability to play well with others is essential if you hope to enjoy healthy relationships, emotional well-being, and the benefits that come from networking and collaboration. Not to mention the obvious—making a great first impression!

Showing that you are easy to get along with and a valuable team player will improve the energy, synergy, and interactions with everyone around you. Once people earn a reputation for being hard to get along with, others often respond by avoiding, ignoring, and merely tolerating their presence. Who wants to be in that position? None of us wants to be around people who are difficult and challenging.

15 Ways to Be a Great Team Player

Whether you are in a work team, sports team, family dynamic, friendship circle, church family, professional organization, or school project, adapting the qualities of being a great team player will help you get along and **play well with others.** Rather than putting your welfare above that of others, do your best to create a sense of esprit de corps.

1. Show genuine commitment.
2. Be fully present and engaged.
3. Volunteer to help and contribute.

4. Care about the people around you.
5. Express gratitude and appreciation.
6. Nurture a sense of belonging for all.
7. Be dependable and take responsibility.
8. Avoid gossip, politics, and picking sides.
9. Participate, cooperate, and collaborate.
10. Be readily available and easily accessible.
11. Remain flexible and agile as changes occur.
12. Treat others with respect and consideration.
13. Promote positive and uplifting communication.
14. Work to resolve conflicts and reach agreements.
15. Hold others accountable and set boundaries when needed.

We are social creatures with tribal instincts. Making the effort to play and cooperate with others could possibly be one of the most important things we do to make our relationships work.

"The way a team plays as a whole determines its success. You may have the greatest bunch of individual stars in the world, but if they don't play together, the club won't be worth a dime."
—Babe Ruth

Team Work and Dream Work

"Teamwork makes the dream work," shared John Maxwell. He's right. Have you ever seen the word team as this acronym?

T—ogether
E—veryone
A—ccomplishes
M—ore

It makes sense when you look at it that way, doesn't it? Individuals can be brilliant and accomplished in their own right, but a group of individuals—all collectively combining their talents and knowledge can change the world— or at least their corner of it! I love the quote by Ken Blanchard that says, "None of us is as smart as all of us."

To take it a step further, we all bring unique perspectives, history, backgrounds, education, and experience to our positions. In a company culture that celebrates diversity and encourages collaboration, teams thrive because that diversity stimulates creativity and inspires innovation.

No Bad Ideas

Would you like to solve problems in your organization? "Fishbone" it! This strategic team exercise was developed in 1943 by Dr. Kaoru Ishikawa, a Japanese quality control expert. The goal of his "fishbone technique" (also called the "cause and effect" diagram), was to help a team address the heart of a problem rather than create "band-aid" type solutions which often conceal a bigger issue. It has been used by corporations big and small ever since.

- Start with a willingness to be open and allow every team member the opportunity to share their idea in a nonjudgmental environment.
- Download a copy of the Fishbone Diagram to serve as an example.
- Decide how you will conduct the fishbone analysis. You can use white boards, smart boards, flip charts, or block paper.
- Write the problem statement or question in the "head," with a straight horizontal line extending out to represent the "backbone."
- From there create four lines from the backbone and label them as relevant categories which may be contributing to the problem.
- Go around the table discussing each cause and adding "bones" until the root causes have been exhausted.

What you'll find is that with diverse minds, synergy, experience, and perceptions, you'll brainstorm a wider spectrum of solutions. The team effort can reveal potentially missed opportunities which may not have shown themselves in a more singular problem analysis. This method unifies people to seek robust solutions together.

Trust, Respect, and Communication are Key

If you are a leader, ensure that your team members feel seen, heard, and respected. You can help do that by recognizing good work, encouraging idea-sharing, collaborative conversation, and team-building efforts.

You'll find many organizations are moving away from team members being confined to cubicles into a more open space design to encourage synergies between people. It's a smart strategy that is quite literally breaking down barriers in the workplace. Try it. You might find it does the same for your team.

"Synergy is what happens when one plus one equals ten or a hundred or even a thousand! It's the profound result when two or more respectful human beings determine to go beyond their preconceived ideas to meet a great challenge."

—Stephen Covey

6. FOLLOW-UP & FOLLOW THROUGH

*"Understand it takes more than one conversation to influence change—
an initial conversation is a great start, but the real change comes from the
ongoing follow-up conversations. Make time to make change happen
100 conversations at a time."*

—Jimmy Casas

You may have an excellent product, a great service, great intentions, and unlimited possibilities, but without follow-up and follow through, they can all become irrelevant and lead to wasted opportunity, not to mention damaged relationships. Failure to follow up is one of the fastest ways to turn a positive impression into a negative one, especially when people are depending on you.

More business is lost every year from neglect (abandoning and overlooking) than from anything else. As a matter of fact, the National Sales Association reports that:

- 48% of salespeople never follow up with a prospect.
- 25% of salespeople make a second contact and stop.
- 12% of sales people make three contacts and stop.
- 80% of sales are made on the twelfth contact.

With statistics like this, half of success is achieved by simply showing up and following through. Approximately twenty percent of sales people close eighty percent of the business. This truth offers a ripe opportunity for the most diligent and persistent people to win the business.

If follow-up and follow through are so valuable to keeping a first impression positive and making you successful in business, why do so many people fail to do it? Failure to follow through seems more commonplace than not in our busy and too often disconnected society.

9 Reasons Why People Don't Follow-Up. They . . .

1. forget.
2. make false assumptions.
3. lack motivation or interest.
4. don't care or want to be inconvenienced.
5. do not have a system to record and track.
6. don't want to appear too pushy or imposing.
7. don't realize the significance of perseverance.
8. have never learned how to follow up effectively.
9. expect the client to get back in touch with them.

Keeping Promises

When you do what you promise, you are demonstrating the spirit of excellence and integrity. People will appreciate your conscientious dependability. When you don't do what you promise, others may lose confidence, lose trust, lose respect, and doubt your reputation.

If you promise to do your best, *do your best!* If you promise to send your proposal by Tuesday, do it! Great follow-up is the mark of sensational customer service and how you will earn the right to ask for referrals and repeat business.

16 Best Practices for Follow-up and Follow Through

1. When you say you are going to do something, do it!
2. Return phone calls and emails within 24 hours.
3. When you get a business card, call them back, touch base, send an email, or write a note.
4. Contact referrals as soon as possible.
5. Clean up past commitments.
6. Connect on LinkedIn.
7. When you reconnect with a new contact, remind them where they met you. Include something positive which you remember about them.

8. Send articles or links which you think they would enjoy.
9. Commit thyself, and don't back out.
10. Create a "reconnect" file to help you remember who, when, where, what, and why to call.
11. Offer various methods for people to contact you (email, text, phone, fax, in-person, instant messenger).
12. Send handwritten thank you notes.
13. Ask for their preferred method of communication.
14. Remember birthdays, anniversaries, and reasons to celebrate and acknowledge.
15. Maintain a simple, easy-to-type, easy-to-remember email that you can duplicate with personalization.
16. Follow up creatively multiple times in multiple media.

Does Persistence Pay Off or Push Away?

Let's look at follow-up from the other direction. What if a lack of follow-up is not the problem, but overkill is? Can it get to be irritating, bothersome, and annoying? Absolutely. Many times I have unsubscribed to emails or requested to be removed from phone lists because the sales person wouldn't take no for an answer. How can you be persistent without being a pest?

- Touch base within the week and send an email every two weeks thereafter.
- Ask them directly if you can continue touching base or if they would like or you to stop.
- Send them interesting information to keep them in the loop without asking anything in return.
- Respect their wishes if they ask you to stop following up. If they do, receive their response on good terms.

Recommitment Conversations

"Commitment means staying loyal to what you said you were going to do long after the mood you said it in has left you."

—Unkonwn

Life can be so busy and filled with distractions that you may forget to follow-up or simply run out of time. When this happens, take responsibility and recommit.

"I had all the intention of getting back to you, but life kept happening. Here is the commitment that I made, and I would like to make it up to you." Recommitting can thereby help you retain the relationship, hit the restart button, make up for lost time, and demonstrate that you can be counted on to keep your word.

Stand Above the Crowd

As a young, energetic, ambitious, and eager financial advisor, Chassidy knew that the success of her business would largely be determined by the assistant whom she hired. She needed someone who was not only smart and detail oriented, but intuitive and dependable. After interviewing numerous candidates, she had a talented pool of prospects from which to choose. One day before making her final decision, she went to her mailbox and found a thank you note.

One of her applicants had written a brief note of gratitude for being considered for the opportunity. Her follow-up was so impressive that she was hired immediately. Now, ten years later, this amazing assistant has helped drive the success of the business and is still a part of their family. Her original initiative to follow up and follow through helped her stand above the crowd to create a rewarding career.

"Diligent follow-up and follow-through will set you apart from the crowd and communicate excellence."

—John C. Maxwell

The Lifetime Value of a Customer

If you are in service or sales, would you like to know the real value of follow-up? Do a little research into your client relationships. Consider your best clients—the ones you can count on to send you referrals or do business with you in the future—then do a little math.

The folks in your sphere of influence (those who know you, like you, and trust you), you can expect one person in twelve to either do business with you or send a referral your way every year.

The key is in the consistency. 89% of home sellers say they would use their agent again, but only 11% did. Why? They forgot the name of their agent!

When you consider the National Association of Realtors tells us that homeowners move, on average, every nine years—can you imagine the missed opportunities for those who allowed their names to be forgotten? If someone moves every nine years and they called the same agent to sell their home every time, at an average commission of $6,000, that's a VIP you'd want to take care of, right?

The same is true in other industries. When we look at how valuable our customers are, we start to realize the value we must bring back to them. Follow-up doesn't have to be "do you want to buy now?" Follow-up is staying connected, offering value, finding out if people need questions answered, or simply asking how you can be of service.

Consider that value. Then, for as long as you are in business, stick to that follow-up plan. It will not only improve your bottom-line, but leave an ongoing positive impression.

7. REPUTATION & RESPECT

"Character is like a tree and reputation like a shadow. The shadow is what we think of it; the tree is the real thing."

—Abraham Lincoln

The quality of your first, last, and continuous impressions serves to build the quality of your reputation. Your good name is priceless. Impressions made greatly influence the respect (or lack of) which people have for you. The wonderful news is that you have the power to make them amazing! By being aware, deliberate, and proactive, you can influence the outcomes and make your reputation sterling.

Reputation

The dictionary defines **reputation** as the beliefs or opinions generally held about something or someone. Hence our reputation determines our standing, status, and esteem in the eyes of others. Whether deemed good or bad, fairly or unfairly, your reputation provides people with a reference point for judging your character, behavior, and personality.

Think of a person you have known and how you know her or him. Does your memory of this person invariably evoke an emotional connection or cognitive response?

Flip it around and realize the same thing happens when people think of you. Your reputation is the memory they've filed away in the reference section of their brains and it will be the first thing they think of when your name comes up.

ASK YOURSELF: How do you make people feel? Have you lived in such a way as to make it positive? What lingering impression are people left with after they have spent time with you? Is your reputation working for or against you?

Character Counts

"There are two ways of establishing a reputation, one to be praised by honest people and the other to be accused by rogues. It is best, however, to secure the first one, because it will always be accompanied by the latter."

—Charles Caleb Colton

Character generates reputation. Live long enough and you will encounter people who are conniving, manipulative, and outright mean. They will not think twice about sullying the reputation of another to elevate themselves and win business. Or in the following example—to save business.

Years ago, I had a fabulous position as a consultant. A strategic part of growing my territory was delivering *Lunch and Learn* programs to empower my prospective clients with tools for success. Helping them succeed helped me succeed. My top prospects became my best clients who began using my company for their services—which meant that the competition was losing business.

An individual who held my position with another company went on the warpath to bring me down. My loyal, new-found customers would share with me the horrible things she was saying about me on the street. It was such a surprise. Many a night I cried myself to sleep because her words were unfounded, untrue, and outright rude.

The ironic turn is that her efforts backfired. The clients could see through her motives and she ended up hurting her reputation more than mine.

---

66 *There will always be naysayers and critics, so brace yourself. Be a good person, do the right thing, and know that if you take care of your character, your reputation will take care of you.* 99

Respect

"Show respect even to people who don't deserve it, not as a reflection of their character, but as a reflection of yours."

—Dave Willis

Respect comes from honoring yourself in the other person. Your success in this lifetime will largely be determined not by how much you achieve and accumulate, but by how many people respect you. We all want to be respected—by our spouses, friends, families, bosses, co-workers, and more. Even though being respected is a core desire within us all, how many people continue doing exactly what it takes to undermine it?

If you want to be loved and respected by most people, you must first offer respect in word, deed, and favor. Consistently demonstrating respect with conscientious sincerity will foster trust and a worthy reputation.

14 Ways to Build Reputation & Respect

1. Live in integrity.
2. Encourage others.
3. Play fair and be just.
4. Keep your promises.
5. Think before you speak.
6. Provide value to others.
7. Be who you say you are.
8. Always do the right thing.
9. Consider how others feel.
10. Respect yourself and others.
11. Catch people doing things right.
12. Combat negativity with positivity.
13. Treat others as you would the ones you love.
14. Do not condemn, criticize, gossip, or complain.

8. Make Moments Memorable

"Great moments make great memories; so be you, be great, and make memorable moments."

—Ricardo Housham

Celebrate the moments of your life is more than a corny cliché or advertising jingle. It is a reminder that time is precious, valuable, and to be appreciated. The moments of our lives happen in an instant, yet their memories may last a lifetime. Literally, a series of moments—equals your life. The seconds tick into minutes . . . and so on.

First impressions work the same way. A moment in time can last mere seconds, yet its memory has the power to shift the trajectory of your future and your outcomes.

These critical moments occur any time we are engaging with people regardless of the setting. Whether professional—networking, branding, meetings, conferences, sales calls, serving customers, and making presentations OR personal—recreation, making friends, dating, travel, adventures, shopping, or family reunions, moments are being made all the time and accumulating into a life well lived.

Think of people you have met only once. Who, in that single fleeting moment, made such a memorable impression you will never forget them. Think of the businesses which stand apart from their competitors because their level of service is extraordinary.

---

66 *Making moments memorable will give your positive impressions staying power and resonance.* 99

ASK YOURSELF: What about you is remarkable and memorable? How can you be remembered in a positive way for years to come? Do you make a lasting impact? What unique qualities do you have that can differentiate you from others? How can you make moments memorable?

Memorable Moments . . .

- Touch our hearts.
- Make us laugh and cry.
- Make our days more special.
- Help us learn, grow, and thrive.
- Provide comfort, joy, connection, and meaning.
- Inspire us to give more, be more, and share more.

Be the Master of Your Moments

In her new book, *Master Your Moments, Master Your Life,* my friend Susanne Gaddis (CommunicationsDoctor.com) shares the importance of making the moments of your life matter. She states that it only takes one to three seconds to create a new moment and each one can be graded with a value of a positive one, negative one, or zero.

---

66 *These mere moments have the power to bring you up, bring you down, or leave you feeling indifferent.* 99

After all, the neurons in your brain don't rest. Regardless of whether it involves a person, a thought, a feeling, a memory, or a situation, pretty much every moment in your life can be deemed as being positive, negative, or neutral.

Think about the relationships you now have and where they fall on this scale of engagement. The "positive ones" energize you with optimism and enthusiasm, and bring out the best in you. The "negative ones" cause you to feel resistance, drain your energy, and leave you feeling frustrated. And then there are the "zeros" that inspire no participation, engagement, or involvement. Nothing—nada!

You know which relationships fit these descriptions, don't you? The more important questions, however, is what kind of relationships or moments are you engendering or bringing about for others? Are you creating positive moments, negative impressions, or being so neutral that you are easily forgotten? You get to pick!

14 Ways to Create Memorable Moments

1. Lighten up with love, laughter, humor, and fun.
2. Celebrate the moments in your life with appreciation.
3. Be disruptive; be original; be innovative and outrageous.
4. Be amazing.
5. Seek to surprise or delight.
6. Deliver 'service beyond self.'
7. Create a meaningful experience.
8. Start with the heart and bring love.
9. Engage, empower, and inspire others.
10. Give without expecting anything in return.
11. Surpass expectations and go beyond delight.
12. Make moments sweet, simple, and enjoyable.
13. Perform unexpected random acts of kindness.
14. Be personal, proactive, passionate, and productive.

Unplug and Be Present

Our world is overflowing with distractions and interruptions—where people are connected to their smart phones, media, alerts, likes, comments, and notifications 24/7. Although this is now the new norm, we can and should step away for a spell or two when we are in the presence of the people who matter most.

Your presence—the full and attentive kind—is your present to others and theirs to you. Be in those moments with people. Speak and listen to one another. Enjoy the meal in front of you, or the conversation around the cocktail table, or backyard fire pit without continuously checking the status of your smart phone. It will make you more conscious of your moments and improve the quality of the time you spend with others.

"As soon as you honor the present moment, all unhappiness and struggle dissolve, and life begins to flow with joy and ease. When you act out the present-moment awareness, whatever you do becomes imbued with a sense of quality, care, and love—even the most simple action."

—Eckhart Tolle

Relationships Matter More

Business is business, no doubt. But human interaction is the driving force of memory making. While it may seem counter-intuitive to success to let a call go to voice mail or leave an email unanswered for an hour or two, believe it or not, when you set those expectations, people will respect them.

Some of the smartest and most successful business people I know are unabashedly unapologetic about being completely present when they are with loved ones or with clients. They have "away messages" on their email that let people know when they will be answering back.

They have reputations for recognizing the absolute value of those face-to-face (and voice-to-voice) encounters. Does it hurt their business? Not even a little bit. Because clients, customers, and leaders know that when it's THEIR time to be connected to that person? They too will have undivided attention.

How can you unplug and be more present in your daily life? The answers could change the way you make moments memorable. If you want to have a more positive life, create more positive moments! The better your moments, the better your memories, your relationships, and your outcomes.

8 WAYS TO **MASTER**
The *Art* of a **POSITIVE**
LASTING IMPRESSION

1. *Happy Endings.* How you end a conversation is as important as how you began it. Learn to exit with comfort, grace, and ease.

2. *Share it Forward.* Create your own movement of paying goodness forward. Live it daily, doing for others without expecting anything in return.

3. *Humility & Gratitude.* A humble spirit does not participate in one-upmanship, but rather, enjoys sharing the limelight and encouraging other people to shine brightly.

4. *Class, Tack & Diplomacy.* These fine qualities demonstrate a personality of refined presence and distinction. Acting with thoughtful deliberation and calm composure is a fine reflection of character.

5. *Play well with others.* Showing that you are easy to get along with and a valuable team player will improve the energy, synergy, and interactions with everyone around you.

6. *Follow up & Follow Through.* Diligent and dedicated follow-up communicate your dedication, reliability, and spirit of excellence.

7. *Reputation & Respect.* Elevate your standing, status, and esteem in the eyes of others by being your best, doing the right thing, taking care to live in integrity.

8. *Make Moments Memorable.* Making your moments memorable will give your positive first impressions staying power and resonance.

8

The Art *of*

NURTURING
YOUR
NETWORK

8 WAYS TO CULTIVATE
YOUR CONNECTIONS TO
CREATE FRIENDSHIPS FOR LIFE

The *Art* of NURTURING YOUR NETWORK

How can you stay connected, cultivate your connections, and nurture your network to enrich your life experience? Would you like to win friends, influence people, and grow your territory?

Your networking relationships can enrich, support, and inspire your personal growth and professional success to build a life filled with opportunity and balance. Since your network is an intrinsic part of building momentum, your ability to turn new acquaintances into rewarding business contacts, and possibly lifelong friendships, can define your sense of success and impact your overall well-being.

In *The Art of Nurturing Your Network,* we will travel past initial encounters and learn how to continue the great flow of feelings to help you win in business and in life. By beginning to cultivate your connections, give and get warm and fuzzy referrals, volunteering your time and talent, help others achieve their goals, and joining new organizations you can expand your opportunities greatly. When you come to life diligent and dedicated to making a great first impression, you just might be rewarded with the greatest gift of all . . . amazing friendships for life.

1. *Cultivate Your Connections*
2. *Warm Referrals & Repeat Business*
3. *Networking to Expand Your Influence*
4. *Join New Groups & Organizations*
5. *Volunteer Your Time & Talent*
6. *With a Little Help from Your Friends*
7. *Make Deposits in the Love Bank*
8. *Friendships for a Lifetime*

1. CULTIVATE YOUR CONNECTIONS

"To be kept strong, a relationship must be attended to regularly, like a plant. It doesn't need constant attention, but it does need regular attention. If not, it will wither after a while, but can be revived. If neglected too long, then no matter how much water you put on it, or how much you care you show, it's just not coming back."

—Unknown

Throughout *The Art of First Impressions for Positive Impact* you have learned valuable tools and enlightened mindsets to create impressive and lasting impressions. Whether you apply a few ideas or many, they will all help you move in a positive direction toward transforming your relationship results.

Once you have succeeded in creating a positive first impression, a new relationship, or a valuable contact, what are you going to do with it? What are your next best steps? How can you nurture your network to expand your influence and make friends for a lifetime?

Remember, You Reap What You Sow

"When I feel very loved, when I nurture and support people, my experience is deepened. I feel connected to a larger purpose and meaning."

—Warren Farrell

Now that you have planted social seeds for positivity and influence, it is time to nurture, fertilize, and tend to the tender new relationships. There are unlimited ways for you to cultivate your personal and professional relationships, but here are a few . . .

12 Ways for You to Cultivate Your Connections

1. Send them a referral.

2. Make an introduction.
3. Volunteer your assistance.
4. Drop them a note or send them a text.
5. Call to simply touch base and say hello.
6. Connect, follow, and friend on social media.
7. Keep yourself present and in their mind's eye.
8. Discover shared interests and take action to connect.
9. Send an article which you think they may be interested in.
10. Invite them for lunch, coffee, wine, dinner, or even a walk.
11. Include them in e-zines, email blasts, updates, and marketing.
12. Acknowledge special occasions like birthdays, anniversaries, and holidays.

Stay in Touch

In her online training website, WritingSpree-A-to-Z.com, author and speaker Judy Dippel says:

"My writing life can leave me feeling isolated. I get tired of hearing my own voice and seeing my own face. I learned early on that real life, face-to-face networking was a must—and the effort extremely valuable!"

Freelancers, entrepreneurs, or the career minded can unintentionally become isolated trying to keep up with all the demands and goals. The hats we must wear to be successful are too many to mention! Networking refreshes and invigorates us on all levels. Face-to-face is the perfect venue to enjoy new professional relationships, invest in others, and share connections, experiences, and expertise. It is invaluable.

Customer Relationship Management (CRM)

Business owners, salespeople, customer service, coaches, representatives, non-profit organizations, consultants, and more, must build, organize, manage, and nurture their lists of contacts and clients to optimize their success in these competitive times. Powerful software programs exist to make relationship management simple, powerful, efficient, and effective. Cultivating connections has never been easier.

CRMs enable you to customize information, populate areas of priority, track sales, note conversations which took place, and create reminders for when you need to speak with your contacts again. You can also take notes to remember their specific needs and challenges so that when you do follow-up you can provide personalized solutions.

Countrywide Connections

"Never ignore a person that loves you, cares for you and misses you. Because one day, you might wake up from your sleep and realize that you lost the moon while counting the stars."

—Unknown

I am grateful to have lived in various places and made friends who are scattered across the country. To keep these friendships alive, it is crucial that I have occasional touchpoints so they know they matter. It is too risky to rely on auto-pilot and take friendships for granted; they may simply disappear. Whether I post a birthday greeting on Facebook, send a card at Christmas, call them out of the blue, surprise them with a visit, or even text them 'hello,' each effort cultivates and nurtures our friendship.

---

66 *When you treat people with love, respect, empathy, interest, and understanding, relationships feel like a continuous, unending conversation. Even if you're separated for 5, 10, 15, or 20 years, you can reconnect and start again where you left off.* 99

I had not seen my godmother, Barbara Morelock, for 15 years, yet we never missed sending a Christmas card or exchanging letters. When we were finally reunited in person, we greeted each other with unconditional love and acceptance as if we had never been apart—easy affection and lifelong friends—an incredible payback for nurturing and cultivating our connection well.

Stoke the Fire

Stay in touch with 'warm contacts' and find ways to stoke the fire so they don't turn cold. Most relationships will not prosper and grow when neglected or left unattended. Consider a campfire as a metaphor: when you add a few twigs at a time, the fire will keep burning and the flame will stay alive. Keep the relationship spark ignited to feed the warmth of friendship, trust, and rapport. Then, when you do decide to reconnect to ask for business, or ask for a referral, they are happy to help.

The Magic of Manners

Please and thank you are magical words indeed. They elicit feelings of acknowledgment, worth, gratitude, and acceptance. They are not only two of the simplest words in any language, but they are also powerful people connectors.

When someone asks "please," your response to their request will naturally be more positive. When you hear "thank you," you are gratefully acknowledged with appreciation.

In the absence of these two simple words, trust and the genuine connection may erode over time. A feeling of entitlement can easily slip into their place. Whether you are two or 102, manners matter. And in a world where kindness is a valuable commodity, they are differentiators which can set you apart to cultivate your connections with grace and class.

Become a Bridge Builder

In our everyday lives, we come across a multitude of people with a wide spectrum of talents, interests, and passions. Begin seeing yourself as a connector who builds bridges and connects people to one another. This thoughtful shift will enable you to look at your relationships from a proactive perspective that can make a positive impact.

"When you actively take part in connecting people, you strengthen your connections and bring value to other relationships."

Imagine introducing one friend who loves art and music to another friend who shares the same interests. Upon learning of a colleague's passion for a specific cause, you could connect them to a person whom you know has the same convictions.

Bridge builders are the encouraging souls who genuinely want to see others thrive, prosper, and succeed. And they take deliberate action steps to help make that happen by connecting folks with each other. When you create opportunities for people to meet each other, you inspire a positive lasting impression!

Six Degrees of Separation

Some say that we are all connected by six degrees of separation. This is the theory that every person on the planet can be linked through their friends and acquaintances in six or fewer connections.

Social media has proven the six degrees theory to be even shorter. Facebook recently reported that their social networking site had reduced the length of this chain to three-and-a-half connections. It seems the world is getting smaller every day!

Why take a passive role in your connectivity when it can reap you such rich rewards? Those people who seek to find mutually shared threads to make relevant introductions are the influencers who can change the world.

Reach Back and Forward

I respect and admire the dedication certain people extend to their own mentors and protégés. The truth is, we all—every single one of us—have both something to teach and unlimited things we can learn.

A beautiful symbiotic relationship occurs when you consider those who are coming up in the ranks behind you—and reach out to help them streamline their journeys. By sharing your expertise, you can warn them of pitfalls, help them avoid costly mistakes, and teach them the tools to succeed.

In turn, when you have the opportunity to learn from someone who has already been in the trenches, their wisdom and experience can enrich your life and simplify your journey greatly.

I believe there are honor and reward on both sides of this equation. It's a privilege to teach others what we know and an honor to learn from those who've already traversed the terrain before us. It reminds me of the Maya Angelou quote, "When you learn, teach. When you get, give." She was a true master at being both a mentor and a protégé.

Ask Yourself: Who would benefit from your wisdom and experience? Who could you encourage to help foster their success? Do you have a respected role model who would be willing to share their hard-earned wisdom with you? Be bold enough to ask these questions—and then take ACTION! It could be a life-changer for everyone involved.

2. Warm Referrals & Repeat Business

"People influence people. Nothing influences people more than a recommendation from a trusted friend. A trusted referral influences people more than the best broadcast message. A trusted referral is the Holy Grail of advertising."

—Mark Zuckerberg

Warm Referrals

Warm referrals are one of your best opportunities to give and receive good will, mutual respect, and rewarding support. Whether you are referring a friend to a trusted professional or asking an acquaintance to help you grow your influence, referrals are a golden source for enriching your own life and that of others. Regardless of how your referrals are given, they are born from making positive and lasting first impressions.

The reciprocity for warm referrals is fortified by being positive, diligent, helpful, loyal, honest, dependable, competent, caring, and all of the other fabulous qualities listed in this book. Do these and you will definitely make a positive impact. When someone has a constructive experience with you, and you excel at what you do, there is a higher likelihood they will want to send you business and help you succeed.

Trust by Association

"All things being equal, people will do business with, and refer business to, those people they know, like, and trust."

—Bob Burg

Take a moment to think about how you met your Realtor, your doctor, your banker, your accountant, your insurance agent, your veterinarian, your hairdresser, or even your fitness trainer. More likely than not, you had a friend who was so pleased with their services that they recommended them to you, right? By the same token, if any of these professionals have done an excellent job for you, you may have already bragged about them to other people.

"Trust by association" implies, "If she did a great job for them, she'll do a great job for me!" It is obvious that you must have positively impressed them to begin with; otherwise they would not be calling.

My brother-in-law, Charles Dixon, is the owner of Pablo Beach Mortgage, Inc. in Jacksonville, Florida. Having been in the industry for over twenty-five years, he regularly receives phone calls from complete strangers who say, "My (sister, friend, nephew, realtor, etc.) says you are the best mortgage broker they ever worked with and I should call you first to arrange home financing." Rather than having to invest in advertising or go out and find business, he lets his business find him.

_____

66 *Wouldn't you love to build such a solid reputation that the world beats a path to your door? You can.* **99**

_____

Repeat Business

Over and over and over again . . . it takes less money and less effort to keep an existing customer than it does to create a new one. Nurturing your relationships builds friendships, earns referrals and repeat business, and should be one of your most strategic marketing efforts.

My friend Virginia Glass has been a top producing Realtor in Tallahassee, Florida for over thirty-five years. Not only have her customers become her good friends, but she's become a part of their families. Families whose homes she listed or sold decades ago continue to refer their children, grandchildren, and great-grandchildren to her. From a lifetime of service and helping others she has established a solid network of quality associations who continue to send her referrals. Her entire business is relationship based, saving her thousands of dollars per year in advertising. Being a good person has a multiplier effect. When you live right and you do right by others, warm referrals and repeat business will be one of your many sweet rewards.

From Cold Leads to Hot Buyers

The mere term "cold calling" conjures frigid visions of being rejected, ignored, verbally abused, or hung-up on. It is one of the most challenging strategies for finding prospects and gaining customers in business. When I am training sales teams, many people will confess that "sales call reluctance" keeps them stuck in fear and procrastination because they are worn down from getting beat up. I encourage them to apply the acronym of "QTIP" to inspire them. When "Quit Taking It Personally" is applied, prospecting calls are made easier. **Rather than trying to *sell* anything, reframe your approach by offering ways to *help people buy.*** It's a brilliant and effective mindset—and remember, it's all about them.

Remove the "sales" speak from your presentation when making phone calls. If you make the "do you want to buy?" pitch—the answer will usually be a yes or a no.

A "no" can feel like failure. Who wants to set themselves up for that kind of rejection? It's no wonder salespeople experience sales call reluctance! Focus instead on your sincere effort to build a relationship.

When you make a call to offer service, see if you can answer questions, and let people know you're there when they need you— you are building trust, nurturing a healthy relationship, and staying in the forefront of their minds. Using this approach can remove the angst from the equation and make picking up the phone a pleasure. It's all about the connection.

8 Ways to Turn Cold Leads into Hot Buyers

1. Focus on building a quality relationship first.
2. Give service beyond self.
3. Ensure they have a great experience.
4. Earn their trust and build rapport through best practices.
5. Meet new people through networking opportunities.
6. Ask for referrals from happy customers and people who love you.
7. Provide something of value, such as an introduction, information, free tips or tools, or gratitude and appreciation.
8. Utilize LinkedIn to search for connections and request introductions.

Do everything in your power to make a positive and lasting first impression. Then rock their world with excellent communication, genuine caring, promises kept, and sensational service. Doing these will melt the ice and warm up the new relationship.

Asking for a Referral

"Referrals aren't given easily. If you don't take the time to establish credibility, you're not going to get the referral. People have to get to know you. They have to feel comfortable with who you are and what you do."

—Ivan Misner

Many people find asking for referrals extremely difficult. Do you think it is due to embarrassment, awkwardness, or fear of looking needy? Once you have made a stellar impression, done an incredible job, and customers are happy with your service, you are in the ideal position to ask; they've already seen you deliver!

The perfect time to ask for a referral is when clients are delighted with your product or services. Strike when the iron is hot. You can ride the wave of enthusiasm because they want their friends and acquaintances to experience the same excellence they did.

The first imperative, if you are to receive referrals, is to do the best job possible. Stand out above the crowd!

The next crucial step is to articulate *where* and *how* you fulfill specific needs. What work do you want to be referred to do? Expressing your intention clearly, from the beginning of your conversation, will help you avoid getting junk referrals that waste your time, energy, and effort.

It is also easier to ask if you approach someone with an open heart and ask what you can do for them. You'll begin making friends all over the place.

---

66 *Master the art of asking for referrals and you will never make a cold call again!* 99

---

3 Ways to Ask for Referrals

1. "I love helping people like you. If you were in my position, what would you recommend I do to find more clients like you?"
2. "I love working with people like you! Do you have a friend who is also in need of _____?"
3. "It has been such a pleasure working with you. Do you know of anyone else who would benefit from my services?"

Third Party Testimonials

ASK YOURSELF: When you are ready to make a purchasing decision, do you first read product reviews to see if other people were happy with their decision? Do you read a movie review before going to see it? Do you seek references before doing business with people? Favorable third party opinions and experiences give you reassurance that you are heading in the right direction.

People are more likely to buy your product or service when other people are bragging about how wonderful you are. Letters of reference, referrals, recommendations, Google business page reviews, LinkedIn endorsements, Angie's List and Thumbtack, and more, would never display glowing reviews about you if you had not already made a positive and **lasting first impression.**

Helping Each Other Succeed

"Relationship Selling transcends the sales transaction and looks beyond it to the ongoing relationship built between the buyer and the seller."

—Jim Cathcart

Keynote speaker Ed Robinson (edspeaks.com) has devoted his career to teaching professionals how to become serious rainmakers for growing their business, profitability, and success. A couple of years ago, Ed and I shared a business strategy session and found powerful ways to help each other.

Ed has a loyal and happy client who hires him every year to speak at their national conference. As they were preparing their speaker line-up for their 2016 program, they asked him to refer a talented speaker who could present on the topics of thriving in change and relationship selling. He graciously gave them my name, for which I am deeply grateful. Based solely on his recommendation, they hired me to keynote at their conference. It was a matter of friends helping friends and I hope that sometime soon I can return the favor.

I love seeing my friends thrive and succeed. Whenever I can help them achieve their goals, I will do my best to share it forward. When you help others, they will want to help you too.

Asking Permission

My friend Adrianne Machina (tornado-marketing.com) is an internet marketing guru. Before she gives a referral, she will first ask for permission from the person for whom she is sending it. As an example, if I wanted to send a referral to her, I would do so by stating, "I know Adrianne would do an incredible job helping you optimize your marketing strategy. May I have your permission to give her your phone number?"

Adrianne advises, "When you want to give a referral, help the involved parties make their connection. It could be done with a three-way call, a joint email introduction, or even a coffee date. Don't just throw it over the fence and hope it's going to be fine. Instead, make it a two-way street to help people help themselves. They will be so impressed by your attentive diligence that they will want to do the same for you."

Gratitude

Thank you for your business! People want to be appreciated and made to feel important. When you demonstrate gratitude for their loyalty and business, they are happy to send you more.

My lifelong friend Cindy Cooper is a mega-producing Realtor in Tallahassee, Florida. Every year she sends Happy Home Anniversary cards to her loyal buyers who have purchased homes through her in the past. Not only is she expressing genuine gratitude, but it helps her stay in the front of their minds if they learn of anyone who could use her services. When it comes time for them to sell their home, Cindy will be the first person they think of. Demonstrating gratitude and appreciation creates and leaves the lasting positive impressions we are hoping for.

Action Begets Action

For most business people, referrals are the lifeblood of their business. I've always been a firm believer that action begets action. If you want more referrals for your business—refer business to other people.

While that may sound counter-intuitive, it activates the Law of Reciprocity. When we do for others, they are compelled to return the favor.

I know speakers who are fabulous about referring other speakers to their clients for the following year's annual conferences. Those speakers, in turn, send referrals back their way. As Tony Robbins says, "The path to success is to take massive, determined action." And spreading goodwill by sharing business with others is a powerful way to cultivate your connections.

Million Dollar Referrals

In his classic bestseller *Million Dollar Consulting: The Professional's Guide to Growing a Practice,* internatonal consultant and bestselling author Alan Weiss shares that enduring relationships are key for succeeding in consulting and business.

He writes, "My credo is 'Always help the other person get rich.' This applies no matter what relationship or fee system you prefer. I don't just want the project to be successful, I want the relationship with my client to be enduring, whether small business referrals, situational alliances, reliable sub-contracting, or large scale collaborations. This is why you can use a reward system for others to dramatically grow your business."

Nurture your network well and you will find that warm referrals and repeat business are a rewarding result of your efforts. Helping other people achieve their goals will help you achieve yours.

3. NETWORKING TO EXPAND YOUR INFLUENCE

"I believe networking gives you confidence to interact with others, teaches resiliency, and helps you overcome challenges in life. The concept of engaging others with an attitude of giving, not getting, will enrich your relationships."

—Joe Sweeney

Business thought leader and financial strategist Peter Drucker once said, "More business decisions occur over lunch and dinner than any other time, yet no MBA program exists on the subject." Isn't that astonishing? Professional networking is the heartbeat of business, and as a result, it deserves your focused attention.

As a business school graduate, I have seen "Sales" as a college curriculum in only the past twenty years. It is about time it be included, considering that our great nation was founded upon and flourishes because of a system of free enterprise. Networking is an integral and essential part of every venture.

In this chapter, we will discuss how you can make networking a lifelong activity to create personal and professional opportunities to expand your influence, make friends, and to succeed in life and in business.

ASK YOURSELF: What is my objective for networking? Am I hoping to make new friends? Do I want to get more involved in my community? Am I marketing my services to make more sales and build my business? Do I need customers? What is the driving motivation behind my networking? Being mindful of these questions will help you thrive in social settings to become a savvier networker.

Nurture Your Network

My friend Joe Sweeney is the author of *The New York Times* Bestseller *Networking is a Contact Sport.* He once reminded me of a powerful fact which we often forget. He said, "80% of everything you need already exists in your network."

How often do you make life harder than it needs to be by thinking it is "me against the world?" Or that you must continuously re-create the wheel? Or that you must endure the stinging rejection of cold calls? Or that you should chart your course alone?

You know plenty of somebodies who know somebody who can help you on your journey. The more networking you do, the more somebodies you will have! The key here is that if you have grown and nurtured your network, you will have a rich reservoir of relationships to tap into that are more than happy to help you succeed.

Benefits of Networking

"Networking is the art of building and maintaining connections for shared positive outcomes."
—Devora Zack

Everything you want to achieve in life is at stake! Even if you feel shy, lack social confidence, or are a self-affirmed introvert who hates networking, please consider how your positives can far outweigh your hesitancies. Why should networking be a part of your life? Because networking . . .

- helps you achieve your goals, purpose, and potential.
- brings new relationship opportunities for making friends.
- creates new opportunities which you would not have otherwise.
- increases your understanding for your industry and the marketplace.
- encourages collaboration and participation.
- is a rich reservoir for referrals, recommendations, and word-of-mouth advertising.

- energizes, synergizes, and unifies people.
- improves your communication skills through practice, engagement, and interaction.
- connects you with mentors, decision makers, and colleagues.
- makes you feel more confident, tapped in, and tuned up.
- enables you to expand your influence and know more people.
- generates new ideas, perspectives, and innovations.
- leads to the discovery of new experiences and enrichment.
- helps you build strong alliances.

Even if you only received three of the benefits from the list above, you would be richly rewarded for your initiative and effort.

15 Ways to Begin Networking

1. Value quality over quantity.
2. Seek events, opportunities, and venues where you can meet, greet, engage, and connect with others.
3. Just show up!
4. Take the initiative to introduce yourself first and begin a new conversation.
5. Ask open-ended questions and become a great listener.
6. Acknowledge and nurture your existing relationships to reap the benefits gained from helping each other.
7. Make eye contact and use positive body language.
8. Learn to enjoy meeting new people.
9. Move beyond your comfort zone to engage with people who are different from you in personality, cultures, or positions.
10. Offer to be of service; how can you help others succeed?
11. Act as though you are the host of the party to help everyone have a wonderful time.
12. Exude the confidence (real or imagined) that you belong there, no matter where you are.

13. Find others who share your interests and passions.
14. Realize the benefits of enlarging your network.
15. Use *The Art of First Impressions for Positive Impact* as your networking mastery manual!

Where Can You Network?

Madison, Wisconsin continues to amaze me. There is always something special and unique happening. The networking opportunities to make new friends, create new business connections, and fill your social calendar are endless. Some of my closest friends today were made at networking events I attended years ago. I cannot imagine where my life would be if I had not taken the initiative to step up, step out, get involved, and make an intentional effort. Networking success will not happen without this effort.

- Professional membership and association events
- Conferences and continuing education venues
- Social settings and mixers
- Your gym, sports, or place for recreation
- Your church, temple, or place of worship
- Social media connections
- Eventbrite invitations
- The community calendar in your local newspaper's Lifestyle section

7 Things NOT To Do at a Networking Event

Yes, there are people who attend networking events with the sole intention of receiving free food and drinks. While they may *show up*, they have no desire to *get in the game.* They couldn't care less about making introductions, speaking to strangers, meeting new people, or making a great first impression. That's okay. They are not the folks who will be reading this book. Bless their hearts!

However, for the rest of us, we can maximize networking events so well that it leads to new business, new friends, and unlimited opportunities. When you set your intention to have a productive event and make a positive impact there are certain things NOT to do:

1. Do not sit only with people you already know.
2. Do not wait for others to make the first move.
3. Do not leave your business cards at home.
4. Do not avoid eye contact and smiling.
5. Do not gossip or speak ill of anyone.
6. Do not go alone if you are shy and need a buddy to your bolster confidence.
7. Do not wait to be introduced to people you'd like to know.

Like-Minded Online

Today's technology tools and social media platforms make networking possible in the "virtual space" on high levels. From Facebook groups to LinkedIn communities you have a wide-open opportunity to reach beyond borders and connect with like-minded professionals across the globe.

It's incredible to realize how you can share ideas, insights, and even send referrals to one another in a forum that links an unlimited number of people.

- Search Facebook and LinkedIn for groups with similar interests.
- Be a valuable contributor—share insights and ideas when possible and join in the conversations in meaningful and engaging ways.
- Give kudos and share the valuable ideas and content of those in your network – so that you can expand their networks.
- Be careful to comply with the group standards, most will have a list of "rules" for posts within the group.
- Be respectful.
- Don't "overshare."
- Steer clear of "too hot topics" in a professional setting such as religion and politics – networking is about finding the connections – not the divides.

- While online networking and social sharing isn't everyone's cup of tea, there is no denying that it is a huge success factor for those who use it effectively.

Be of Service

For some, the idea of networking in a social setting is the stuff of nightmares and anxiety. What if you turned the table on the experience by offering to help with the event? Being in a position of volunteering or service completely changes the dynamic. You'll still get to meet a wide variety of people, make new connections, and create conversations. However, it will feel less like selling yourself—which is usually at the heart of networking angst. Instead of standing in a corner, waiting for an opportunity to converse, you could . . .

- Offer to help with registration—where you'd literally be the gatekeeper as all the fine folks you'd like to meet come through!
- Offer to be the liaison to the speakers and presenters for the event. That's instant access to the power players in the room.
- Let the event organizers know you're there to help, and to learn—they'll be instant ambassadors for helping you make connections.

As you help, ask for business cards, jot a note down on the back with a hint as to your interaction (carry a sharpie with you – some cards are hard to write on with a pen), and follow up after with an email. You'll be memorable for your acts of service. Your detailed follow-up will help you stand out and be memorable – all without the awkward exchanges. How's that for a win-win? Give it a try.

Set your intention, take deliberate action, and follow through. You'll be amazed by the difference it makes in your networking results.

4. Join New Groups & Organizations

"Joining a band of brothers together, a group with one common interest or mission, whether as a company, a team, or a motorcycle club, requires not only a commitment to loyalty but an understanding of self-preservation as well."

—Sonny Barger

By nature, we are social creatures with a tribal instinct to gather and grow. Joining new groups and organizations is one of the fastest and most proactive ways for you to expand your network, grow your territory, enrich your relationships, further your career, enjoy a hobby or group activity, or simply make new friends.

Your options are unlimited when you consider local, national, global, and online options. Choosing a valuable group inevitably depends on what your goals may be. It's important to find a group that is a good fit for your interests, in its purpose and style, and in the commitment required. Choose a door and walk through it! The variety is endless, but a few of the most popular are . . .

Mastermind Groups

Thought leader and businessman Jim Rohn once said, "You are the average of the five people you spend the most time with." How is it working for you? Do your closest relationships lift you up and inspire your best? Or do they bring you down with drama, conflict, and discouragement? Take an inventory to consider how you are being impacted by others. Since your lifestyle and attitude generally reflect your choices – choose wisely, my friend, choose wisely.

That is the beauty of a mastermind group—you get to pick! Surrounding yourself with people who raise your standards and help you achieve your goals is a powerful and worthwhile endeavor.

Mastermind groups can be instrumental in helping you achieve your goals.

Mastermind Groups Can . . .

1. Keep you emotionally invested in your own success.
2. Shorten your learning curve by teaching each other best practices and methods.
3. Stimulate new opinions, perspectives, tools, and ideas.
4. Help you run a faster race by running with faster runners.
5. Hold you accountable for accomplishing your objectives.
6. Give you the opportunity and satisfaction of helping others.
7. Share best practices and a better way to approach activities.
8. Provide you with valuable feedback and solutions.
9. Enrich your relationships to form deep, meaningful, and long-lasting friendships.

My friend Peggy Brockman (peggybrockman.com) launched a public forum for her local business community. She wanted to bring people together to collaborate through leadership training, hot topic expert panels, networking, and social media classes. It has been a powerful way for her to expand her influence and serve her community. Apparently, she has tapped into a great need, because her Mastermind events have been well received and wildly successful. She indeed filled a need. Join a Mastermind group or start one yourself to enjoy the synergy and resources which come from the combined brilliance of various individuals.

Nonprofit & Community Service Organizations

Charitable organizations and non-profit groups are always in need of volunteers who will bring their time, talent, energy, experience, money, efforts, and more. There are so many important causes and valuable places where your contributions would be greatly appreciated and well-utilized. In addition to giving back and serving a bigger vision, it a wonderful place for meeting like-minded people, giving you common ground as you build new friendships.

Support Groups

Have there been times in your life when you felt lost and alone, or endured challenging trials and tribulations? Rather than continuing to feel that the road to recovery, resilience, or well-being is a painful path, join a support group to help you achieve faster healing. Being surrounded by caring, compassionate, and supportive people who can empathize with your struggles will give you strength and vitality for renewal and rejuvenation.

Recreation & Hobbies

What do you do for fun? What are your hobbies or passions? When Teresa and Doug Turner moved from Tallahassee to Destin, Florida, they were leaving behind a lifetime of friendships, thriving businesses, and a wealth of connections. Wanting to design a new life in a new town, they each chose a group to join for fun, recreation, and friendships. Teresa chose a running group and Doug chose a biking club. Now, several years later, the new friendships formed in their respective groups laid the foundation for their new lives and made their entire transition easier and more rewarding.

Chambers of Commerce

Local Chambers of Commerce are wonderful places to meet new people, promote your business, build friendships, volunteer your time, learn new skills, and enjoy a fun social life. Whether you jump in with both feet, volunteer to be an ambassador, join an action committee, or sit quietly in the back of the room, your local Chamber of Commerce is a great venue in which to make a fabulous impression, catch the synergy, and find connection and happiness. These serve a variety of purposes and offer myriad programs, specific to various groups—great education, opportunity, and professional contacts are the return for money spent to join.

Professional Associations

What business organizations will help you fast forward your own business? What network would provide you with a bounteous referral base for new opportunities and increased sales? Many types of businesses have national and state associations who serve their industry. A few favorites include:

- Alumni organizations
- Local Chamber of Commerce
- LinkedIn
- MeetUp.com
- Execunet
- Netshare
- ChiefExecutiveNetwork.com (paid site)
- Executive Networking Groups
- BNI International

13 Reasons to Join a New Group or Organization

1. It's fun.
2. It gives you the chance to share what you know and learn from others.
3. It creates a social outlet for personal and professional relationships.
4. It bonds you with your peers who share similar goals, challenges, situations, and career paths.
5. It helps you make new friends.
6. You're able to give back to your community.
7. You will learn more about what is happening all around you.

8. It can broaden your knowledge and keep you informed.
9. It can enrich your network to grow your connections.
10. It brings credibility and status to your resume.
11. You can develop leadership skills.
12. You will have new opportunities for new experiences.
13. It will help you stay engaged, inspired, and motivated.

Taking the initiative to volunteer or join a new organization creates a ripple effect that will bring great satisfaction and fulfillment that you would not have otherwise. You never know how enriched your life will be by taking that first step. This week, seek out one new organization, club or group to visit.

5. Volunteer Your Time & Talent

"We make a living by what we get, but we make a life by what we give."
—Winston Churchill

Volunteering to serve a cause above and beyond yourself reflects your heart, character, work ethic, and convictions. As you give, it feeds your spirit in return. Your actions speak louder than words and on your behalf to illustrate what is important to you and what you truly care about. Along the way, you may earn the respect and garner the admiration of other people when they recognize your vision to be of service. And that makes a very positive impression!

Aligning Your Purpose and Your Passion

Aligning your purpose and passion with your volunteer service may open the door to opportunities you may never have imagined and create a life-changing experience. This alignment will enable you to use your talents, build upon your strengths, enjoy intrinsic rewards, know profound fulfillment, and receive the staying power to stick with it once you make a commitment. Your passion will fuel your efforts as a volunteer. The greater reward? Your ability to make a huge impact in the lives of others.

In his 2015 *Forbes Magazine* article, Mark Horoszowski shared four benefits of volunteering your time, skills, body, and experience. He wrote, "Volunteering your time makes you feel like you have more time; volunteering your skills helps you develop new skills; volunteering with your body helps you have a healthier body; volunteering your experience helps you gain new experience." The benefits are many.

5 Reasons Volunteering Can Enrich Your Life

1. **Experience personal happiness and fulfillment.**

Those who volunteer have a greater sense of well-being, involvement, and happiness—and science confirms—they live longer! Doesn't it feel great to do a good deed? Whether your giving is acknowledged or anonymous, volunteering will leave you with a smile on your face and a sense of purpose and contribution.

2. Create new opportunities to make new friends.

Reflecting upon my own friendships, I came to realize that many of these valuable relationships were forged through our mutual volunteering. Not only will you get to make new friends, but you will enjoy the company of others while expanding your circles and influence.

In the early 2000s, I volunteered to write a newspaper column for the *Destin Log* entitled "Motivation Station," in which I shared weekly tips and inspirations for being your best and living a life that demonstrated love. Since I was new to the area, writing this column positioned me as a speaker and writer.

As I gained loyal readers, several people reached out to meet with me and start new professional and personal friendships. I will never forget the day Karen Baker called to schedule lunch to introduce me to one of her best friends, Marnie Tate. For the next seventeen years, the three of us would have lunch, share life, shed tears, support each other's dreams, and celebrate our successes. Our connection surpassed making a great first impression and became a sisterhood which I'll cherish the rest of my life—all because I volunteered to write a newspaper column.

3. Boost your resume.

Sometimes people lack job experience or have gaps in time when they were out of the workforce all together. Rather than worrying about how this will impact your competitive edge for career opportunities, utilize your volunteer experience to boost your resume. I've learned many a skill through volunteering that I would not have had the opportunity to take on in the workplace.

Whether it is a young person who is new to the workforce, a young mother who has been busy raising her family, or a seasoned professional who is bored with retirement, experience gained from volunteering is a powerful indicator of your continuing professional engagement and capabilities.

When people have acquired leadership experience, engaged in creative problem solving, participated on teams, helped raise money or reach goals, and demonstrated responsibility, sacrifice, and reliability through their volunteer service, their resumes are enriched. It is most impressive. If you were an employer and saw this kind of initiative on a candidate's part, wouldn't you consider giving her or him a chance for a new opportunity?

4. Support your favorite organizations to keep them viable.

Do you enjoy museums? Love your church? Feel grateful for how local sport leagues engage children? Value the social services available for the elderly? Many valuable organizations exist only because of the kindness, generosity, and involvement of committed citizens who recognize their value. Rather than taking them for granted or relying on the efforts of others, get involved to ensure their sustainability.

5. Meet people who share common interests.

By volunteering, you're creating a relationship with those who support similar causes—not to mention the value in connecting with those you're helping. Years ago, I served on the Board for the Boys & Girls Clubs of the Emerald Coast in Florida. Regardless of our backgrounds, educations, businesses, or experience, we were all unified by the same mission to enhance the lives of children and provide them with a safe and supportive place to grow, thrive, and succeed. This shared camaraderie and commonality extended past our board activities and into helping each other succeed in business. Without question, we love to do business with people who are most like ourselves.

Volunteering Unifies People in Times of Crisis

My life love, Daniel, was raised in Mississippi, though his career led him to Madison, Wisconsin twenty-eight years ago. Being so far away from home and missing his family was a sacrifice he made for a wonderful career opportunity. His longing for loved ones has never ceased regardless of the success he has enjoyed in the Midwest.

When Hurricane Katrina hit the Gulf Coast in 2006, Southern Mississippi was devastated. For days, Daniel could not reach family members to be assured of their safety. He made the announcement at work that he was going to rent a truck, gather supplies, and drive to Mississippi to help his family and their community.

The word got out and before he knew it, volunteers at Group Health Cooperative (ghcscw.com) had rented a 26-foot Penske Truck and filled it with supplies: water, diapers, formula, non-perishable food, and anything else they could think of for people who had lost everything. Donations poured in from the Madison community.

Two of Daniel's friends and co-workers, Jon Bowman and Dennis Spoerl, threw their hats in the ring to volunteer for the journey. No one knew what they would find when they arrived in Mississippi, but it didn't matter—they were on a mission.

As the three men drove into Pascagoula, Mississippi, the natural disaster was evident and it looked like a war zone. Having learned of rampant robberies and high-jackings, they cautiously made their way through debris and devastation. Once they made sure Daniel's family was safe, they proceeded to the local hospital. The hospital was using emergency generator power and was running low on everything they had brought. The humble thanks and deep gratitude from the community he was raised in was beyond words and made the men's journey there more than worthwhile.

Volunteering May Help You Grow Your Business

Have you ever enjoyed an unexpected payback for volunteering your time or talent? One in which your efforts created a ripple effect for secondary gain?

Several my best clients have come from the selfless gift of donating my time and my talent. One day I volunteered to deliver a motivational speech for a high school leadership class's graduation ceremony. Unbeknownst to me, there was a mother in the audience whose son was in attendance. She and I became friends and our new relationship led me to not only empower the youth group at her church, but it opened the door for me to become a Leadership Development Trainer at the Doolittle Institute that serves the Air Force Research Labs (AFRL) at Eglin Air Force Base. Denise Wagner and I have remained good friends to this day, and I will be forever grateful to her for bringing me and my programs into the United States Air Force.

In the early 2000s, I reached over fifteen-thousand children by speaking in local schools to empower them with tools for success to create happy lives. It was some of the best work of my life, though I made the least amount of money. On one occasion, with the help of my amazing friend Teresa Pipper, we provided an all-day empowerment workshop for middle-school girls at a local hotel in Destin, Florida. It turns out that there was a beautiful young lady in the group named Ashley, whose family owned a large McDonald's franchise. They generously donated lunch, drinks, and snacks for the girls.

Move forward eleven years. Ashley's parents hired me to work with their organization to design and deliver customer service hospitality training for all their McDonald's restaurants. You never how your charity and generosity will be remembered and come back to reward you years later.

Giving Back to the Community

Henry Ford once said, "To do more for the world than the world does for you—that is success." Individuals and wise corporate leaders understand the value of giving back to the communities where they do business. It fosters good will, improves their reputation, connects them with their customers, and it's a great strategic move.

Realizing the importance of community involvement and employee engagement, TASC, a third-party administrator for employee benefits based in Madison, WI, provides their employees with paid volunteer time each year to get out and serve their communities. They want to help support causes which are important to their employees and provide the time and money to make it possible. They lead by example by encouraging their people to make a difference in the lives others.

Costa Enterprises (mcdmc.com) owns and operates the large McDonald's restaurant franchise in the Florida Panhandle which I mentioned above. They created a service campaign in all their restaurants named, "Coffee for a Cause." On the designated volunteer days, fifty percent of their profits are dedicated to supporting local charities. Their initiative has been met with an outpouring of gratitude as they are committed to improving the community in which they live.

These brief examples represent the heart of corporate philanthropy and how their mission benefits the people involved on both ends of the giving and the receiving.

❝ *How could you not want to do business with a company who puts their money where your heart is?* ❞

Sharing Hands Network

In their commitment to volunteering their time, talent, money, and energy, my special friends Esther and Jon Hemphill became deeply aware of disconnects that occur when volunteers want to help, but don't know where to begin. When donations go unused because channels don't exist for distribution. When food rots in the field while children go to bed hungry at night.

The disconnect became so alarming they founded the nonprofit organization SharingHandsNetwork.org to close the gaps to **connect those in need with those who can help.** By providing a robust resource and database, when a person in need plugs in their need, Sharing Hands Network will tell him where he can go and who he can call to get the assistance he needs. Volunteering does indeed change the world for the better. Very impressive!

What Is Right for You?

How can you decide where to begin and how you want to contribute? Some folks have no clue as to how they can get started. Ask yourself a few questions to clarify where your interests may lie . . .

- What do you do for fun?
- Do you enjoy working with people or animals?
- Would you like to get physical or use your intellectual abilities?
- Do you enjoy being indoors or outdoors?
- Who can learn from your knowledge, skills, and experience?
- If you had a million dollars to give away, whom would you like to help?

Do yourself a favor and explore the unlimited opportunities available for you to enrich your life by enriching the lives of others. Don't just view it, do it—at volunteermatch.org.

Choosing the right volunteering opportunity will not only make a positive impression on others, but it will also help you optimize your experience to more fully live out your life's calling.

6. With a Little Help from Your Friends

"Be strong enough to stand alone, smart enough to know when you need help, and brave enough to ask for it."

—Ziad K. Abdelnour

When you have made a great impression on others, forged meaningful relationships, been in service, and cultivated your connections, you will have done more than make a positive lasting impression. You will have created a rich resource which you can tap into to help you achieve your personal and professional goals. Asking for help is easier when you feel mutual respect, emotional safety, and genuine friendship with one another.

ASK YOURSELF: Do you often get frustrated trying to do everything yourself? Are you ever involved in projects that simply require more hands or experience than you have within your scope of time or expertise? Do you have tasks which overwhelm you because you don't know how to finish them? Are continuous steep learning curves running you ragged? ? Perhaps it is time to call upon others to help you.

---

66 *Everything is better in life when people come together to care for and help one another.* 99

Why Ask for a Little Help from Your Friends?

"I would rather earn 1% off of 100 people's efforts than 100% of my own efforts."

—John D. Rockefeller

- You procrastinate on handling a task because you lack the energy, time, or skills to do it yourself.
- You have strengths that are better used elsewhere.
- You would love to delegate areas of weakness or inefficiency to ensure the job is done right.
- You want to grow your business and need personal introductions to meet key decision makers.
- You are overwhelmed by doing something alone and genuinely need assistance.
- You are more productive and fulfilled by synergy and collaboration as a team player.
- You can multiply your efficiency, effectiveness, and productivity exponentially.
- You may fulfill a long-desired goal—together!
- You may be faced with physical, emotional, or mental limitations.

This is a concise list indeed; however, it begins to reveal how you can make your life easier and your workload lighter when you merely ask other people for their assistance. Even Winnie the Pooh said, "Life's easier with friends."

The Gift of Asking

Asking for help is paradoxical. Will you gladly give the shirt off your back to help another, but be reluctant to ask someone to help you? Do you feel like you would be imposing, causing inconvenience, or risking someone's feeling that you are taking advantage of them? The irony is that your hesitation to ask for help may be denying the other person the generous gift of giving. Not only will their help make a valuable difference for you, but you may actually make the other person feel valued, trustworthy, generous, and happy in the process.

Stubborn Pride

When I graduated with my Master's Degree, the economy had crashed, the speaking industry had come to a complete standstill, and there were no jobs to be found. I had sent my resume to over 100 employers who had posted available positions, but was rejected or ignored at every turn. I began to feel as though my talents were irrelevant and that I wasn't good enough because no one wanted me. Month after month, I lived in fear and anxiety. As a single mother, I simply wanted to provide a sustainable income for my children and me. After everything we had been through with a divorce and the death of my ex-husband, I was already beaten down. So, this continuous failure was salt in the wound.

---

66 *I felt alone, ashamed, and lost. I stayed stuck in silent suffering much longer than I needed to because I did not reach out to ask for help.* 99

Why couldn't I just pick up the phone and shift everything for the better? I know thousands of people, have wonderful friends, and my network of contacts is rich and plentiful. I had nurtured my network for decades BUT I never reached out to ask for guidance, referrals, or recommendations. WHY? I was too embarrassed and humiliated that my life had become shattered and unrecognizable. I felt like Oliver Twist holding out an empty porridge bowl saying, "Please Sir, I want some more." Any one of my friends in my network would have gladly helped me, but I didn't know where to begin.

Colleague and good friend, Judy Dippel (and co-author Debra Whiting Alexander, Ph.D.), address a situation in their book, *Friendship Interrupted:*

"I have a friend who is so independent that even when she clearly needs my support, I am not free to offer it. She pushes people away during the time she needs them most. Unfortunately, because of her fierce self-sufficiency, she won't let her guard down and I lose the opportunity to be of help."

They advise: "There is an alternative way of relating. **Interdependence** is a healthy combination of dependence and independence—it balances both extremes and allows you to be self-reliant while exercising a healthy dependence on others at the same time. Imagine an emotional teeter-totter, moving comfortably together—one may be up, the other down, but both friends enjoy a steady, balanced give and take."

Why Don't We Ask for Help?

- Fear of judgment, rejection, or being turned down
- We don't want to appear weak, incompetent, or needy
- We are very private and don't want others to know our business
- We don't want to bother or impose
- To project and protect our reputation and confidence

Reach Out and Touch Someone

"We can't help everyone, but everyone can help someone."
—Ronald Reagan

How many times have you found yourself lost, confused or overwhelmed? Were you reluctant to call someone and ask for help or did you reach out? Remembering that 80 percent of everything you need already exists in your network can take a lot of pressure off and dispel your belief that you are alone, life is a struggle, and you have to do everything yourself.

Winning Ways to Ask for Help

In her book, *How to Ask for Help and Increase Your Chances of Getting It,* Susanne Gaddis, PhD (www.communicationsdoctor.com), teaches that there are direct and indirect ways to ask for help, depending on your situation. She says there are "words to use" and "words to lose" to ensure your requests are well received. There is definitely an art to the asking. Susanne shares that a few winning ways to ask for help include:

- Please show me how to . . .
- Do you think you could help me with . . . ?
- What ideas do you have regarding . . . ?
- What contribution would you like to make . . . ?

Susanne teaches, "Whether you are a new or seasoned professional, knowing when, how, and who to ask for help can prove to be extremely beneficial. By learning how to ask for help and enlisting the support of others, you will see an increase in your motivation, productivity, self-esteem, and self-confidence."

Once you receive the help you requested, provide sincere appreciation. There's nothing worse than helping someone and not being acknowledged for it. Susanne suggest three steps to offer proper praise:

1. Say thank you.
2. Tell them specifically what they did to help you. Here, include the specific behaviors that made a positive difference for you.
3. Tell them how their help impacted you, the team, the organization, etc.

Give People a Chance

"Refusing to ask for help when you need it is refusing someone the chance to be helpful."

—Ric Ocasek

Think about how good it makes you feel to be in service to others. Your mood is lifted, your own challenges seem lessened, and all those wonderful endorphins fill up your happiness quotient.

When we allow others to be in service, we give them the opportunity to experience those positives as well. It makes both our friendships and our business connections feel less one-sided.

Do you know of someone who always insists on picking up the check when you are out to lunch? Once or twice may feel all right and perhaps even generous. But if you're never allowed to reciprocate their generosity, it can begin to feel uncomfortable quickly. To the point, where you might not want to accept another invitation.

Can you see how one-sidedness might erode a relationship rather than help it grow? Giving people an opportunity to reciprocate is a balanced blessing for you both.

Your Village, Your Tribe

It is gratifying to get to a point in life where your friendship circles become your tribe. A place where you have each other's backs and know each other well enough that you intuitively know how and when you can help one another.

Creating relationships with this depth of insight, compassion, and closeness is the kind of "friendship goal" most people strive for. These are the friends who will tell you what you need to hear, rather than what you want to hear. They will dispense honest, tough love without hesitation—especially when it is in your best interest. And your lives are more enriched because of it.

Not asking someone in your circle for help, in this case, is not an option. Just as if you knew one of them was in need, you'd move heaven and earth to help them, wouldn't you? Would you think less of them for asking for help? Of course not. Keep that in mind when you are closing the door to the help you need by simply not asking.

Ask Outrageously

My friend Linda Swindling (lindswindling.com) is a negotiations expert who coaches executives and organizations on how to communicate powerfully so others will listen.

In her new book, *Ask Outrageously*, Linda acknowledges that asking is a brave act. She shares, "Asking outrageously requires vulnerability and giving up control. Sometimes you have to risk looking stupid or hearing the word "no." However, when you learn to ask outrageously you can avoid wasting time, create shockingly good outcomes, and receive even more than originally requested.

Be as Kind to Yourself as You Are to Others

It is disheartening to see people deny themselves the help they need because they feel unworthy, under-valued, or are too afraid to impose on others. If that sounds familiar, please, please—be as kind to yourself as you are to others.

Would you think for a moment to berate a friend who asked for help or tell them they aren't worth the time? No. So, why would you say those things to yourself? We are all worthy. We all have times in our lives where we could use a helping hand. That's one of the many reasons friendships are such a blessing.

We lift each other up, help each other out, push each other forward, and bring value to one another. Be a giver and a receiver. That's a meaningful part of bringing your friendships full circle.

7. Make Deposits in The Love Bank

"If I make deposits into an Emotional Bank Account with you through courtesy, kindness, honesty, and keeping my commitments to you, I build up a reserve. Your trust toward me becomes higher, and I can call upon that trust many times if I need to. I can even make mistakes and that trust level, that emotional reserve, will compensate for it. When the trust account is high, communication is easy, instant, and effective."

—Stephen Covey

Imagine this scenario. You go to a bank to open a new account. You make a substantial deposit to ensure the account is well-funded so it will be stable and secure. As you go about your activities, you will occasionally make withdrawals from your account, however, you know that in order to keep the balance reconciled and healthy, you must continuously make fresh deposits. If you don't, the account will be overdrawn. And in the worst case—the account will be closed. Even though we all know this, it doesn't mean all people choose to make deposits to cover all their withdrawals.

This metaphor aptly illustrates every relationship in your life. When your relationship bank is overflowing with love, generosity, service, kindness, connection, intimacy, and understanding—the relationship feels sterling, doesn't it? It's well-supplied and healthy.

In a perfect world, this would be the happy reality and state of our existence, don't you agree? We both know, however, that different relationships require different levels of maintenance depending on their level of importance and priority.

Once you have made a positive first impression and have come full circle to create an ongoing relationship, how can you continue to invest in it wisely so that it matures into a treasured and long-term experience? Make deposits in their Love Bank!

Love Languages for Life

In his book, *The 5 Love Languages,* Dr. Gary Chapman shares that we all learn how to give and receive love in childhood. As our 'love language' develops, it defines how and what we need to feel appreciated, respected, and loved. A challenge that occurs in relationships, however, is that we end up speaking different languages! What might make one person feel loved and appreciated may leave another feeling overlooked and neglected.

Learning your primary love language, and the ones of the people around you, will provide you with an enlightened awareness for better understanding yourself and others. Once you do, you will realize that a person's love language is the currency for making deposits into their love bank! The 5 Love Languages are . . .

- Words of Affirmation
- Acts of Service
- Giving and Receiving Gifts
- Physical Touch
- Quality Time

Dr. Chapman says, "Love can be expressed and received in all five languages. However, if you don't speak a person's primary love language, that person will not feel loved, even though you may be speaking the other four. Once you are speaking his or her primary love language fluently, then you can sprinkle in the other four and they will be like icing on the cake."

To take a free assessment and learn how you can communicate with others from a place of empathy, understanding, and compassion please visit www.5LoveLanguages.com. Applying these amazing concepts will help you laugh, and love, all the way to the bank!

10 Ways We Make Withdrawals

"If you allow people to make more withdrawals than deposits in your life, you will be out of balance and in the negative. Know when to close the account."

—Unknown

When more withdrawals are being made than deposits, relationship bankruptcy ensues. At this unfortunate—and often preventable—stage, feelings are hurt, friendships end, business is lost, and divorces happen. We could write volumes on the many reasons that relationships fail, but the following name a few . . .

1. Breaking promises.
2. Dismissing another's ideas, dreams, or contributions.
3. Reacting with anger, sarcasm, and impatience.
4. Behaving rudely.
5. Cheating, lying, and living without integrity.
6. Making excuses or blaming others.
7. Spreading rumors, gossip, whining, and complaining.
8. Forgetting important dates, birthdays, anniversaries.
9. Neglecting to acknowledge milestones and accomplishments.
10. Being insensitive to another person's feelings.

Make Deposits with Generosity

Generosity in spirit and action are powerful ways to make great impressions and fuel solid relationships. We've shared some ways to make withdrawals, let's now look at some wonderful ways to make "deposits" . . .

1. Be fully present in their presence.
2. Leave distractions at the door.
3. Take an active interest in what others are interested in.
4. Always give the benefit of the doubt.

5. Practice grace and forgiveness.
6. Listen intently.
7. Keep your promises.
8. Show up on time.
9. Practice random acts of kindness.
10. Tell others what you appreciate about them.
11. Show others how you appreciate them.
12. Be respectful.
13. Be accountable.
14. Give freely without expecting anything in return.
15. Take responsibility.
16. Speak their "language"— touch, service, kind words, quality time, or gifts.
17. Keep learning about them.
18. Look for and celebrate attributes, not flaws.
19. Show faith and belief in the goals and dreams of others.
20. Remain faithful.
21. Include your relationships in daily acknowledgments of gratitude.
22. Take ownership when you're wrong and apologize.
23. Practice open communication.
24. Be a safe space.
25. Don't judge.
26. Show empathy by making an effort to "walk in someone's shoes" and see things from their perspective.
27. Before you act, think – how will that affect my partner, friend, family, colleague, or team.
28. Pitch in.
29. Change things up – don't let routine create stagnation.
30. Check in regularly to let people know they matter.

There are literally millions of ways we can help make the people in our lives feel cared for, important, valued, and loved. Take up the challenge with a sense of wonder and creativity and you'll see your relationships not only survive the test of time, but thrive in incredible, life-affirming ways.

Get Creative

There are times in every relationship where one or the other needs an extra boost of self-worth and appreciation. These are the time to add a little creativity to your deposits.

A gratitude journal. I once read a story of a husband whose marriage was in trouble. Through counseling and therapy, they found that they, as many do, had been focused on the flaws in their relationships rather than the things that they fell in love with. (Where our attention goes, our energy flows, right? So, they were getting more of what they were focused on (the flaws) rather than the things they loved (the attributes). The husband, unbeknownst to his wife, decided to get a notebook and for the next three months, he wrote down five things every day that he was grateful for about his wife, or something he appreciated about their relationship that day. After three months, he surprised her with this gift. As you can imagine, it was a thoughtful stepping stone in the salvation of their marriage.

A memory jar. For a friend's husband's 50th birthday, she collected fond memories from some of his closest family and friends and wrote them all down on slips of colored paper and filled up a jar. It is to this day, one of the most treasured gifts he's ever received.

What can you do to make a big impression on a loved one in your life? Consider their love language, then get creative!

Appreciation

"I consider my ability to arouse enthusiasm among my people the greatest asset I possess. And the way to get what is best from a person is through appreciation and encouragement."

—Charles Schwab

The word love not only applies to romance and intimacy, but to the meaningful connection and goodwill that flows between you and everyone you know.

After the worldwide success of Dr. Chapman's, *The 5 Love Languages*, he and Dr. Paul White explored how the same love languages apply to empowering people professionally. In their book, *The 5 Languages of Appreciation in the Workplace,* they teach practical steps for making any work environment more encouraging, productive, and successful.

Would you like to enjoy a higher ROI (return on your investment) in your professional relationships for improved communication, collaboration, engagement, performance, and loyalty? Make deliberate deposits in your team and customer 'love banks.'

---

66 Seek to nurture your network, and make consistent, accurate deposits, and you will be rewarded with lasting positive impressions and meaningful relationships—which only appreciate in value. 99

---

8. $\mathcal{F}$RIENDSHIPS FOR A $\mathcal{L}$IFETIME

Friends at First Sight

There was a time when every one of your closest friends was still a stranger. A time when you had little or no awareness of each other and had yet to cross paths. Then, as fate would have it . . . you met.

Each one of these encounters experienced a single moment in time for a first impression to be made between the two of you. For every one of these close friends, you probably remember when, where, and why they had a positive impact in your life—and how it opened the door to explore, as a lifetime relationship began.

What got your attention and made you take notice? What made you interested enough to learn more about them to keep the conversation going? What was the attractor factor that magnetized you together? Whatever you've been doing, keep it up!

Obviously, your first encounter made a memorable impression to still be in each other's lives today. It is exciting to realize that on any given day someone new may arrive who becomes a significant and valuable part of your life. Make your impressions awesome!

As Chance Would Have It

As I have been writing this book, I have reflected upon the amazing friends who are in my life and retraced how I met them. I've shared many of them with you throughout this book. Whether they came to me for a reason, a season, or a lifetime, there was a first initial contact that changed the trajectory of our lives. How did I meet each one of these incredible people? Their first impressions had staying power that grabbed me and made me want to take another step, find common ground, and share ordinary and extraordinary moments together.

Within a couple of months of moving to Madison, Wisconsin I attended the Middleton Chamber of Commerce Christmas Party. I walked into a room full of strangers and saw a vision of light in the smile of a beautiful woman wearing a bright red dress. Her positive energy was captivating and reassured me that if I approached, I would be greeted with enthusiasm and interest. After introducing ourselves to each other, we could not speak fast enough. She was so filled with love and caring for others, her joy and enthusiasm bubbled over.

I knew instantly upon meeting Deborah SuZan, that I wanted her in my life far into the future. Now, two years later, she is one of my best friends. I have no doubt that she will be in my life for the rest of my life. In your quest to master the art of first impressions, untold gifts and amazing people will walk through the door and into your life when you create the space for it to happen.

Make Room

There's a time in our youth where most of us hope to accumulate the largest possible circle of friends. Call it status, ego, insecurity, or the simple desire to be liked—it's more about quantity than quality.

Similar to when Facebook first became popular and it limited individuals to 500 friends. The race was on to see who could get to that magic number first, only to "turn people away" because of their perceived popularity.

However, what we learn—both in life and in social media connectivity—is that it's much more fulfilling to have true-blue authentic friends. Relationships built on quality rather than quantity.

We can reach immeasurable financial success in life and yet still be poor of spirit and connection if we fail to make friendships a priority in our lives.

The truth is, the people who enrich our worlds, make us laugh, and support us without question, are the main course in this banquet of life. They should be treated as such. Move relationships closer to the top of your daily to-do lists. Make room for the ones who matter most.

Multiply and Divide

I love the reminder by Spanish Philosopher Baltasar Gracian, "True friendship multiplies the good in life and divides its evils. Strive to have friends, for life without friends is like life on a desert island . . . to find one real friend in a lifetime is good fortune; to keep him is a blessing."

When we recognize that having true and genuine friendships in our life is one of the greatest blessings we can manifest, we can cherish and nurture them for all they are worth.

A great friend multiplies our joys, our celebrations, our milestones, and lifts us higher than we could ever go flying solo. True friends do, indeed, divide our grief—as they support us in times of strife or struggle.

If a relationship is not true, mutually beneficial, respectful, reciprocated, or life-lifting—be grateful for its place in your journey. Appreciate the lessons it has brought and taught, then with love, set boundaries or let it go. It is the equivalent of saying no to the things in your life that do not serve you—so you can say yes to opening new doors for things that do.

Lamp Lighters

Most everyone experiences moments in life where we let seeds of doubt creep in. Where we become stuck in ruts of negative thinking and give more focus to worry than wonder. These dark valleys can leave us feeling low on light and short on faith.

True friends are the lamp-lighters. They shine a spotlight on the faith they have in us and remind us of our ability to shine. Their light can help lead us out of the dark corners. Treasure these people, and hone your best scouting skills to be a lamp lighter for the people in your life.

Ann Landers summed it up quite nicely when she said, "Love is friendship that has caught fire. It is quiet understanding, mutual confidence, sharing and forgiving. It is loyalty through good and bad times. It settles for less than perfection and makes allowances for human weaknesses."

Here are 30 ways to fan those friendship flames and make the VIPs in your life know that you care:

1. Each week, calendar calls with friends to simply check in. It could be the best part of their day.
2. Each week, send at least one handwritten note to someone who has made a difference in your life. It might take you ten minutes, but it will be a thoughtful treasure for a friend.
3. Schedule a friend gathering at least quarterly, if not every month. (Don't fall into the "I'm too busy" trap.)
4. Each week, like and comment genuinely and fondly on the posts of at least five friends on social media.
5. Send at least two "thinking of you" texts to family or friends per week.
6. Look people directly in the eye and tell them you appreciate them.
7. Finish a great book that was hard to put down? Pass it along to a friend with similar tastes.
8. Remember and acknowledge their birthdays and important occasions.
9. If something catches your eye, (a meme, article, picture, etc.) that reminds you of someone, don't wait. Send it to them and let them know!
10. Notice their challenges and acknowledge their strengths.
11. Invite them to a meal, a movie, or both!
12. Say thank you, often.
13. Support them in their beliefs.
14. Put down your phone and listen.
15. Ask them to teach you something you know they are good at, which helps them see their value.
16. Pay a kind compliment.

17. Do something in their honor.
18. Care for the people they care about.
19. Pat them on the back when they've had an accomplishment.
20. Remember their favorite things – flowers, meal, wine, dessert, and surprise them with it once in a while.
21. Share your vulnerability about something – it will let them know they don't have to be guarded either.
22. Make every exchange a standing "no judgment zone."
23. Be the person whom they can call when they aren't doing well or need a confidant.
24. Jot a memory on a postcard and send it to them to make them laugh.
25. Spotlight their wins and create a celebration.
26. Share honesty.
27. Ask their opinion – and really listen.
28. Share resources which you believe they would enjoy.
29. Always give the benefit of the doubt.
30. Contribute to their success by referring them, spotlighting their talent, lending a hand – or all of the above.

Life gets busy. No doubt. Regardless of your business level or family responsibilities, begin to make friendship a priority in your life. The rewards are priceless.

Grounded in Gratitude

"Make new friends, but keep the old. One is silver and the other gold."
—Unknown

Loving, loyal, and rewarding friendships take tender loving care and attention. How many times have friendships evaporated or drifted away simply because of neglect and disconnect? Or perhaps because we took them for granted and assumed they would always be there? Gratitude for them and their friendship can help prevent that from happening.

It is amazing how much the laws of attraction and reciprocity play out in our friendships. When I am grateful for the friends in my life, more new friends show up. When I acknowledge, celebrate, and thank friends for their presence in my life, it makes rich deposits in their love banks to keep our fires burning.

As you apply the golden nuggets which you have learned in this book, you will soon see that the art of first impressions is about so much more than making a sale, getting a job, or building a business. It's about your ability to create, maintain, and nurture rewarding relationships that help you enjoy a life of significance and satisfaction.

8 WAYS TO **MASTER**
The *Art* of NURTURING YOUR NETWORK

1. *Cultivate Your Connections.* Now that you have planted social seeds for positivity and influence, it is time to nurture, fertilize, and tend to the tender new relationships.

2. *Warm Referrals & Repeat Business.* Warm referrals are one of your best opportunities to give and receive good will, mutual respect, and rewarding support.

3. *Networking to Expand Your Influence.* Set your intention, take deliberate action, and follow through. You'll be amazed by the difference it makes in your networking results.

4. *Join New Groups & Organizations.* Your options are unlimited when you consider local, national, global, and online options. Choose a door and walk through it!

5. *Volunteer Your Time & Talent.* Volunteer to serve a cause above and beyond yourself, it is a reflection of your heart, character, work ethic, and convictions. Giving feeds your spirit. The needs are great and the choices are many.

6. *With a Little Help from Your Friends.* Make life easier and your workload lighter; ask others for their assistance.

7. *Make Deposits in Your Love Bank.* From first impressions to full circle friendship, continue to invest in it wisely; it will mature into a treasured, secure, long-term experience.

8. *Friendships for a Lifetime.* Seek to nurture your friendships and be grateful for their presence in your life. You never know when a new connection will become a lasting one.

Bringing It Full Circle

Thank you for reading *The Art of First Impressions for Positive Impact.* While I don't know what specific impact this book has made on you, my hope is that it has, and will continue to guide your inner confidence and the first impressions you make. I hope it will influence how you meet people and positively impact the many facets of the relationships that are important in building the life you desire— personally and professionally.

I encourage you to remember to live this very moment—to be your best; to make preparation a habit; to continue to grow in awareness of your body language, as well as the words you use; to take action on all you have learned within this book; to be generous, gracious and grateful, and I hope those you care about return the same. Enjoy skillful, authentic communications that leave you at ease, as you make new connections that go full circle to leave a lasting impression—some for a season, some for a lifetime.

At this time, I may not be able to look you in the eyes as we talk, but when the day comes that I'm speaking in your city, it would be a pleasure to meet you in person. Speaking from the bottom of my heart, it has been my sincere honor to have written this book for you! I've shared it all to the best of my ability and now I pass the baton—be your own best friend and live life to the fullest, in whatever endeavors lie before you.

Let me know if you have questions, comments, or speaking invitations I look forward to the day we perhaps meet. In the meantime, be happy; know you are significant as you step out in all you can be—and do all that you are meant to experience on this earth. And remember . . . life will bring you full circle when your positive first impressions become your lasting impressions.

In Friendship,

Acknowledgements

Thank you . . .

To the man I love, my life-mate and partner Daniel Futch, for believing in me and providing me with the space, place, freedom, love, and commitment to help me live my dream.

To my brilliant sister and editor Elizabeth Dixon for helping me enrich my message by editing every word, concept, and idea. Your loving hands and profound guidance have made this book truly special. You have been incredibly patient and consistently loyal in the process—from its original inception five years ago to the final manuscript.

To my talented graphics designer and friend Kendra Cagle (5LakesDesign.com) who helps me make an outrageously positive impact with her cutting-edge designs, colors, creativity, and innovation for my books and professional branding.

To my content development editor and friend Judy Dippel (jldwrites.com) for helping me to expand my message and further enriching the importance of making a positive first impression.

To my wonderful family, including mother Ann Cullison, aunt Marjorie Jane Chandley, son Nick Young, daughter Ally Christman, sisters Elizabeth Dixon, Jane Cullison Vosser, Christine Collins, and Farrell Hendricks.

To cherished friends Marnie Tate, Tina Hallis, Cheri Davis, Natalie Leon, Cheri Neal, Susanne Gaddis, Amy Tolbert, Laura Wells, Cindy Cooper, Nancy Fox, Jon & Esther Hemphill, Joy Todd, Monika Moritz Klam, Shep Hyken, Joe Anheier, Adrianne Machina, Ed Robinson, Julie McCarthy, Deborah Suzan, Michelle Reddington, Denise Pedersen, Peggy Libson and Julie Cleghorn.

Thank you to the fellow speakers and writers whom I have quoted for their inspired insights, words of wisdom, and dedication to be messengers of hope—life-changers and world-changers!

About Susan Young

Susan runs the speaking and training firm, Susan Young International. She helps organizations leverage the power of change to improve positivity, engagement, and communications. Her keynotes and workshops empower people with tools to move from transition to transformation. She holds her Master's Degree in Human Performance Technology.

As a result of her work, people share that they are able to shift their mindsets, shed what is holding them back and reach a new level of potential to live a life they love. When she is not speaking to audiences across the country, training global sales teams, or motivating the masses, she enjoys dancing, biking, movies, and spending quality time with loved ones.

Susan is a grateful mother to her young adult twins, Nick and Ally and grandmother to Jace. Though a Florida native, she currently resides in Madison, Wisconsin with her true love Daniel Futch. She is a world traveler, scuba diver, interior designer, painter, avid reader, cyclist, and beach lover.

Please visit:

www.SusanSpeaks.com

to invite Susan to speak at your next event, join her community, or discover ways to move from transition to transformation. We look forward to seeing you there!

Additional Books by Susan

When the main book, *The Art of First Impressions for Positive Impact*, was finally finished, it was almost 100,00 words and over 400 pages! With 8 content-rich chapters that could make complete stand-alone topics, I decided to showcase each one and give it its own book! In your busy life with everything vying for your attention, I wanted to make it easy for you to enjoy this valuable content in whatever form worked best for you. Whether you read the main book, one of the 8 small books, or all nine, these valuable lessons are timeless, true, and ready for you. Please visit Amazon.com or SusanSpeaks.com to buy your copies today.

The Art of
BEING

The Art of
PREPARATION

The Art of
BODY LANGUAGE

The Art of
ACTION

The Art of
COMMUNICATION

The Art of
CONNECTION

The Art of a
POSITIVE LASTING IMPRESSION

The Art of
NURTURING YOUR NETWORK

Release the Power of Re³
Review, Redo & Renew for
Postive Change & Transformation

Now Available on Amazon

- Do you embrace change with optimism and resilience?
- Or do you resist it with fear, denial, and frustration?
- Are you at a loss for how to move past adversity and challenge?
- Would you like to create more positive change in your life?

Then this book is for YOU! Change isn't going anywhere and will continue to happen again, again, and again . . . with you, without you, for you, or against you. That's life.

They why do some people strive and thrive, while others flop and flounder? You have the power to choose. In *Release the Power of Re3: Review, Redo & Renew for Postive Change & Transformation*, Susan Young shares her 3-Step Formula for harnessing the power of change, being exponentially resilient, and optimizing your outcomes in life and in business. Whether you hope to navigate change more successfully, create something brand new, or improve upon the past, Susan Young will help you make the right choices for the right changes.

Please Leave a Review on Amazon

Thank you very much for reading *The Art of First Impressions for Positive Impact*. If you enjoyed reading it and sharing our journey together, please be so kind to post a short review on Amazon. Your support really does matter and I deeply appreciate your feedback. Thank you!

Let's Stay in Touch and Connect on Social Media

susanyspeaks

SusanYoungSpeaks

susanyoungmotivationalspeaker

+SusanYoungMotivationalSpeakerMadison

52156908R00261

Made in the USA
Columbia, SC
27 February 2019